# Important Themes in
# BIBLICAL
# THEOLOGY

## Canice C. Njoku, C.S.Sp

**Spiritans**

ISBN 978-1-0980-0264-0 (paperback)
ISBN 978-1-0980-0265-7 (digital)

Christian Faith Publishing, Inc.
832 Park Avenue
Meadville, PA 16335
www.christianfaithpublishing.com

Printed in the United States of America

# CONTENTS

Acknowledgments ....................................................................5
Preface................................................................................7
Abbreviations .........................................................................9

Chapter 1:   The Development of Christian Canon ...................11
Chapter 2:   The Pharisees of Our Present-Day
             Religion: Contextualizing Mt 23:2–3 ...................19
Chapter 3:   The Influence of Hellenism on the Socio-
             Cultural and Religious Lifestyle of the
             Jewish State: 400 BC–6 BC ..............................30
Chapter 4:   The Medieval Spirituality: AD 500–1500............36
Chapter 5:   What Defines Perennial Philosophy? ....................50
Chapter 6:   Modern Philosophers and the Implications
             of their Philosophies on Exegesis..........................60
Chapter 7:   A Comparative Evaluation of Tradition and
             Magisterium in Richard Gaillardetz and
             Lawrence Feingold................................................69
Chapter 8:   Where Tradition Meets Liturgy: Their Relationship ... 76
Chapter 9:   The Biblical Foundation and the
             Fundamentality of Sacraments................................85
Chapter 10:  The Biblical Root of the Divine Sonship of
             the *Totus Christos* ...........................................93
Chapter 11:  The Eucharistic Relationship between
             Ecclesiology and Eschatology................................110
Chapter 12:  An Analysis of the Mosaic Covenant
             Ratification in Ex 24: 3–10.................................123

Chapter 13:   The Davidic Covenant (2 Sam 7): Literary
              and Theological Fulfillment....................132
Chapter 14:   Development of Prophecy in Israel: The
              Relevance of Prophet Amos ....................142
Chapter 15:   Evaluating the Messianic Prophecy in the
              Book of Zecharias................................150
Chapter 16:   Wisdom Literature in the Canon of the
              Old Testament....................................159
Chapter 17:   The Sapiential Literatures: Exploring the
              Book of Proverbs ................................165
Chapter 18:   An Overview of the Book of the Psalms................184
Chapter 19:   Psalm 149: The Song of the Redeemed and
              the New People of God..........................191
Chapter 20:   The Women's Post-Resurrection Visit:
              Discrepancies in the Synoptic Gospels?................198
Chapter 21:   Christ's Death and the Inauguration of the
              New Temple Theme in John's Gospel....................210
Chapter 22:   The Three Divine Persons: One Essence,
              One Mission in John's Gospel..............................221
Chapter 23:   A Catholic Perspective on Pauline Gospel
              and Theology........................................235
Chapter 24:   Catholic Epistles and Letter to the Hebrew:
              A Very brief Excursus............................250
Chapter 25:   The Significance of Κοίνωνιά in
              Johannine Community: 1 Jn 1:1–4 ....................260

Bibliography........................................................271

# ACKNOWLEDGMENTS

I am greatly indebted to all my professors who moderated these papers and gave their valued corrections and advice. These include my professors during my studies for MA in divinity: SIST, Enugu/ Duquesne University, Pittsburgh, Pennsylvania; and MA in biblical theology: John Paul the Great Catholic University, Escondido, California. Some of them include Fr. Dr. Munchi Ezeogu; CSSp (of blessed memory), Fr. Dr. Charles Ebelebe, CSSp; Sr. Dr. Mary-Sylvia Nwachukwu, DDL; Fr. Dr. Cosmas Uzowulu OFM Cap; Fr. Dr. Philip Igbo, CFM; Most Rev. Dr. John Okoye (bishop of Ogwu); Most Rev. Dr. Gabriel Mendy, CSSp (bishop of Banjul, Gambia); Fr. Dr. Bona Ugwu, CSSp; Fr. Dr. Bede Ukwuije, CSSp; Fr. Isidor Nkwocha, CSSp; Dr. Michael Baber; Dr. John Kincaid; Jackie Wakelin; and Luke Heintschel. Finally, I am grateful to all my valued classmates at JP Catholic, especially Fr. Jude Thaddaeus Langeh, CMF.

# PREFACE

What I have decided to put down here is not the thesis of my post-graduate studies. Rather, it is a collection of twenty-five papers that I have personally written both in the course of my studies for my MA in divinity and MA in biblical theology. They are made up of important themes in biblical theology. They consist of themes which were actually suggested, assigned, and moderated by seasoned professors and biblical scholars in various aspects of biblical theology. Although in some cases I have modified the themes, yet, I tried as much as possible to remain focused on the objectives of the papers.

One very interesting point to note is the treatment of most of these themes basically from the biblical perspective. This is mostly with regards to themes drawn from courses which are not "strictly scriptural courses" rather are more of theological courses, but nonetheless, form an integral part of the study of biblical theology. So, in addition to the core scriptural courses, I have featured themes from fundamental theology, ecclesiology and eschatology, sacramental and liturgical theology, trinitarian theology, etcetera.

Also, it suffices to note that this work is not a commentary on the Bible, nor is it a comprehensive approach to all the courses in biblical theology. Rather, it is a treatment of some important themes scholars or students encounter in the course of their study of biblical theology. This is simply meant to give one an idea of how these themes together shape biblical theology, and most importantly, how to approach some of these themes. While their treatment might not be perfect here, there is always room for further readings and improvement on them. Also, as is usually the case in biblical theology, where new discoveries continue to emerge, thus giving room for improvement of knowledge and ideas, so there is room for improvement on these themes.

# ABBREVIATIONS

| | |
|---|---|
| AD | *Anno Domini* |
| BC | Before Christ |
| Ca. | *Circa* (approximately) |
| CCC | Catechism of the Catholic Church |
| DV | *Verbum Dei* |
| Gk | Greek |
| Hb | Hebrew |
| LG | *Lumen Gentium* |
| NIV | New International Version |
| NRSV | New Revised Standard Version |
| NT | New Testament |
| OT | Old Testament |
| SC | *Sacrosanctum Concilium* |
| ST | *Summa Theologiae* |

# The Development of Christian Canon

*Early Christian Fathers and formation of the Christian Canon*

## Introduction

The development of the Christian canon has a very long and perhaps complex history. Strictly speaking, Christian canon of the Scripture contains the Old Testament (OT) and the New Testament (Harrington 2006, 156). This work will, therefore, try to trace the development of the Christian canon starting with the Christian OT canon. However, it will focus more on the development of the New Testament (NT) canon. This is in order to highlight the role played by the Church Fathers in the development of the Christian canon.

## Canon: Etymology and Meaning

The term *canon* (Greek, Κανων and Hebrew, *Kaneh*) according to Metzer B. (1978, 289) was derived from a Semitic root (Heb *qaneh*, Assyrian *qanu* [i.e., Sumerian, Akkadian *qin* and Ugaritic *qu*). It was passed into Greek as *kanna* or *kane* into Latin as *Canna* and English as *Cane*. It originally meant "reed" and came to mean something firm and straight. However, in time it came to be used as standards, rules (2 Cor. 10, 13), precedents, and guidelines, or in the case of the early church, setting forth the essentials of Christian preaching, as in the rule of faith. When used in connection with the Bible, the word *canon* refers to the collection of books that are acknowledged to be authoritative in the church and by which the church's faith can be measured. It was not until the fourth century that the church began to refer to the Scriptures of the OT and NT as "ho kanon" (the Canon). Canon came to mean "a list of sacred writings" (Harrington 2006, 156).

## The Development of the Christian Old Testament Canon

Before this brief look at the Christian OT canon, it suffices to bear in mind that the Bible of Jesus and his disciples was the Hebrew Bible, while the Bible of Paul and his converts was the Greek LXX. James A. Sanders (1987, 834) notes that several factors contributed to make the Alexandrian LXX canon more acceptable to Jewish writing than the Palestinian official Bible. Palestinian Jews made a sharp distinction between inspired scripture and human writings; canonization was a solemn recognition that certain books were divinely revealed to prophets. "Traditionally, the 'final canonization' of the whole Bible was accomplished by men of the 'Great Synagogue' (Assembly) in the time of Ezra and Nehemiah." In Alexandria, on the contrary, the Jews tended to accept as scripture any writing in Hebrew or Aramaic which came from Palestine. They tended to regard all books translated into Greek from Hebrew as divinely inspired as opposed to those written originally in Greek. Although Sanders may be referring to the ancient Jewish Scriptures as they were originally, Ellis E. E. (1988, 653-683) tells us (and may be right) that "the development of the final closed Canon of Scripture (i.e. Jewish) was the work of a pharisaic and rabbinical Judaism which came to prominence after the fall of Jerusalem in 70 C. E."

When Christianity moved away from the significant influences of Judaism, the church continued to appeal to religious literature that was popular in Palestine before AD 70. Melito (Ca. AD 180) reports a Jewish canon of twenty-two books, which is the equivalent of the present Jewish and Protestant canon except for Esther. In the fourth and fifth centuries, however, apocryphal and pseudographal writings were still found in Christian list of OT canonical scriptures. Athanasius for e.g., in 367 listed in his OT canon both Baruch and the epistles of Jeremiah, but omitted Esther. Also, many of the lists include one or more of the apocryphal writings (e.g., Origen, Cyril of Jerusalem, Hilary with Epiphanius, and others), but codex Sinaiticus and Gregory Nazianzus omitted Esther. G. W. Anderson (1970, 113) notes that the content of the Christian Protestant OT is identical with that of the Jewish canon, but the material is divided into thirty-nine books and arranged in a different order.

The canon of OT books traditional in Catholicism contains all the books of the Hebrew Bible along with the seven more books that were part of the Greek translation known as the Septuagint. The additional books in the Catholic canon are sometimes called the apocryphal or deuterocanonical. The canons of the various Orthodox churches contain some material beyond what appears in the Catholic canon. George J. Reid (2007) surmises that the most explicit definition of the Catholic canon is that given by the Council of Trent. The order of books copies that of the Council of Florence (1442), and in its general plan is that of the Septuagint. The divergence of titles from those found in the Protestant version is due to the fact that the official Vulgate retained the forms of the Septuagint.

## The Development of the New Testament Canon

To appreciate the development of the NT canon, it will be very necessary to look at the contributions of certain individuals who played key role in the process. Philip Igbo (2010, 36) is of the opinion that it was from this early period that the Christian community began to recognize the NT writings as being revealed and equal in authority to the OT. However, it is important to note also that the canonization of the NT books took a gradual process. It was not until the end of the fourth century AD that the NT books were recognized as canonical.

With one exception (Rev 22:8–19) as Ferguson et al (1990, 169) posits, the NT writings appear not to have been written as sacred literature, but by the end of the first century, NT literature was frequently used to settle disputes and address the life and ministerial needs of the church. The formal recognition of NT literature as scripture is first attested by Irenaeus of Lyons (ca. 130–200), who was also the first to use the terms *OT* and *NT*. After him, there was widespread acceptance of NT writings as scriptures, especially by Clement of Alexandria (born ca.140–150), Tertullian (ca. 160–220), and Origen (ca. 185–25). Finally, one fact which is inalienable is that even though the NT writings themselves were not generally called "scripture" before the time of Irenaeus, they often quoted words, ministry, passion, and resurrection of Jesus. E. Ferguson (1978, 677–83) gives the following as example of such books quoted: (1 Cor. 1:10–17; 11:23; 1 Thes 4:15; Mt 28:18; but also, 1 Clem 1:1–4; Ignatius, Philad. 8, 2; Polycarp, Phil 2:2–3, etc.).

## Marcion (ca. 100–160)

The role played by Marcion in the development of Christian canon cannot be overlooked. Marcion was the son of a bishop and a brilliant theologian, who, however, fell to heresy for rejecting the OT entirely and held that the God of the OT was an inferior being—"a demiurge" who insisted on strict justice. He was the first to have a formal canon list, which contains only Luke's gospel and only ten Pauline epistles (Philip Igbo 2010, 36). Although Marcion was excommunicated, his continuous impact led to lengthy refutations from Irenaeus and Tertullian. Ferguson et al (1990, 176) strongly believes that although establishing a closed canon of scripture was not Marcion's primary aim, his canon did have the effect of spurring the church into considering which Christian writing best defined its faith and mission. Marcion's canon evoked lots of responses.

# Irenaeus of Lyons (ca. 130–200)

Irenaeus accepted all four of the canonical gospels and urged that only those four be accepted as authoritative in the church (Haser, 11, 8–9). These four gospels he held corresponds to the four ends of the world. However, he did not quite accept the letter to the Hebrews. He accepted thirteen Pauline epistles but rejected the shepherd of Hermas. It was also not clear if he accepted the catholic epistle (except 1 Peter, 1 and 2 John). Tertullian (ca. 160–220) also accepted all four gospels; Matthew and John as coming from the apostles, while Mark and Luke as presenting the teaching of Peter and Paul (Mark 4.2.5). He equally accepted Acts, thirteen Pauline letters, 1 Peter, 1 John, but he refused to recognize Hebrews as authoritative. Origen (ca. 185–254) is the next writer for whom there is a list of canons, but this list may have been an invention of Eusebius of Caesarea. The simple reason for this is that it is found in Eusebius's writing (HE 6.25. 3–14) and only in Rufinus (345–412). Origen's canon contains twenty-two books: four gospels, the Pauline epistles, 1 Peter, 1 John, and Apocalypse.

# The Emperors and the Development of the Christian Canon

Two emperors are worth mentioning here. While Diocletian's (245–313) reign spelled doom for Christian writings, that of Constantine (306–337) was exactly the opposite. In 303, Diocletian's persecution demanded the destruction of the church, the confiscation and burning of sacred scriptures. Many Christians were persecuted to death because of their refusal to hand over their sacred books, and one can assume that the churches had already identified which books were demanded. Although the churches were not in complete agreement on which books were sacred, it is likely that most of them had by then decided the broad parameters of their biblical canon.

Constantine's conversion brought many benefits to the church. Apart from the cessation of persecution and restoration of property, his reign (306–337) was characterized by the pursuit of social and religious conformity (Eusebius, V.C, 2.65, 68). During his reign, there was a move in the church toward unity in theology and biblical canon. Constantine requested Eusebius to produce fifty copies of scriptures for use in the new capital city of Constantinople (Eusebius V. C.3. 37). Which scriptures to be included in those copies was probably decided by Eusebius, but his choice was accepted by the emperor, a fact that probably influenced other Christian's decisions on the matter.

## Other Major Key Players

Eusebius, bishop (ca. 260–340) of Cæsarea, was one of Origen's most eminent disciples. In imitation of his master, he divided religious literature into three classes: those "accepted" as scripture, those that were "questionable" or "disputed," and those that were "spurious." He included in the first group twenty of the current NT books (four gospels, Acts, thirteen Pauline epistles, 1 John, and 1 Peter). The "questionable" group included James, 2 Peter, Jude, 2 and 3 John. The "spurious" group was rejected outright and included such works as the gospel of Peter, Thomas, Matthias, Didache, etc. In time, the middle group was accepted by most churches, but the latter failed to find acceptance (Reid, 2007).

Athanasius's (295–373) list is contained in his thirty-ninth festal letter of AD 367. J. C. Turro and Raymond E. Brown (1965, 354) writes that "Athanasius was the first to name as exclusively authoritative and precise the 27 documents that finally came to constitute the NT as we know it. Some of the criteria used to biblical canon include: i.) Apostolicity, i.e., the writing was accepted if it is believed to have been written by an apostle. ii.) Orthodoxy, i.e, if the writing coheres with the teaching that was believed to have been passed on to the churches by the apostles through their successors. iii.) Public Lection, i.e., the book must have been in use in the public worship of a prominent church or a majority of churches. iv.) Catholic, i.e., it has to be relevant to the church at large."

In 1740, L. A. Muratori (1672–1750) discovered what has been referred to as the "oldest canon" in the Ambrosian library in Milan. It is a seventh- or eighth-century translation of a list of sacred scriptures, mostly believed to have originated near Rome ca. 180–200. The list, according to Ferguson et al (1990, 172), approximates the current NT collection, with the exception that 1 and 2 Peter and Hebrews are omitted, but the apocalypse of Peter and Wisdom of Solomon are included. There is no agreement on the dating of the fragment. However, some scholars hold that it belongs to either the second or third. The value of this canon lies in the fact that it indicates the book's availability in the second century.

## Canonical Lists and Council Decisions

It is also worthy of note that there were other canonical lists that existed in the fourth century. The following stand out: Codex Sinaiticus is one of the oldest and most valuable of ancient MSS of the Greek NT. It was discovered in Mt. Sinai in 1859 by Dr. Tischendorf. It contains twenty-seven books of Athanasius, the epistle of Barnabas and Shepherd of Hermas. Codex Vaticanus is considered the oldest extant vellum manuscript. It is placed in the Vatican Library at Rome by Pope Nichols V in 1448. It was the decision of councils that helped in streamlining the canons although no conciliar decision reversed the list set forth in the canon of Athanasius. Some of these councils include Council of Laodicea (AD 363), which accepted twenty-six books while omitting Revelation; Synod of Rome (AD 382), which recognized twenty-seven books as canonical; Council of Hippo (AD 393) and Carthage (397), which named twenty-seven books; the Council of Trent (1546–1563), which made the final determination of the canon as we have it today.

The Tridentine decree defining the canon affirms the books to which proper names are attached, without however including this in the definition. The order of books follows that of the Bull of Eugenius IV (Council of Florence), except that Acts was moved from a place before Apocalypses to its present position, and Hebrews put at the end of St Paul's epistles. The Tridentine order has been retained in the official Vulgate and vernacular Catholic Bibles. The same is to be said of the titles, which as a rule are traditional ones, taken from the canons of Florence and Carthage (Reid, 2007).

## Conclusion

Following the progress made so far in tracing the development of the Christian canon, which is the objective of this work *ab initio*, it is, therefore, important at this juncture to draw the following conclusion. The following facts emerged clear through the course of this work. The earliest and primary canon of the early church was the life, death, resurrection, and teachings of Jesus. The theology of the earliest Christians was informed by an array of writings wider than that included in the present-day Protestant or Catholic churches of the fourth to sixth centuries were in wide but not complete agreement on either their Old Testament or New Testament canons. It is very important to note that although the church rejected Marcion's truncated canon, his became a factor that pushed and woke up the churches to the need for a canon of their sacred scriptures, especially the New Testament. Finally, the Christian canon as we have it today been not the product of any individual, but a product of centuries and the effort of many protagonists especially the Church Fathers who worked hard to make sure that the church persevered her sacred writings through canonization.

# THE PHARISEES OF OUR PRESENT-DAY RELIGION: CONTEXTUALIZING MT 23:2–3

*Introduction to the New Testament*

## Introduction

The scribes and the Pharisees (γραμματεις και οἱ φαρισιοι, *grammateis kai oi Pharisaioi)* are associated because almost all scribes were of the sect of the Pharisees. The scribes, the Jewish scholars, the theologians and lawyers would naturally be of the religious sect. The scribes and the Pharisees are represented as the pious and zealous official representatives of Judaism. Knowledge of the opinions and practices of the Pharisees at the time of Christ is of great importance for entering deeply into the genius of the Christian religion. Christ denounced them in the bitterest language because they were rigid interpreters of the letters of the Mosaic Law but frequently violated the spirit of it by their traditional and philosophical interpretations.

This paper seeks to employ Mat 2:2 as a basis for discussing the importance of the Pharisees during the time of Jesus, and to highlight the present Pharisees of our Christian religion. In light of this, the writer will in this paper trace the etymology of the name *Pharisees*, their origin, their position in the Jewish state of Jesus' time.

Furthermore, their importance during the time of Jesus would be critically explored, while the implication of the phrase "Sit on Moses' seat" (NRSV Catholic Edition) would be briefly and exegetically expounded. Finally, great effort would be made toward identifying the present Pharisees in our Christian religion.

## Etymology of the Word *Pharisee*

The etymology of the word *Pharisee* is not crystal-clear. However, efforts have been made to come close to it. The word Pharisees is rendered in Greek as φάρισάιος (*pharisaios*), and in Hebrew, *fair'uh-seez*, meaning separated. Hence, they may be referred to as separatists (Heb. *Persahin*, from *parash*, to be separated). They are a Jewish sect during the time of Jesus. The group was active from the late second century BC through the destruction of Jerusalem in AD 70 (Richard 1989, 999).

Concerning the derivation of the name Pharisees, there is even less agreement among scholars than in the case of Sadducees. One plausible hypothesis derives the name from a Hebrew word meaning "separatist," as already mentioned above. However, it is uncertain whether this was a self-designation or a derogatory label of their opponents. The problem of determining specifically what it was from which they were separated is likewise difficult (Brown et al 2007, 41–77).

## Origin of the Pharisees

Howard Clarke records notes that the origin of the Pharisees was in some way related to the revolt of the Hasidim in the Maccabean period. The Hasidim in the second century BC sources, and the Pharisees as depicted in later sources, were both rigorous supporters of the Torah. According to their traditions, they looked back to the time of Ezra as the formative period for their group's ideal aspiration. Another account by Easton (1897: Power Bible CD) has it that the Pharisees were probably the successors of the Assideans (i.e., the "pious"), a party that originated in the time of Antiochus Epiphanes in revolt against his heathenizing policy. The first mention of them is in a description by Josephus (37–c.100) of the three schools into which the Jews were divided (145 BC); the other two sects were divided into the Essenes and the Sadducees (*Antiquities of the Jews*, 17.42).

The Pharisees in the words of Josephus (probably a Pharisee himself), "is of the kin to the sect of the stoics as the Greeks call them." They believed with the Stoics that all things and events were controlled by fate, yet not so absolutely as entirely to destroy the liberty of the human will. One certain feature of the Pharisees, however, is that they were politically involved in the dynastic struggles at the end of the second century BC, as Josephus attests. However, their strategy seems to have been to acquiesce in whatever foreign power that dominated their land so long as they could shape the lives of the Jewish people. This goal was to be achieved by political involvement that could coerce Jews to obey the Torah. Josephus informs us that when Alexandra became queen (76–69 BC), she turned over to the Jewish state "if she ruled the nation, the Pharisees ruled her." He further describes them as "having a reputation for excelling the rest of their nation in the observance of religious piety and as exact exponents of the law" (Whiston 2006, 52–54). They were able to manipulate the queen to preserve the façade of her royal authority, while actually controlling the lives of her subjects by forcing conformity to their interpretation of the Torah.

## The Pharisees and the Torah (Law)

Like the Scribes, the Pharisees looked upon the Torah of Moses as the definitive revelation of God's will. Unlike the Sadducees, they also venerated the prophetic writings, and another group called holy writings (Hagiographa) that were eventually to be accepted as authoritative. Indeed, it was the Pharisees who finally (about AD 90) determined the contents of the Hebrew Bible; they went a step further because they also stressed the existence and validity of an oral Torah (Howard, 52–54). If the Mishnah portrays faithfully what the Pharisees were like even with minimum accuracy, then we can see that although God has fully revealed his will in the written Torah, new rules of conduct had to be worked out if the written Torah were to be understood and obeyed in the face of ever-changing external circumstances. It would have been their firm conviction that every decision in life must be governed by the Torah that led them to develop elaborate principles of specific rules to govern conduct in every conceivable situation. A rule or instruction so derived to set forth the relevant meaning of the written Torah was called a Halakah.

Through the oral tradition, the Pharisees found outlet for their religious imaginations always of necessity oriented toward the written Torah. It, among other things, enabled them to incorporate into their thinking the apocalyptic and eschatological insights which became increasingly important during the second century BC, and later. Such expectations as the victorious coming of God's kingdom, the coming of the messiah, and the resurrection of the dead, assumed an important place in pharisaic thought (Howard, 44–49).

## The Meaning of *"Sit on Moses' Seat"* (Mt 23:2)

In Greek, this phrase from Jesus' warning reads, "ἐπι τῆς Μωῦσεως καθεδρας εκαθισαν" (epi tês Môuseôs kathedras ekathisan). The genomic or timeless aorist tense, εκαθισαν (ekathisan), is not the aorist "for" the perfect. The "seat of Moses" is a brief form for the chair of the professor whose function it is to interpret Moses. "The heirs of Moses" authority, by an unbroken tradition, can deliver ex-cathedra pronouncements on his teaching (Robert 2008). Manson T. W. (1975, 227–39) discloses that recent archeological work in Palestine shows that the seat of Moses was no mere figure of speech but part of the furniture of the synagogue. The first seat of Moses was unearthed at Hammath by Tiberias and was followed by another in Chorazin (Manson 1975). The scribes and the Pharisees sit on Moses's seat, as teachers or doctors of the Law (νομοδιδάσκάλος, nomodidaskalos) of Moses; they were the only religious guides whom the people had. So they were obliged to follow them as expounders of the law but were by no means to look to them as living exemplifications of that law.

By the beginning of the Christian era, major political changes had taken place in Palestine that directly contributed to the transformation of the Pharisees and their history, and of the subsequent history of Judaism as a whole. This was basically the coming of Pompey in 63 BC and the installation of the Herodian family as puppet king of the Jews, which resulted in the political impotency of the Jews, and the Pharisees in particular. The gospels, though hostile to the Pharisees, picture them as primarily concerned about purity issues: personal purity, food laws, sacrificial offerings, Sabbath observances that emphasis is discernable in the oldest layers of the rabbinic traditions. Though they were written down in their present form, centuries later they reflect the concern that dominated the pharisaic movement in the period before AD 70 (Howard 1997, 53–54).

## The Importance of the Pharisee during Jesus' Time

Easton (1897, 53–54) reports that during the time of Jesus, the Pharisees were the popular party (Jn 7:48). They were extremely accurate and minute in all matters appertaining to the law of Moses (Mt 9:14, 23:15; Lk 11:39, 18:12). Paul, when brought before the council of Jerusalem, professed himself a Pharisee (Acts 23:6, 26:4–5). There was much that was sound in their creed, yet their system of religion was a form and nothing more. Theirs was a lax morality (Mt 5:20, 15:4.8, 23:3, 14, 23, 25; Jn 8:7). On the first notice of them in the New Testament (Mt 3:7), they are ranked by Jesus with the Sadducees as γεννήματα εχιλνων (gennêmata echidnôn, "generation of vipers"). They were noted for their self-righteousness and their pride (Mt. 9, 11; Lk 7:39, 18:11, 12). They were frequently rebuked by our Lord (Mt 12:39, 16:1–4). From the beginning of his ministry, the Pharisees showed themselves bitter and persistent enemies of Jesus. They could not bear his doctrines, and they sought by every means to destroy his influence among the people. Herein lays the importance of the Pharisees during the time of Jesus.

Jesus' polemic against the Pharisees, "hypocrites" (Mt 23:13, 16, 23, 25, 27, 29) is noteworthy. They are attacked for their failure to practice Judaism sincerely, guide others to live Judaism correctly, interpret the scriptures, and attend the major principles of the law and Jewish way of life. They are used as negative examples for how a community leader should act (Mt 23:4–7) and are contrasted with Christian leaders who should be characterized by lowliness (Mt 23:8–12). The Pharisees comprise the most constant opposition to Jesus in Galilee. They challenge Jesus' authority as a religious and social leader by assaulting its divine source (Mt 9:32–34, 12:22–30) and argue with him concerning divorce (Mt 19:3–9 in Judea). After Jesus attacks the Pharisees with series of parables which they perceive as directed against them (Mt 21:45–46), they plot against Jesus (Mt 22:15), and their hostility brackets the crucifixion of Jesus. The Pharisees are not only part of the local leadership whose influence over the people, and power over social norms, are being challenged and diminished by Jesus, but they are also in direct contact with the more powerful forces of the Jerusalem leadership who condemned and crucified Jesus.

The importance of the Pharisees during Jesus' time, therefore, is enshrined in the fact that they constituted a great opposition toward the ministry of Jesus and virtually opposed every teaching of Jesus. They were his achrival, and the teachings of Jesus were contrary to most of theirs.

1. While it was the aim of Jesus to call men to the law of God itself as the supreme guide of life, the Pharisees, upon the pretense of maintaining it intact, multiplied minute precepts and distinctions to such an extent that the whole life of the Israelite was hemmed in and burdened on every side by instructions so numerous and trifling that the law was almost, if not wholly, lost sight of. These "traditions" as they were called had long been gradually accumulating. Of the trifling character of these regulations, innumerable instances are to be found in the Mishna. Such were their washings before they could eat bread, and the special minuteness with which the forms of this washing were prescribed; their bathing when they returned from the market; their washing of cups, pots, brazen vessels, etc.; their

fasting twice in the week, Lk 18:12, were their tithing; Mt 23:23 and such, finally, were those minute and vexatious extensions of the law of the Sabbath, which must have converted God's gracious ordinance of the Sabbath's rest into a burden and a pain. These Jesus condemned.

2.  It was a leading aim of the Redeemer to teach men that true piety consisted not in forms, but in substance; not in outward observances, but in an inward spirit. The whole system of Pharisaic piety led to exactly opposite conclusions. The lowliness of piety was, according to the teaching of Jesus, an inseparable concomitant of its reality, but the Pharisees sought mainly to attract the attention and to excite the admiration of men (Mt 6:2, 6, 16; 23:5, 6; Lk. 14:7). Indeed, the whole spirit of their religion was summed up not in confession of sin and in humility, but in a proud self-righteousness at variance with any true conception of man's relation to either God or his fellow creatures.

3.  With all their pretenses to piety, they were in reality avaricious, sensual, and dissolute (Mt 23:25; Jn 13:7). They looked with contempt upon every nation but their own (Lk. 10:29). Finally, instead of endeavoring to fulfill the great end of the dispensation whose truths they professed to teach, and thus bringing men to the hope of Israel, they devoted their energies to making converts to their own narrow views, which with all the zeal of proselytes were more exclusive and more bitterly opposed to the truth than they were themselves (Smith 2008).

Josephus (*Antiquities of the Jews*, bk XVIII) compared the Pharisees to the sect of the Stoics (Whitson 2006). He observed that they lived frugally, in no respect giving in to luxury. We are not to suppose that there were not many individuals among them who were upright and pure, for there were such men as Nicodemus, Gamaliel, Joseph of Arimathea, and Paul.

## Against the Pharisees

Jesus' anger, which could be sensed throughout his encounters with his enemies, now breaks forth in a magnificent and terrible diatribe as he excoriates their perversion of Israel's religious spirit. Addressing the crowd and his disciples, he warns them that while obedience is due to their religious leaders insofar as they are authentic and authoritative witnesses of Mosaic traditions, their hypocrisy, lack of charity, love of ostentation, and pomposity are not to be imitated (Mt 23:3). It is, however, important to note at this juncture that Jesus in his condemnations of the Pharisees recorded in the New Testament is in fact referring to the hypocritical Pharisees (David 1960, 73–74). Among the five classes is the "shoulder Pharisees" with his good deeds on his shoulder; there are also the God-fearing Pharisees, like the Hebrew patriarch Job; and the "God-loving Pharisees." These last appear even in the Gospel as sympathetic to Jesus (see Lk 7:37, 13:31), if not to his ideas (Perlewitz 1988, 148–156).

Against the Pharisees or pharisaic lifestyle, Jesus pronounces seven judgments, one antithesis of the beatitudes. They refused to enter the kingdom and yet prevent others from entering; contemporary Jewish proselytizing (then in a flourishing state) results in perversion not conversion; pharisaic casuistry exemplified by excusing from vows to God in order to destroy the essence of the Old Testament religious spirit (the basis of the religious life); they confused external religious observances with the spirit of the Mosaic code (justice, mercy, and good faith); formalism has strangled the interior religious spirit; hypocrisy cloaks the absence of virtues, and though they honor the prophets with shrines, they equivalently admit decent from the prophets murder.

The fierce crescendo is reached as Jesus predicts the awful destiny of these traducers of Mosaic institutions. The importance of the Pharisees during the time of Jesus cannot therefore be overemphasized, for one can conveniently assert that all through his ministry, the Pharisees presented a stumbling block and stiff-neck opposition, and Jesus spent a great deal of his lifetime trying to counter their influences on the people, and also to teach the people the right religious piety and the best way to keep or observe the laws of Moses (Harrington 1980, 50–125). However, Jesus had no problem with their authority but with their way of life, which culminated to oppression of God's people.

## The Pharisees of the Present-Day Religion

In order to understand who the Pharisees of the present Christian religion are, it will be necessary to highlight in brief the characteristics, function, and position they occupy in the Jewish setting. First and foremost, they were a special people who opted to live and uphold Judaism in a more radical way than the rest of the Jews. Secondly, they occupy "the seat of Moses"; hence, they were in charge of the law, and the onus lied on them to teach it and teach it very well. Pejoratively speaking, the Pharisees were seen during the time of Jesus as hypocrites and those who make life more difficult for people. From the ongoing so far, one can succinctly figure out that the "religious men and women" (i.e. the pope, the cardinals, the bishops, the priest/pastors, religious men and women under vows, etc.) of today are the Pharisees of our time. The reason is not far-fetched; they are "the separated" who "vowed" to follow Jesus Christ more closely and radically. By virtue of this closeness as in the days of Jesus, they are "teachers" or "doctors of the Law" (νομοδιδάσκάλος, nomodidaskalos). The rest of the Christians learn from and look up to them for interpretation of the message of Christ. They sit on what one could reframe as "the chair or seat of Peter (the Moses of Christians era)," to whom the Lord entrusted the keys to the kingdom of heaven (Mt 16:17–19). They are the direct successors of Peter, the first pope. They are also the champions of religious piety by their constant prayers, habits, and study of the scriptures.

However, all true Christian in a sense could be said are Pharisees. This is because all true Christians (baptized though) share in the royal priesthood of Christ (1 Pt. 2: 9) (basileion hierateuma, cf. Ex 19:6; Rev. 1:6, 5:10). The official in Christian churches is πρέσβυτέρος, presbuteros (episcopos), not hiereus. We are all hiereis, priests, (cf. 1 Pe 2:5, Robert, 53–54). By virtue of this baptism, the Christian has accepted to become a partaker in the life of Christ and of the Church founded by him. Thus, every Christian is to be an *"auta Christus,"* living out the word and law of God. Having expanded the pharisaic scope to include all baptized Christians, it is however important to stress that the greatest burden and onus of Pharisaism rests with and hovers around the pastors and religious of the Christian religions of our time. The obvious cannot be overstressed here because they are the ones judging from every ramification, who are occupying the "the seat of Moses" (i.e., the mantle of leadership). They epitomize the law and religious piety. Vatican II Council (CCC 77) speaking on the authority for transmission and authentic interpretation of divine revelation asserts that in order that the full and living Gospel might always be preserved in the church, the apostles left bishops as their successors. They gave them their own position of teaching authority, but the task of giving an authentic interpretation of the word of God, whether in its written form or in the form of Tradition, have been entrusted to the living teaching office of the church (the Magisterium) alone. Its authority in this matter is exercised in the name of Jesus Christ (Flannery 2007, 666–75).

From the above excerpt, one can conveniently infer or conclude that the Magisterium has the sole authority of interpreting the scripture. However, this authority extends to the pastors and whomever she (the Magisterium) has empowered to exercise it, and all these holistically viewed, are the Pharisees of our time.

## Conclusion

Although the literary understanding of the meaning of Pharisees or who the Pharisee is has been very pejorative (especially in this present age), it is evident that the term has been wrongly employed and used only to denote a hypocritical way of life. The lay persons (lay faithful) are not to blame for this. First, it could be due to their level of understanding of the scriptures. Second, it could perhaps be attributed to the way Jesus Christ Himself employed or used the term when warning his followers. However, it suffices to note here that Jesus had no quarrel with one being a Pharisee, rather he advocated for justice and the right use of the position. He never condemned the office of the Pharisees, but he condemned the way of life of the occupiers of the seat, which is supposed to be an honorable seat (for to occupy the seat of the man of God, Moses, one must be prepared to live an honorable and impeccable life).

The lesson here is that we ought to listen to whatever we are truly taught from the word of God, even by "wicked teachers", but in a way so that we abstain from their evil behavior. Also, because God appointed the order, the Lord would therefore have his word to be heard even from the mouth of hypocrites and hirelings. Paul admonishes us thus on this issue: "Some indeed preach Christ even of envy and strife; and some also of good will, but the other of love... What then? Notwithstanding, every way, whether in pretense, or in truth, Christ is preached; and I therein do rejoice, yes, and will rejoice" (Phil. 2:15–18).

Finally, the foregoing discussion on the Pharisees challenges the religious of today to live above par in order to be truly what we preach to and teach the people of God who to look up to us for good examples. As the Pharisees of our time (who "sit on the chair of Peter"), we have a great task ahead of us. We are like a house built on the hilltop, like one living in a glass house, who must not cast stones. The people of God are ready to listen to us like humble sheep. If we live like the Pharisees of Jesus' time rather than like Jesus Himself, then we are like salt that has lost its taste and only good to be trampled upon by the people of God (Mt. 5, 13). Of course, they will not hesitate to trample upon us, as experience has already proved. On the other hand, if we live out in spirit and in truth what we profess, preach, and teach the people of God, then we can say with Paul the true apostle, the repented and rejuvenated Pharisee, "I have fought the good fight, I have finished the race, I have kept the faith" (2 Tim 4:7–8.)

Finally, the problem is not sitting on the "seat of Moses" or being the "successors of Peter" but being faithful to what it takes to occupy such an exalted position without abusing it. There is nothing wrong in being a Pharisee, but everything will be wrong if we live and fashion our lives on that of the Pharisees of Jesus' time.

# THE INFLUENCE OF HELLENISM ON THE SOCIO-CULTURAL AND RELIGIOUS LIFESTYLE OF THE JEWISH STATE: 400 BC–6 BC (VIS-À-VIS AD 1)

*The Close of the NT Era*

## Introduction

In the second half of the second century BC, the Jews and Judaism went through a serious crisis. The outcome of that crisis shaped the development of all latter Judaism and so determined in part the setting for the emergence of the Church. When the Persian king Cyrus overthrew the Babylonian empire in 539 BC, he gave permission for the captive Jews in Babylonia to return to Palestine (Ezra 1). Even before these Jews returned from exile, Greek wares and culture had begun to make their way into Palestine. When Alexander the Great (356–323) invaded Near East and took over Palestine, the impact of Greek culture on the Jews increased (Filson 1952, 3). Sean Frayne (1980, 9) notes that:

Mention of the Greek world naturally brings to mind classical Athenian life and culture that has given such a lasting legacy to mankind and which Christianity has done so much to foster… However, the Greek world that contributed enormously to the development of Christianity was a different character to that classical high point that was Athens. It is usually designated "Hellenistic" and its beginning is associated with the conquest of Alexander the Great of Macedon, the powerful king of great might who does as he pleases.

Alexander himself did not live long to enjoy the fruits of his great conquest that took him from his barren homeland in Northern Greece to the Indus River in the space of ten short years (333–323 BC). However, those conquests had set in motion cultural, social, and religious trends that could not be reversed despite the splitting of this empire among various generals and bitter rivalries that marked the relationships between them: the Ptolemies in Egypt, the Seleucids in Asia, and the Antigonids in Macedonia. After centuries of struggle in which the political empire of Alexander was never reunited, each kingdom fell in turn to Rome. Macedonia felled in 146 BC, Syria in 64 BC, and Egypt, finally, in 30 BC.

## What Is Hellenism and Its Significance?

From the first usage of the term, Hellenism has meant a variety of things generally pertaining to Greek world after the conquest of Alexander the Great. Love for things Greek is often called Hellenism, after the name that the Greeks called themselves, Hellenes. But Greek influence in the other countries of the ancient world is usually referred to as Hellenistic, especially after the time of Alexander the Great. The mixture of Greek and North Eastern ideals produced a combined culture in most places. This is especially in Jewish territories. It should be noted that Judah and the rest of Palestine had

31

already known much Greek influences before the time of Alexander. Attic pottery from Athens area had reached Judah as early as the seventh century BC, and Greek money was in common use after the fifth century. Greek styles in furniture and bronze were popular among the wealthy in the post-exilic period as a whole (Boadt 1984, 496–7). From the discussion so far, it is now obvious that the word Hellenism is not to be taken in the sense of classical, literary, or intellectual training. It refers to something vaster, more human, and more complex: a type or a form of civilization which was the product of the "Greek genius," Alexander the Great.

## Influence of Hellenism on the Socio-Religious and Cultural Life of the Jewish State

The conquest of Alexander and the policies of the Ptolemy's government after him established certain official practices aimed at turning the Jewish way of life more toward a Hellenistic culture. The Greek rulers set up a large number of new towns populated entirely by pagan Greeks and others; they organized and fostered trade with the Greeks in the West. The new cities had Greek temples, gymnasiums for leisure and sports stadiums for horse racing, youth centers for the cultivation of health and education, and of course, theaters. Knowledge of Greek became very important for anyone who dealt with the government or traveled to other cities and regions. Greek education's stress on scientific and philosophical knowledge created a natural superiority complex over "barbarians" who held on to the older ways of Israelite life. The strong attraction for Greek ways and Greek education, however, only took hold among the upper class in Judah (Boadt 1984, 496–7).

That Hellenism had a great influence on the religious lifestyle of the Jewish state during the period is in fact as obvious as the air we breathe. Hans Dieter (1965, 127) comments that: "The Judeans were not immune to this impact, and consequently Hellenism had some impact upon Jewish religion." One of the greatest influences was the importation of foreign gods, ideologies, and religion as a whole into the Jewish territories, and forcing the Jews to worship them. Worthy of note is the case of the profaning of the temple in Jerusalem by Antiochus Epiphanes (c. 215–164 BC) who coveted and looted the temple treasury (1 Mac 5:15–16); prohibited the Jewish worship; introduced the worship of Zeus and also replaced the Levitical ordinances with the cult of the Olympian Zeus and Hellenistic way of life (2 Mac 6:1–6). Hellenistic altars were built, and the worship of Zeus was instituted in Jerusalem. The climax of this abomination came in 167 BC and is referred to as "the abomination of the desolation" (cf. Dan 11:31, 12:11; cf. Mk 13:14) when Antiochus Epiphanes built an altar of Zeus right upon the Altar of Sacrifice in the temple of Jerusalem. According to Raymond Brown (2007, 57), in principle, the sacrifices were offered to him. Robert A. and Feuillet A (1965, 14) capture the resistance that followed in the following fashion:

> In the face of the threat which Hellenism posed for the monotheistic faith and the national tradition, Palestine Judaism braced itself and rebelled: in the fight-to-death which took place between Antiochus IV of Syria (Antiochus Epiphanes) and the Maccabees (167-141) the foreigner was conquered and the mounting tide failed to engulf the little Jewish island by Jerusalem.

Alexander's campaigns had opened up new trade routes never before explored, and the riches of the East began to flow westward in the preceding centuries. The new wealth was mainly concentrated in trade and commerce. Therefore, everywhere one finds the emergence of a wealthy middle class who were able to profit in some way from the new possibilities. Among the Jews, the Sadducean priestly aristocracy that had ruled the temple state of Judea since Persian times had to make way for the Pharisees who, Josephus tells us, were particularly popular with the townspeople (i.e., the middle new class), even in matters pertaining to temple worship. Though the differences of religious point of view were operative, there were also very definite social implications in this shift in the balance of power, even in religious community (*Complete Works of Josephus*, 1862). While the Jewish Hellenistic towns were bursting with a new vitality, the countryside still remained the backbone of all Hellenistic economies (Frayne 1980, 9). However, this did not necessarily mean that the lot of the country people improved. Inevitably, the slide into brigandage was easy and frequent, and one meets highway robbers everywhere in the countryside of the ancient world eking out an existence by attacking the trading and other caravans away from the more protected areas.

Among the Jews, there was a great tension between those who believed in a future under Hellenistic culture and those who resisted it as pagans and unfaithful to Israelite religion. Many young people enthusiastically adopted Greek fashions and custom. Also, along with the Greek education came a lifestyle that was often fixed on material pursuits, idleness for those with the money to afford it, and a sensual orientation that was foreign to Israelite ideals expressed in the prophets and the book of Proverbs. There was also an ambitious greed in the Greek way. In the words of Lawrence Boadt (1984, 687):

> On the other hand, the free movement in the Hellenistic world also allowed customs and ideas to flow the other way as well, and many oriental beliefs from Persia and the East began to influence Jewish thought in the late Old Testament period. Apocalyptic language, concepts of heaven and hell, and a more positive view of afterlife all entered biblical books in this period, probably mostly from the East. It was an age of syncretism, in which peoples took in new ways of thinking from both West and East.

A remarkable influence of Hellenism on the social and economic life of the Jews is the taxation system. This had undergone far-reaching changes as a result of the economic and commercial developments in the wake of Alexander's conquests. Tax, and tax collections, played quite an important role in the NT. Jesus was born according to Luke, as the whole world was being enrolled (Luke 2, 1). The early Hellenistic monarchies left the taxes of particular areas or countries to certain individuals who were responsible for the amount of the tribute that had been levied on the area in question. That such a position was extremely lucrative can be seen from a story in Josephus which tells of the keen bidding that went on for the right to gather the taxes of Palestine. Naturally, such an alien system caused great bitterness, since the native (Jew) who engaged in tax collecting was regarded not just as financial oppressors but also as collaborationist with the enemy. The tribute in question could be based on a land tax or a poll or head tax or both, so that nobody was likely to escape the net. So Jews were in a particularly unfavorable position in regard to taxes because of the sacred obligation their religion imposed on them to provide for their temple and its priesthood (Frayne 980).

## Conclusion

The small island of Jews in Palestine could not keep out Greek influence even if they wanted to. Egypt and Syria were Greek states, and the Negev desert, Palestine territory, Galilee, the states across the Jordan, and Phoenicia were all filled with Greek cities. Even Samaria became more a Greek city than Jewish. The Decapolis, the league of ten Greek cities in Galilee and Trans-Jordan, which is mentioned in the NT, was already flourishing in the second century BC. This early Greek period also gave rise to a number of Jewish writings in the style of short novels: Esther, Judith, Ruth, and Tobit. In AD 1, Jesus started his movement. In the eyes of Jesus, Hellenism was represented in Palestine by Roman occupation and by the Jewish authorities imposed on the Jews by Rome.(cf. Mk 12, 15–22, 8, 15, 12, 13; Luke 13, 31–33). The influence of Hellenism on Christianity is remarkable in that the NT was written in Greek language spoken and understood most by Christians, a majority of whom lived in the gentile territory, with Greek as the official and "one-world language" of Hellenism.

# THE MEDIEVAL SPIRITUALITY: AD 500–1500

## *Christian Spirituality*

### Introduction

Our concern in this work or brief exposition is primarily with a period of Western Europe, which has had a deep impact upon modern Christian thought. Middle Ages or Medieval spirituality is therefore used to refer to Western European spirituality of the era. During this time, the precursors of many modern institutions, such as universities and bodies of representative government, were created.

### Clarification of Terms

Defining periods in history is notoriously difficult. Part of the problem lies in the absence of universal agreement on the defining characteristics of eras. This is especially the case with the Middle Ages, Renaissance, and the modern periods (McGrath 2001, 33). The term *Middle Ages* is a period in the history of Europe that lasted from about AD 350–1450 (Microsoft Encarta, 1993–2008). This term (Middle Ages) was invented by writers of the Renaissance and seems to have come into general use toward the end of the sixteenth century. The writers of the Renaissance were anxious to discredit the period intervening between the glories of classical antiquity and their own time. They thus invented the term Middle Ages to refer to an uninteresting and stagnant phase separating two important and creative periods. The adjective *medieval* means "relating to the Middle Ages." Therefore, the term *the Spirituality of the Middle Ages* or *medieval spirituality* has passed into general use and can generally be interpreted to mean "Western European Spirituality in the period between the end of the dark ages and the 16th century" (McGrath 2001, 33). It must, however, be appreciated that the term is imprecise, disputed, and open to various interpretations. When the so-called Dark Ages finally lifted from Western Europe, giving birth to the Middle Ages, the scene was set for revival in every field of academic work.

## Movements During the Middle Ages

The Middle Ages gave rise to two of the most important intellectual movements in the history of thoughts: scholasticism and humanism (though toward the end of this era). An understanding of the nature of both movements is essential to any attempt to make sense of the development of Christian spirituality during the period, or to understand the religious and intellectual pressures which eventually gave rise to the Reformation. The two movements are related, in that the latter is generally regarded as being a response to the cultural poverty and theological overprecision of the former. We will, therefore, dwell briefly on these movements.

## Scholasticism

Scholasticism is probably one of the most despised intellectual movements in human history. It derived its name from the great medieval *scholae* (schools), in which questions of theology and philosophy were debated, often with a degree of intricacy which has astonished as much as amazed later historians. The very word *scholasticism* could be argued to be the invention of humanist writers anxious to discredit the movement which it represented. The Middle Ages were seen as little more than an intermezzo between the cultural magnificence of antiquity and its rivals during Renaissance (Alister 2001, 36–37). Similarly, the term *scholasticism* (scholastic) was used by humanist to refer equally disparagingly to the ideas of Middle Ages. Scholasticism is best regarded as the medieval movement, flourishing in the period 1200–1500, which placed emphasis upon the rational justification of religious belief and systematic presentation of those beliefs. It does not refer to a specific system of beliefs, but to a particular way of doing and organizing theology.

As early as the ninth century, Dun Scotus Erigena (+870) had tried to introduce Platonic philosophy into traditional study of sacred doctrine, but he was condemned for his efforts. Theology continued to be a study of scripture interpreted according to the fathers of the Church. In the eleventh century, however, two factors contributed greatly to the rise of scholasticism: the concordance of the patristic texts on theological questions and the bitter dispute concerning the respective roles of faith and reasons, revelation and speculation, theology and philosophy. It was immediately evident from the compilation of patristic teaching that many of the texts were incompatible with one another, if not contradictory. It was also evident that human reason must have some role to play in the understanding and development of the truths of faith (Aumann 2006, 13).

## Humanism

The term *humanism* has now come to mean a worldwide view which denies the existence or relevance of God or which is committed to a purely secular outlook. However, this is not what the word meant at the time or period of the Middle Ages. Most humanists of the time were religious and concerned to purify and renew Christianity rather than eliminate it. In the recent past, two major interpretations of the movement were predominant. According to the first, humanism was a movement devoted to the study of classical languages and literature. According to the second, humanism was basically a set of ideas comprising the new philosophy of the period. Humanism was concerned with how ideas were obtained and expressed rather than with the actual substance of the ideas.

## Spirituality

What is now called spiritual theology has been designated by various names throughout the history of theology. Some have simply called it spirituality; others have named it spiritual life, devout life, supernatural life, interior life, mystical evolution, and theology of Christian perfection. In its widest sense, spirituality refers to any religious or ethical value that is concretized as an attitude or spirit from which one's actions flow. The concept of spirituality is not restricted to any particular religion or even age; it applies to any person who has belief in the divine or transcendent and fashions a lifestyle according to one's religious convictions. In this context, one can speak of Zen, Buddhist, Jewish, Muslim, Christian spirituality, as well the spirituality of a particular age or epoch. Spirituality does not become an area of theological study and investigation until it fits this description given by Paul Evdokimov (1966, 17): "The life of man facing his God, participating in the life of God; the spirit of man listening to the spirit of God."

During the medieval era, two distinct levels of spirituality were evident: popular and professional spiritualities. Popular spirituality could be distinguished from professional. Mass conversions, low levels of general education, and pastoral neglect promoted religious experience characterized by cult of relics, magic under the guise of sacraments, pilgrimages simply for the sake of travel, and thinly veiled paganism. Professional spirituality was informed by study and guidance. This distinction does not intend to overlook the uneducated saints, nor self-righteous monks and nuns.

Medieval spirituality would be examined here according to two levels that may be distinguished, the real or existential level of individual spiritual experience and the spirituality of social group and varying spiritual traditions. It suffices to note here that the easiest way of accessing the spirituality of individuals on existential levels is by examining their autobiographies, personal letters, prayers, sermons etc.

## Some Medieval Schools of Spirituality

Due to the fact that the Holy Spirit moves in a variety of ways to lead individuals to perfection, with the result that saint differs from saint in glory, there are styles of Christian spirituality sufficiently diverse to be classified as schools of spirituality. The cause of the diversity as St. Thomas Aquinas (1225–74) states is that God dispenses his gifts of grace variously so that the beauty and perfection of the church may result from these various degrees. The schools of spirituality are thus an indication of the diversity of the ways of the spirit, proof of the Church's respect for personal freedom in following the impulses of the spirit, and a corporate witness to the variety of ways in which the mystery of Christ is imaged in the mystical body of the Church (Downey 1995, 1035).

One of the main sources of the various schools of medieval spirituality was the rise of different monastic traditions and, later, of religious orders. An exceptionally influential monastic movement was that derived from Benedict of Norcia, whose famous *Rule* became the guide for most western monks from the ninth century onward (Conn 2006, 975–77). In the medieval period, the monastic life and ideals were the guiding principles of the Church. It was in the monasteries that Christian virtues were arranged for the external use. Promotion of spiritual welfares was also directed by the monks. In fact, some held that life in the monastery was the inspiration of Christianity in the West. Some held that it was religious arrogance, but the monks refuted that this is not true. Nevertheless, some monastic writers held that life in the monastery was indeed the realization of the Christian life. That is, being Christian is being a monk. This notion was based on the biblical injunction in Acts 4:32, where the Christian community shared things in common, *"they are one in heart and soul."*

In the medieval period, the monastic life was marked with communal life. This was their spiritual and material values which some writers held to be the mark of the Christians in the medieval period. They abandoned private ownership for community. For them, this manifested what the church should be, that is holiness of God mediated by human beings, a holiness separated from the world. This is what Saint Augustine of Hippo (354–430) demonstrated in his division of the world into two cities, the city of God and the city of man. (*The City of God, Civitate Dei*, AD 246). The spiritual yearning of this time was the restoration of paradise so that monks through prayer enter into contemplation. For the monks, the spirituality of the lay or laity was pointless or unnecessary because for them, the life in the monastery is the locus of grace and the taste of paradise (Aumann 2006).

## Religious Orders

Despite the prohibition by the council of Lyons in 1274 of new religious institutes, two new orders came into existence in the thirteen century, the Franciscans and Dominicans. As mendicant orders, they both emphasized a strict observance of poverty. As apostolic orders, they were dedicated to the ministry of preaching. The mendicant orders were not simply a development of monasticism; much more than that, they were a response to vital needs of the church: the need to return to Christian life of the gospel *(vita apostolica);* the need to reform religious life especially in the area of poverty; the need to extirpate the heresies of the time; the need to raise the level of the diocesan clergy; the need to preach the gospel and administer the sacraments to the faithful. This was especially true of the Dominicans, who were consciously and explicitly designed to meet the needs of the times and to foster the "new theology," scholasticism.

## Secular Clergy

The spirituality of the secular clergy (what most of us popularly known today as diocesan priests) often suffered from their being poorly educated and from abuses such as simony, lay investiture of unworthy persons, and other forms of control by feudal lords. The Gregorian reform of the late eleventh century fought the sources of this decline, sought to establish clerical celibacy, and began to promote clement life in communities of canons guided by the rule attributed to Augustine of Hippo.

## The Laity

In the history of Christian spirituality, there was a shift from life in the monastic environment to what is called "the marketplace." That is, the life in the secular or unenclosed setting. The shift was based on the understanding of where grace worked and of where Christian life was lived. During this period of what may be called spiritual revolution, many writers were of the opinion that monastic life was the true pattern of life for the church. For instance, Rupert, abbot of Deutz (+1130), in his treatise on monastic life entitled *De vita vere apostolica* (on the truly apostolic life), asserts that if you desire to consult all the testimonies of scripture, they seem to say nothing other than that the church originated in the monastic life. He also affirmed that it is evident that monks, insofar as they are monks, take their form of life from the apostles. There all apostles were truly monks. This implies for him that every life that is not centered on the monastic way of living will not be called spirituality or Catholic Christian spirituality, forgetting that there are other forms of vocation with their way of doing things. Gerhoh of Reicherberg (+1169), who seem to be more embracing reacted by saying that whoever has renounced at baptism, the devil and all its trappings, even if that person is not a cleric or monk, has nonetheless definitely renounced the world, whether rich or poor, noble or self, merchant or peasant, all who are committed to the Christian faith reject everything hostile to this name. By implication, he holds that both monks and lay faithful can achieve salvation outside the monastery as far as that person abhors those things that are negative or unfriendly to Christian teaching and faith.

In fact, what this two contenders advocate for is the dissimilarity. While Rupert champions the life in the monastery to be the true Christian vocation, Gerhoh on his own side advocates for a change in Christian awareness, which is one of the basic contentions of the medieval Christian thinkers. That is, the life of lay Christian, as well as the life of the monks or cleric, would emerge as the sphere in which salvation was worked out. This is what prompted James of Victory to observe that clerics, monk, and lay faithful who serve the

Lord under the gospel rule and live by the authority of the Church participate in Christian life. The shift of Christian life from the monastery to marketplace, that is, secular life, signed a new perception of the laity and their spirituality in the medieval church (Downey, 1034). Beguines (women) and Beghards (men) were mostly middle- or upper-class persons from northwestern European cities who led lives of chastity, poverty, and devotion without belonging to a religious order. Beguines first appeared in the late twelfth century and were much more numerous than their male counterparts, the Beghards, who first appeared in the early thirteenth century. In fact, the movement was not only predominantly female, but it is noteworthy for being the only medieval female religious movement not inspired or guided by men. The spirituality of these women and men seems to have been analogous to that of the mendicant orders. That is, it grew from a desire to follow the gospel ideal by lives of simplicity and piety without cloistered separation from the world.

Third orders were another manifestation of lay spirituality. In the twelfth century, lay penitential groups sought Christian perfection and life of penance while carrying on their life and work in the world. With the rise of the Dominicans and Franciscans in the thirteenth century, some of these groups sought links with these orders for spiritual guidance and help. They were gradually organized in to third orders of the Dominicans and Franciscans, sharing the spiritual benefits of these communities, seeking to live their spirit, and imitating their practices as much as they could while remaining in the world. According to Michael Downey (p. 1034), other important sources of lay spirituality include guilds (association of merchants and craftsmen); *devotion moderna* (the brethren of the common life and the sisters of the common life). Thomas a Kempis (1379–1471) belonged to this group.

## Spiritual Crisis of the Medieval Period

In the medieval period, there was exclusion of social dimension of grace by the monks who held that monastic life is the model for Christian life. This made Church's holiness not to be found in catechesis, preaching, or celebration of the sacrament among the people. Rather, it was placed in being virtuous and living more humbly than anyone else. Another thing that led to spirituality crisis during this period was rigid penitential code, which led to the reformation of the clergy which was advocated by Pope Gregory VII. In fact, during this period, monastic centers were involved in training theologians, administrators, and missionaries who served not only the church but also in courts and secular administrations. Charitable institutions which serve a number of purposes like care for the sick, distribution of food, clothing to the needy, shelter for pilgrims and travelers were established by the monasteries. In addition, tax system, judicial structures, and the executions of legal decision were often administered by monks. In the medieval period, there was rigidity in spiritual practices which has monks as its leaders and administrators. The society of that time was made up of three traditional structures: the knights (who held sword of temporal power), the priests (who wielded the sword of spiritual power), and the monks (who shed tears of constant prayer).

## Some Key Theologians of the Period

Of the many theologians to have emerged during this period of enormous creativity, some are of special importance and of interest. The early part of the medieval period was dominated by developments in France. Several monasteries produced outstanding Christian writers and thinkers, for example Lanfranc (c. 1010–89) and Anselm of Canterbury (c. 1033–1109), both from the monastery at Bec in Normandy. The University of Paris soon established itself as a leading center of theological speculation with such scholars as Peter Abelard (1079–1142), Albert the Great (1200–80), Thomas Aquinas (c. 1225–74), and Bonaventure (c. 1217–74) (Sudbrack 1975, 1631–32). A central resource to the new medieval interest in theology is also linked with Paris. Some notables include the following.

## Anselm of Canterbury (c. 1033–1109)

While standing at the dawn of the theological renaissance of the twelfth century, Anselm of Canterbury made decisive contributions in two areas of discussion. These include the proof for the existence of God and the rational interpretation of Christ's death upon the cross. One of his work, the *Proslogion* (written around 1079) in many ways anticipates the best aspects of scholastic theology. Anselm's phrase *fides quaerens intellectum* (faith seeking understanding) has passed into widespread use. Anselm is considered the father of scholasticism. Taking Plato and Augustine of Hippo as his guides, he sought to provide a rational basis for that which is believed. Yet, he never failed into the extremes of rationalism, since for him, faith is always the touchstone of theology (Sudbrack 1975, 1631–32).

## Thomas Aquinas (c. 1225–74)

"The angelic doctor" or "the dumb ox" was a Dominican. Despite intense opposition from his family and religious order, he ended up becoming the most important religious thinker of the Middle Ages. Among his works include the *Summa Contra Gentiles* (Summary Against the Gentiles) where he argued in favor of the Christian faith for the benefit of missionaries working among Moslems and Jews, and the *Summa Theologiae*, where he developed a detailed study of key aspects of Christian theology (such as the role of human reason in faith), as well as a detailed analysis of key doctrinal questions (such as the divinity of Christ).

## Dun Scotus (c. 1265–1308)

Dun Scotus, a Franciscan friar was unquestionably one of the first minds of the Middle Ages. Scotus regarded the divine will as taking precedence over the intellect. A doctrine often referred to as "voluntarism." Thomas Aquinas had argued for the primacy of the divine intellect; Scotus opened the way to new approaches to theology based on the assumption of the priority of the divine will. He was the champion of the doctrine of the Immaculate Conception of Mary the mother of Jesus. Thomas had taught that Mary shared the common sinful condition of humanity. She was tainted by sin (*macula*) like everyone else apart from Christ. Scotus, however, argued that Christ, by virtue of his perfect work of redemption, was able to keep Mary free from the taint of original sin.

## William of Ockham (c. 1285–1347)

He is simply and popularly known as Ockham. His razor is often referred to as parsimony (frugality). He insisted that simplicity was a theological and philosophical virtue. His razor eliminated all hypotheses which were not absolutely essential. Earlier medieval theologians had argued that God was oblique to justify sinful humanity by means of what was called a created habit of grace. In other words, an intermediate supernatural entity, infused by God into the human soul, which permitted the sinners to be pronounced justified. Ockham dismissed this notion as an unnecessary, irrelevant and declares that justification was direct acceptance of the individual by God (Alister, p. 64). Ockham was a diehard nominalist (Hahn and Wiker 2013, 47–59).

## St. Bernard (c. 1110–50)

St. Bernard founded "a new kind of militia." The first of the military orders, the Knights Templar was founded in the precinct of the temple at Jerusalem around 1118. Later on, Malta Templar was also founded in Jerusalem. Its mission was to defend Christians in the city of Jerusalem, even by force of arms. The knights observed poverty, chastity, and obedience and were therefore recognized as religious. The problem arises on how to reconcile Christians—indeed men vowed to the evangelical councils—with dedication to war and the necessary killing of the enemy. Yet, even St. Bernard insisted that they are fighting for the Lord, they are to fear neither the danger of being killed nor the sin of killing an enemy. Yet, the crusaders were never considered martyrs, for they were, as St. Peter the hermit (c.

1050–1115) described them, "monks as regards their virtues, but soldiers in their actions (Aumann, p. 113).

## Piety of the Medieval Period

The medieval period witnessed a great deal of religious piety and as such left a great legacy for the Church. Interest in the reading and discussion of the gospel and the reaching of the crusades for the liberation of holy places naturally contributed a great deal to another dominant characteristic of medieval piety. Or better still, spirituality: devotion to the sacred humanity of Christ. This devotion did develop in the twelfth century, however, and because of the worldwide interest in the crusades and the holy land, the devotion of the faithful began to focus more and more on various scenes or "mysteries" of the life of Christ or more on the instruments of the passion and death of Christ. The attention of the faithful was especially fixed on the intensity of Christ's sufferings and, indeed, was preoccupied with that respect.

The name of Jesus was likewise the object of great veneration during this period, propagated by St. Bernard, as was devotion to the sacred humanity of Christ. Also, closely linked to the imitation of Christ was increasing devotion to the Blessed Sacrament. Until the eighth century, Christians firmly believed that the Mass was a continuation of the last supper and that Christ was truly present on the altar. Eventually, theologizing on the Eucharist led to controversy, in the midst of which Bernergure of Tours (AD 999–1088) denied the real presence of Christ in the Blessed Sacraments. The expression *transubstantiation* seemed to have been introduced into the theology of the Eucharist at this time. During this period, a lot of changes were introduced regarding the Eucharist. One of the most notable was the elevation of the host after the consecration of the Mass.

The reception of Communion was infrequent in spite of the great devotion of the people. As a result, the fourth Lutheran Council commanded that Catholics must receive Communion at least once a year, during Easter season. The reason the people seldom received Communion was due to their profound respect for the Eucharist.

They felt obliged to go to confession before Communion even when there was no need to do so. Thus, confession "of devotion" became more and more common. The reservation of the Eucharist in the tabernacle became standard practice, and in 1246, the first diocesan feast in honor of Corpus Christi was celebrated. Later, it was extended and made a universal feast by Pope Urban IV. The pope has hesitated about the promulgation until the clergy and faithful of Orviet brought to him in solemn procession a corporal that was stained red with precious blood that had flowed from a consecrated host. This was on July 19, 1264.

Together with devotion to Christ and veneration of the Blessed Sacrament, the faithful of this period had a filial love for Mary, veneration for the saints and the angels. Marian devotion was promulgated particularly in the monasteries (the Cistercians were called the brothers of Mary). Known prayers and hymns in the twelfth century were "Salve Regina," "Maris Stella," "Alma Redemptoris," and of course, "Ave Maria." However, at this time, the Ave Maria consisted only in the archangel's salutation; the name of Jesus was added in the fifth century. There was also the practice of reciting 50 or even 150 Ave Marias, but rosary was, as we know it, did not come into popular use until later. The angelus was recited only at the ringing of the bell in the evening.

## Conclusion

From the exposition so far, one can conveniently and without much ado describe the medieval spirituality as a spirituality fostered by scholasticism. Other characteristics of the medieval spirituality can thus be recapitulated as including monasticism, which championed prayer (meditation and contemplation); the evangelical councils and asceticism; return to the source of Christian spirituality, which is the scriptures; popular devotions (to the Eucharist, the name of Jesus, the Blessed Virgin Mary, saints and angels, etc); and sacramental spirituality also gained grounds during this period because agreement on the definition of sacraments was reached during this era, likewise the number of sacraments there are.

Furthermore, medieval spirituality interprets its experience of being human as one with God. Thus, it continues patristic themes: grace as divinization; intellect, memory, and will as reflection of the Trinity (e.g., the cloud of the unknowing); the image of God as given from the beginning yet tarnished by sin; and asceticism as the way to develop the true likeness of God (e.g., the imitation of Christ). Finally, this period was innovative, for example, in styles of religious life and art, but it was not revolutionary because it remained firmly rooted in traditions from the previous era.

# WHAT DEFINES PERENNIAL PHILOSOPHY?

*Biblical and Philosophical Interpretation*

## Introduction

In a paper like this one, before examining the various concepts contained therein, it would not be out of place to answer the question which formed the theme of this paper: *"What defines perennial philosophy?"* Or simply put, what is perennial philosophy? Either way, it seems a simple question or rather, a question that is only begging for a mere definition. It is more than this. However, giving the nature and size of this paper, I would give only a brief insight of what perennial philosophy is. Then I shall proceed to treat the following themes: reality and realism; analogy and participation; and divine and human agency. Although other relevant and related sources would be employed to throw more light on issues here, the major source for this paper would be Stephen L. Brock's *The Philosophy of Saint Thomas Aquinas*. Consequently, this means that we shall focus much on Thomas Aquinas's views (and works) on these important themes.

## What Defines Perennial Philosophy?

Perennial philosophy is the belief that at the core of all the great religions and wisdom traditions is the same mystical experience of Ultimate Reality. All the surface disagreements, different names for Ultimate Reality, different myths, etc., are just window-dressing (Nazi 2017). Historically speaking, it has its root in the syncretism of renaissance humanists like Marsilio Ficino and Pico della Mirandola, who suggested that Plato, Jesus, Hermes Trismegistus, and the Kabbalah were all pointing to the same God. Gottfried Wilhelm Leibniz (1646–1716) also championed the *philosophia perennis*, thus coining the phrase "perennial philosophy" (Strickland 2011). The idea then reached a mass-market through Aldous Huxley's 1945 book *The Perennial Philosophy*. For him, it is metaphysics that recognizes a divine reality substantial to the world of things, the psychology that finds in the soul something similar to, or even identical with, divine Reality; and the ethics that places man's final end in the knowledge of the immanent and transcendent ground of all being (Harrod 2010, 2).

Rudiments of the perennial philosophy may be found among the traditionary lore of primitive peoples in every region of the world, and in its fully developed forms, it has a place in every one of the higher religions. However, it suffices to say that perennial philosophy is the ruling spiritual philosophy of our time. It includes in its ranks everyone from Sam Harris, William of Ockham, Immanuel Kant, John Locke, Thomas Hobbs, David Hume, Benedict Spinoza, Descartes, Gottfried W. Leibniz, Machiavelli, Abraham Maslow to Ken Wilber. Perennial philosophy, by being so universalist and essentialist, ends up doing violence to the traditions it tries to cohere. Perennialists tend to rank religions, and even sects within religions. Christianity is usually near or at the bottom. For Aldous Huxley, the Bible was an obstacle to evolution, and Tibetan Buddhism is at the top. Furthermore, perennialists like Huxley, Abraham Maslow, Wilber, or Sam Harris tend to describe this type of philosophy as a "science of consciousness." Thus, they tried to provide empirical certainty for some of the claims of the mystics (Harrod 2010, 2).

## Reality and Realism

Reality is the state of things as they actually exist. Reality includes everything that is and has been, whether or not it is observable or comprehensible. A still broader definition includes that which has existed, exists, or will exist. To say that a thing exists means that it could be both material or immaterial. That is, a "substance" that has its own nature. It could also be a "substance" that cohere in both matter and form, such as human beings and other created things; that coheres only in form, such as angels and spirits, and also, a Being that is in itself without matter or form, God the necessary Being. The axiom of "independent reality" claims that knowledge unconditionally presupposes that the reality known exists independently of the knowledge of it, and that we know it as it exists in this independence.

The most important question that always comes to mind is, can reality be known or can one know the whole of reality? Things do exist, there is no doubt about it. This is because it has to do with the knowledge of the "true existence of a thing." For instance, I know that my mother's name is Anna. Nothing can change this fact. Whether she is alive or dead, her name is Anna. Hence, as Brock L. Stephen (2015, 90), puts it: "Aquinas, thinks that there are many things that we all know and cannot reasonably doubt that we know, even if no formulation of them can preempt all questions." In this regard, the actual knowing of reality depends on the fact that it is knowable, and the knower had the ability or intellect to know or grasp the truth about the thing. I know my mother because she is there;, even when she is not there, I know her, what she looks like. Her picture is not her but only confirms what I know about her. So my knowing her does not depend on her particular picture but on the fact that I have grasped her form and who she really is. "Aquinas argues that by intellect we can know the natures of all bodies or things…it knows them absolutely (Brock, p. 90). Hence, his account of cognition simply takes for granted that we can grasp real things as they really are.

Realism is a position, a mood, a perspective, or a point of view. In effect, it could take different dimensions. Although realism cuts across a board spectrum, it is more common for philosophers to be selectively realist or nonrealist about various topics. Hence, realism is the view that a "reality" of material objects, and possibly of abstract concepts, exists in an external world independently of our minds and perceptions. Historically, realism is a metaphysical claim about this independently existing world. It views knowledge or cognition (knowing) as bearing primarily on representation of things (i.e., ideas, impressions, or external world). Platonic realism abstracts things like numbers, perfect geometric figures, and other things that Plato called forms or ideas that have a real and independent existence, though they are not material objects. Hence, following Plato, some realists think that one can access concrete physical objects directly and fully with only one's perceptual sense data. This realism mistakenly assumes that the information in the perceived sense data or its representation in the mind is quantitatively equal to the information in the physical object (Gallagher 2010, 2).

For Immanuel Kant in *Critique of Pure Reason* (Paul Guyer and Allen W. Wood, eds. 1999, 10–27), these secondary qualities are "phenomena" (things as they appear to one) that could tell us nothing about the "noumena," things as they are in themselves (*das Ding an sich*), which the empiricists called the "primary qualities." These are properties the objects have that are independent of any observer, such as solidity, extension, motion, number, and figure. These qualities exist in the thing itself. Kant thought that some of these qualities can be determined with certainty as synthetic *a priori* truths. Some of these qualities are analytic truths, defined by the logical meanings of linguistic terms. For example, a circle cannot be a square.

Since Aristotle's *Metaphysics*, two kinds of questions (ontological and epistemological) are raised: what exists and how can we know what exists? The ontological status of abstract concepts is a completely different question from the ontology of concrete material objects, though these questions have often been confounded in the history of philosophy. Aristotle believed that to understand an object, its ultimate form had to be understood, which does not change (Michael 2003, 163–83). For example, a rose exists whether or not a person is aware of it. A rose can exist in the mind without being physically present, but ultimately, the rose shares properties with all other roses and flowers (its form), although one rose may be red and another peach-colored.

For Thomas Aquinas, all knowledge originates in sensation, but sense data can be made intelligible only by the action of the intellect, which elevates thought toward the apprehension of immaterial realities. So Thomas's moderate realism holds that true knowledge of things begin with the sense (though not perfect because of its materiality). The perfection of knowledge of things as they are is in the intellect (which has a higher degree of immateriality as well as more cognitive power (STh, 1., q. 80, a. 1). So for him, certainty of knowing or cognizing comes from an experience of the object cognized or known. Our intellect finds its object in something presented by the senses, in particular in what he (Thomas) called *phantasma,* an image produced by the interior sense. It is important to note that even if the external senses are operating, without the phantasma, the intellect cannot work. Thomas often speaks of the intellect "abstracting" its object, which is a nature taken absolutely and universally from the phantasmata (Stephen 2015, 90). This is simply to say that nothing could be in the mind without first being experienced in the senses. Therefore, for Thomas, reliable knowledge of reality beyond the empirical, physical, or concrete world is based solely on experience.

## Analogy and Participation

Analogy is a word with varieties of meanings and, thus, used in different modes. Some of its usage include as a form of reasoning (i.e., reasoning by analogy, which is also called argument from convenience); as a mode of explanation; and as a mode of predication (i.e., analogous predication or making of speeches). Analogy is very important in the study of the mode of being. Aristotle was the first to deal systematically with analogy as a form of predication (Klubertanz 1960). He divides the predicates, according to their modes of signification, into three classes. Aristotle calls the terms of the first class univocal and the terms of the second class equivocal (*New Catholic Encyclopedia*, 2017).

For Thomas Aquinas, all beings are alike, or analogous to, each other in existing. This comparison is the basis of his *analogia entis* (analogy of being). The analogy is said of being in many different ways, but the key to it is the real distinction between existence and essence. Thomas Aquinas (following Aristotle) distinguishes three kinds of predicative analogy. First, attributive analogy. This is when, for example, "strong" is predicated of Samuel, iron, medicine, climate, or color. In this analogy, a quality is predicated properly and intrinsically of the first thing or being, and it is predicated of others because of the relation that they have to the first being. Second is the metaphorical analogy. This is, for example, when "to sleep" is predicated of Jane, and of the sun flower.

In this analogy, a quality is predicated properly only of the first being or thing. While about the other, it is predicated only because of some similarity between their situations, especially that of the first. Third is proportional analogy. This is when, for example, "substance," "nature," "being," "cause" are predicated of man, animals, trees, stones, etc. In this analogy, a perfection is predicated properly and intrinsically of each thing. According to Aquinas, all three kinds of analogy may be used in theology. Attributive and metaphorical analogies help one to talk about God's dynamic perfections. Proportional (and also attributive) analogy enables one to talk about God's entitative perfections (i.e., about God's nature as it is in itself [*New Catholic Encyclopedia*, 2017]).

Participation belongs to epistemology or the theory of knowledge. In Thomas, it is about how the human soul knows and participates or shares in God. "Every creature, of course shares in esse only in a limited fashion" (Brock, p. 90). Thomas takes God to be the efficient cause of human knowledge and the light in which human knowledge partakes by participation (Murdoch, *Pro Ecclesia* vol. XXIII, no. 4:418–34). He notes that God is in all things, not, indeed, as part of their essence, nor as an accident; but as an agent is present to that upon which it works. For an agent must be joined to that wherein it acts immediately and touch it by its power. Therefore, as long as a thing has been, God must be present to it, according to its mode of being. Hence, God is immediately present to all beings as

Creator (Brock, p. 96–97). Yet, there is a special relationship between human beings and God. "Only created rational nature", he writes, "has an immediate order to God." For other creatures do not attain to anything universal, but only to some particular, sharing in divine goodness either by merely existing, as inanimate things do, or also by living and cognizing, as plants and animals do; but rational nature (that is, humans), in as much as it cognizes the universal nature of good and being, has an immediate order to the universal principle of being (STh, II–II, q. 2, a. 3).

So Thomas details three kinds of participation: logical, onto-logical, and that which obtains between an effect and its cause. The last type governs the participation of real beings in the divine *ipsum esse*. Analysis of this third type demonstrates the role that the actus essential plays in Thomas's thought as the "unifying perfection of the universe" (Wippel 2000, 97–99). The purpose of the doctrine of participation in Thomas's thought was for him a way to correlate the one and the many, or the perfection of an attribute and its par-tial concretizations. There is implicit in his theory of participation a relationship of dependence. The participant in the perfection receives this perfection from a higher source. Thomas's understand-ing of participation would seem so far merely a recapitulation of Neoplatonic thought. However, the conjunction of Thomas's view with Aristotelian thought lies in his association of the theory of par-ticipation with an Aristotelian metaphysic of act and potency (Clarke 1952, 147). He writes: "Everything participated is compared to the participator as its act participated existence is limited by the capacity of the participator; so that God alone, who is His own existence, is pure act and infinite. However, in intellectual substances there is composition of actuality and potentiality… Wherefore some say they are composed of that whereby they are and that which they are" (STh. I, q. 7, a. 5). In this, we see that being, therefore, is in finite things not a nature, but is the entitative act of a nature really other than itself (Owens 1985, 103).

The theory of participation in Thomas's system relates to both the creation and the conservation of the created being. Through par-ticipation, the divine *esse* is the act of being of all other beings, and given the convertibility of being and knowing. In his thought, the knowledge of intellectual creatures is also a participation in esse. The recognition of God as both the efficient cause of human knowledge and the light in which human knowledge participates provides the foundation for Thomas's theory of knowledge (Regis 2010).

## Divine and Human Agency

Here, unlike in the previous topics above, I will go straight to treat these two concepts (divine and human agency) together. Agency here could be understood as the principle(s) of causality. Simply put, the divine agency refers to the necessary Being or God. Whereas, the human agency could be conceived as referring to the human causality or the contingent beings. In this regard, God or the Necessary Being is the one who caused the contingent being, who in turn causes other beings or things. On Thomas's view, the highest principle and cause of all, and that about which the metaphysicians chiefly seek to know the truth, is a single being, God. He is one being (Brock, p. 117).

For some in the Middle Ages, any appeal to the autonomy of nature, that is, any appeal to the discovery of real causes in the natural order, seemed to challenge divine omnipotence. Accordingly, events that occur in the natural world are only occasions in which God acts (Marmura 1997). On the other hand, Averroes—Abu-l Walid Muhammad ibn Rusd (1126–98)—a Muslim Andalusian philosopher and thinker, rejected the doctrine of creation out of nothing because he thought that to affirm the kind of divine omnipotence which produces things out of nothing is to deny a regularity and predictability to the natural world. Thus, for Averroes, to defend the intelligibility of nature, one must deny the doctrine of creation out of nothing (Van den Bergh 1987, 173).

Contrary to these positions, Aquinas argues that a doctrine of creation out of nothing, which affirms the radical dependence of all being upon God as its cause, is fully compatible with the discovery of causes in nature. God's omnipotence does not challenge the possibility of real causality for creatures, including that particular causality, free will, which is characteristic of human beings. However, Aquinas also rejected any notion of divine withdrawal from the world so as to leave room, so to speak, for the actions of creatures. Aquinas does not think that God "allows" or "permits" creatures to behave the way they do (Carroll 2000, 319–47). So no creature (not even angels) can be the cause of the very nature of being, nor can it cause everything that pertains to the being of a thing. It cannot produce something ex nihilo or create. Nor can it produce prime matter (Brock, p. 118). Similarly, Aquinas rejected a process theology which denies God's immutability and His omnipotence (as well as His knowledge of the future) so that God would be said to be evolving or changing with the universe and everything in it. For Aquinas, such views fail to do justice either to God or to creation. Creatures are what they are (including those which are free) precisely because God is present to them as cause. Were God to withdraw, all that exists would cease to be. Creaturely freedom and the integrity of nature, in general, are guaranteed by God's creative causality (Russell, p. 119–223).

Aquinas shows us how to distinguish between the being or existence of creatures and the operations they perform. God causes creatures to exist in such a way that they are the real causes of their own operations. For Aquinas, God is at work in every operation of nature, but the autonomy of nature is not an indication of some reduction in God's power or activity. Rather, it is an indication of His goodness. It is important to recognize that divine causality and creaturely causality function at fundamentally different levels. The same effect is not attributed to a natural cause and to divine power in such a way that it is partly done by God, and partly by the natural or human agent. Rather, it is wholly done by both, according to a different way, just as the same effect is wholly attributed to the instrument and also wholly to the principal agent (*Summa Contra Gentiles* III 70.8).

It is not the case of partial or cocauses, with each contributing a separate element to produce the effect. God, as only Creator and Necessary Being, transcends the order of created causes in such a way that He is their enabling origin (Tanner 1988). Yet, the same God who transcends the created order is also intimately and immanently present within that order as upholding all causes in their causing, including the human will. Hence, for Aquinas "the differing metaphysical levels of primary and secondary causation require us to say that any created effect comes totally and immediately from God as the transcendent primary cause and totally and immediately from the creature as secondary cause" (Shanley 1988, 100).

# MODERN PHILOSOPHERS AND THE IMPLICATIONS OF THEIR PHILOSOPHIES ON EXEGESIS

*Biblical and Philosophical Interpretation (2)*

## Introduction

There are many important philosophers who contributed in no small measures to the development and shaping of modern philosophy. This is especially with regards to impacting seriously on biblical exegesis. However, we shall focus on just few of them. This would include William of Ockham, John Wycliffe, Niccoló Machiavelli, Martin Luther, René Descartes, Thomas Hobbes, and Benedict Spinoza. While not taking it for granted that these are more important than those not covered here, it is important to note that most philosophers build their "philosophical castles" on the foundations of their predecessors. For example, in Luther, one finds a synthesis of the "philosophical and political ghosts" of Ockham, John Wycliffe, and even Marsilius. A close look at Locke's political philosophy would reveal the powerful "spirits" of Descartes, Hobbes, and Spinoza in full force. While Hobbes's mechanistic worldview is indebted to Descartes and Machiavelli, and his exegesis supported Henry VIII's state.

In this paper, we shall examine the *impetus agitat* of their philosophical thoughts. Second, we shall point out as precisely as possible the implication of their philosophical cum political thoughts on biblical exegesis. These would be followed by a very brief conclusion. The work of Hahn and Wiker *Politicizing the Bible: The Root of Historical Criticism and Secularization of Scripture, 1300–1700* (2013) is a valuable one. It is well-researched and carefully written. It is one of the most important work to date in the history of modern biblical scholarship. They particularly have in mind the ways in which the interpretation, and the study of Scripture have been secularized over the course of centuries. Thus, they clearly showed how various interests (especially political), and undergirding philosophies shaped and impacted biblical exegesis (Jeffrey 2014, 145–55). Hence, their work would be the primary source for this paper. However, other relevant sources would also be cited.

## William of Ockham (1285–1349)

Although lesser known, yet a quite venerable hypothesis is to blame the plagues of modernity on this fourteenth-century logician, William of Ockham. Ockham's context was the Avignon papacy and the Franciscan poverty debate. Ockham attacked the papacy while seeking to reinstate the medieval view of sacred and secular as two distinct powers. Seeing an extraordinary need for church reform, Ockham argued for the ability and necessity of secular rulers to rule over sinful prelates. Related to this was Ockham's emphasis on the role of biblical specialists who should be in charge of biblical interpretation. "As a philosopher, it was Ockham's privilege to usher into the world what possibly, is the first known case of a new intellectual disease" (Gilson 1937, 86).

The driving force of Ockham's philosophy was nominalism, and he is considered as its founding father. Nominalism will bear much and varied fruits over the next centuries. Although Ockham did not consider himself un-Aristotelian, his rejection of the reality of universals could not but help undermine the final causation, and hence prepare the way for anti-Aristotelianism inherent in the new materialistic reductionist sciences (Hahn and Wiker 2013, 58). Ockham also destroyed the analogy of being on allegorical biblical interpretation. The consequence of this is not little. This is because if nature no longer acts in a real symbolic way, then traditional typology becomes more difficult to maintain. It would either disappear so that only the historical sense is finally tenable or becomes entirely rarified as merely spiritual or literary (Scott and Benjamin, p. 58). Further consequence of Ockham's nominalist philosophy was taken to another level when he laid much emphasis on the authority of experts in the scripture. The implication of this is also quite grave, as it seems to lift exegetes out of the context of the church and into an entirely academic reality, making it a kind of activity unto itself. Hence, the Bible is to be treated like other literary works.

## John Wycliffe (1330–84)

Wycliffe played a great role in shaping the face of future exegesis both in England and the world at large through his participation in English messianic nationalism. Unfortunately, Wycliffe's attack on nominalism inadvertently supported the same sort of exegesis and subordination of the church the same way that Ockham did. Wycliffe passionately argued that the state had an obligation to control the civil realm and should thus take control of the church's temporal goods. "Since the focus is on the English nation, Wycliffe's exegesis in support of a national Church could not help but involve a politicization and secularization of the bible. Hence, If England is the new Israel, salvation history as found in the bible must be interpreted with English history as its culmination" (Scott and Benjamin, p. 113).

Furthermore, Wycliffe's *sola scriptura* is worthy of note because this would also later influence Luther, who was also a strong proponent of sola scriptura. Suffice it to note that his presentation of this was somewhat sophisticated, yet with a careful reading, one would definitely grasp it. His doctrine of sola scriptura could only mean Christ alone, for he, and he alone, is the book of life. So the scripture cannot be destroyed. For Wycliffe, there is no other place through which Christ could be known except through the scripture.

## Niccoló Machiavelli (1469–1527)

As Han and Wiker (p. 117) rightly put it: "It might seem odd to turn to the infamous Machiavelli to shed light upon the assumptions of modern biblical exegesis." This is given the fact that Machiavelli was not a Bible scholar or exegete but a political theorist. Machiavelli's social and historical context was the politics of Florence of the latter half of the fifteenth century and the universally recognized instances of the corruption of the papacy and of some members of the clergy. These are essential to understanding his oeuvre, and thus his contribution to the later development of historical criticism (Jeffrey, p. 147). His magnum opus, *The Prince,* exposed the great hypocrisy and intrigue of Italian political states (including popes, cardinals, and bishops) and promoted a political theory where ends justify means (Stamper and Chalk 2014, 11).

The astute Machiavelli understood how powerful Scripture could be, particularly as a force in political philosophy. So he sought to reinterpret Scripture and reengineer its focus to serve his own political theories. Machiavelli sought to secularize all politics for the very Marsillian goal of terrestrial peace, and in so doing, he effected "a fundamental shift in the treatment of Scripture." He placed the biblical Moses in the context of pagan political leaders. He effectively secularized Moses's role within Scripture and made him "a merely political leader," rather than one called by God to mediate his covenant with the Israelites (Scott and Benjamin, p. 131). Machiavelli was convinced that the biblical account needed this sort of "corrective" to make the Bible's history read more like Plutarch's. With his *Discourses on Livy*, Machiavelli was consciously trying to create a modern critical history where he could recover history "shorn of the Christian overlay and interpretation." Obviously, within this account, Machiavelli shifted the question from religious veracity to political utility as "one of the earliest, and certainly the most influential, sources of the hermeneutics of suspicion" (Scott and Benjamin, p. 144).

## Martin Luther (1484–1546)

We now turn to Luther, one of the greatest forces of modernism and the father of the Reformation. It would not be too blunt to point out that Luther was a nominalist, a self-identified follower of Ockham. He was an advocate of a German national church led by secular authorities and promoted the use of temporal authorities to accomplish spiritual goals. Luther sowed a historical-critical interpretive seed.

Inadvertently, Luther aided in the transformation of the public civic realm into a secular realm, wherein the state controlled the church. As a philosophical disciple of Ockham, he was a nominalist. Hence, he asserted "my master Ockham" to be the greatest dialectician. Luther's impact is still very much with us five hundred years after. This is seen in the different strains and shades of biblical interpretation. He drove the car to a very different and weird direction and, thus, made lots of disciples for himself, as is always the case with reformations and revolutions. One of the most important effects of Luther's impact on biblical exegesis was his *sola scriptura*, which he no doubt picked up from Wycliffe and the from the nominalistic view of his master Ockham.

Also, his declaration of *sola fide* (justification by faith alone) became his hermeneutical key for unlocking Scripture's meaning. Furthermore, Luther's idea of "promise" replaced the traditional role of typology (Pickwick 2016, 26). Upset with justifications of papal authority from spiritual exegesis, against which Ockham had earlier written as well, Luther severed Scripture's intimate bond with the liturgy and erected sharp dichotomies between the "letter" and the "spirit," the "law" and the "gospel," and, importantly, the Old and New Testaments. It is misleading to assume that the importance of Luther as an exegete is his focus on the literal account of Scripture. Rather, his importance consists in substituting the dialectical mode of exegesis for the traditional fourfold meaning of Scripture. In the context of Luther's contribution to later biblical criticism, it is also significant that Luther developed a notion of a "canon within the canon." He explicitly exalted the gospel of John, St. Paul's epistles (particularly Romans, Galatians, and Ephesians), and First Peter, above all other portions of Scripture (Pickwick, p.26).

## René Descartes (1596–1650)

René Descartes was a seventeenth-century French mathematician and philosopher who is now considered the father of modern philosophy. As a mathematician, Descartes is responsible for the Cartesian coordinate system. Descartes is credited at beginning the school of thought called rationalism, which asserted that there was important knowledge that could be gained without the senses but through reason alone (Pickwick, p. 30). Descartes laid the Bible aside in his philosophical program. This set the stage for a secular cosmos devoid of God and the supernatural, and thus the ground was prepared for a folly secular biblical hermeneutic.

Descartes came to view religion as something entirely separate from the methods of reason and objectivity, religion being "beyond our understanding," while the natural world explored through mathematical and scientific research can be known and manipulated with certainty. This hypothesis was also indebted to nominalism, as Descartes determined that mathematical forms rather than Aristotelian universals should govern human conceptions of forms. Descartes is a key figure in the new focus on method that would produce a *mania* for method (Scott and Benjamin, p. 258). The examination of Descartes's method reveals how it shaped modernity: "The mathematization, the mechanization, and the mastery of nature." The habitual posture of doubt ingrained by following Descartes's method will become the unquestioned beginning point of many of the most prominent scriptural scholars toward the biblical texts. Rather than the text having authority, it is the method that is authoritative, judging revelation and reconstructing the text on the basis of methodological conclusions (Morrow, p. 150). His method thus introduced a radical doubt of the senses, as the mechanistic-mathematical ontology replaced ordinary thinking, language, symbols, and metaphors as the means by which the individual can acquire true knowledge. Furthermore, if mathematical philosophy is the means by which the cosmos is to be understood properly, there is little left for the Bible but to serve as a moral guide.

## Thomas Hobbes (1588–1679)

The early modern political philosopher Thomas Hobbes played a foundational role in the emergence of modern biblical criticism. Thomas Hobbes is universally recognized as a political theorist. He represents a synthesis: his secularized exegesis makes sense for a mechanistic worldview and is indebted to both Descartes and Machiavelli, while his exegesis supports the kind of state Henry VIII created (Morrow, p. 33). An examination of his work on the Bible in his book *Leviathan* (1961) shows how his exegesis supported his political agenda. The political context to Hobbes's biblical criticism shaped the way in which he read the Bible, and the method he espoused was an attempt to politicize the modern biblical critical project. Specifically, Hobbes wished to take the Bible out of the hands of the theologians and place it in the hands of state-appointed officials.

Hobbes's influence on biblical exegesis cannot be overemphasized. In addition to his role as a political theorist, Hobbes was also an early modern biblical critic. A number of scholars have noted Hobbes's foundational role in the rise of modern biblical criticism. Hobbes was one of the earliest modern biblical critics to argue that his method was scientific and that it follows the dictates of reason (Morrow, p. 33). In the second half of *Leviathan* is Hobbes's exegetical project wherein he interprets the Bible to support his politics and philosophy, placing all temporal and spiritual power, including exegetical authority, in the hands of the civil sovereign and declawing the church of any real authority apart from the state. "The flow of typology properly understood, is forward in the divine economy, toward the culmination in Christ… Hobbes's typology inverted the order, flowing not toward culmination and spiritual transformation, but backward, toward the reduction to some earthly, original meaning" (Scott and Benjamin, p. 334). Hobbes went further than the Reformers, however, in that he wished to separate biblical exegesis from the Church altogether, relegating scriptural interpretation to the state sovereign. In effect, Hobbes replaces God with the state sovereign (Hobbes 2004, 1651). Hobbes's political philosophy determined the direction of his biblical philology. Hobbes proposed a new hermeneutic for Scripture, which he believed was scientific, for the Bible, he maintained, was easy to understand when one is aided by the proper use of reason (David 1986).

## Benedict Spinoza (1632–77)

Benedict Spinoza (1632–77) is an important figure in the rise of historical criticism of the Bible. He is often considered the progenitor of this approach. A very important point that defines Spinoza's philosophy was its pantheistic nature. Spinoza was indeed a true pantheist who "collapsed God and nature, divinizing nature and naturalizing God" (Scott and Wiker, p. 391). Spinoza was a quintessentially modern rationalist thinker who developed a philological-historical method to interpret biblical texts. According to this line of thought, Spinoza cleared a path for the Enlightenment, supplying ammunition for attacks against religious belief, the Christian church, and the Bible. The impact of Spinoza's *Tractatus Theologico-Politicus* (1670) went far beyond anything previously written; its effects on Western thought about the Bible were to be lasting. Any exegesis of the Bible applying historical-critical methods, henceforth, came under the suspicion of crypto-Spinozism.

Spinoza deals at length with all relevant Bible references. Spinoza's account of the Bible constitutes the heart of the *Tractatus Theologico-Politicus*: chapters 7 (on the exegetical method) to 13 (conclusion: the Bible does not teach philosophy but obedience). His systematic point of departure is that the Bible should be understood from itself alone (*ex sola scriptura*). On the face of it, this looks akin to the Protestant formula of *sola scriptura* (God's word as the only source and measure of faith), but Spinoza's principle aims at something completely different: explaining the Bible through itself is to lay bare the meaning it had for its authors and their audiences (Spinoza 1951).

From that perspective, the biblical message is a purely moral one; it does not teach any philosophical or scientific truths. So rather than overthrowing humanistic criticism and philology, Spinoza's approach to the Bible is firmly grounded in that tradition: The Bible is a text, and it should be handled with the same tools as profane texts. Hence, the claim that scripture may safely be reduced to a merely moral core was rooted in Spinoza's dour assessment of intellectual capacities of the passion-filled, irritational mob which could possibly grasp the mathematical cum mechanical philosophy. The setting up of endless tasks that face exegete before anything of doctrinal certainty can be affirmed from scripture was a clever way to discharge the energy of those who would previously go to battle over different doctrinal interpretations. Ingenuously, it allowed Spinoza simultaneously to affirm sola scriptura and render it harmless.

## Conclusion

Through the study of these philosophers, one point stands out very clearly. This is the fact that they employed the Bible in their different (exegetical) ways in order to achieve or further their goals. While some specifically went on outright and deliberate attack on the scripture in order to settle their scores, and perhaps have their pound of flesh from the religion that has "offended them gravely," others, knowing full well that one of the best ways to superstardom at the time was to take the "negative way," the critic of religion and the Bible. Also, it is clear from the study of these philosopher's biblical perspective that reading the Bible or attempting to interpret it outside the community of faith to which or, within which, it is given to leads one nowhere.

# A Comparative Evaluation of Tradition and Magisterium in Richard Gaillardetz and Lawrence Feingold

*Fundamental Theology and Biblical Interpretation*

## Introduction

Tradition and Magisterium are two important aspects in the Catholic Church's teaching. For a very long time, their nature, duty, and relationship has been the subject of a very strong debate both within and outside the Catholic Church. While Tradition along with Scriptures flows from divine revelation and form one sacred deposit of the word of God, Magisterium is the teaching office of the church whose task is to authentically interpret divine revelation. However, Magisterium is not the third channel of divine revelation (*Dei Verbum*, Dogmatic Constitution on Divine Revelation, 9–19).

Gaillardetz and Feingold have contributed to this ongoing debate on Tradition and Magisterium. Hence, in this paper, we shall compare and contrast their different views and argue that Feingold's presentation aligns more with the Catholic Church's teaching on these subjects. We shall accomplish these tasks by taking a look at, and evaluating the presentation of both authors on Tradition and

Magisterium, respectively. Finally, we shall draw a brief conclusion based on our evaluation of their presentations and views on Tradition and Magisterium.

## Gaillardetz's Presentation of Tradition

Gaillardetz rightly noted that Tradition predates the Bible. The Bible itself is the fruit of Tradition. Before there were written texts, there were stories that were "handed on" from generation to generation and community to community (Dei Verbum 9–19). In his view, there existed a harmony between the two until the Protestant Reformation came and espoused the doctrine of *sola scriptura* (Feingold 2015, 142). He observed the notion of Tradition and traditions in the Vatican II. However, he did not elaborate much on this. Gaillardetz noted that in Vatican II, the ancient unity of Scripture and Tradition was restored. The council wrote that Scripture and Tradition make up a single deposit of the word of God, which is entrusted to the church (DV 10).

In his view, "The dogmatic constitution on divine revelation shifted away from a propositional view of divine revelation." He further observed, that the relationship between scripture and tradition involves both continuity and discontinuity. Hence, he writes that "[c]onsequently, we must recognize that while tradition stands in 'continuity' with the biblical testimony and shares a common source in the living Word of God, it is not strictly identical to it. Tradition also bears witness to real discontinuity with the past (Feingold, p. 195).

## Feingold's Presentation of Tradition

Feingold in his work noted that both scripture and tradition issue from the same source of divine revelation. Scripture and tradition are two channels by which the one deposit of God's revelation is passed down through the ages. Hence, he called it "living tradition which will continue to be transmitted till the end of the world." Feingold also clearly explicated the functions of tradition stating that, contrary to the Protestants view, Tradition was only necessary for the beginning of the church, that it is necessary for the church in all times for many reasons. Some of the reasons being that tradition predates scripture, it is the key for interpreting scripture. Hence, without Tradition, "scripture would be a dead letter." Therefore, Tradition is ampler than Scriptures and contains truths that are not explicitly contained in the Bible (Jn. 21, 25). Yves Congar (2004,102–28) was very clear on this in his reflection on "Tradition as objectively containing things not contained in Scripture." While Gaillardetz glossed over it, Feingold took time to differentiate clearly the difference between Tradition ("T") as the deposits of divine revelation, and traditions ("t") as ecclesiastical issues that are not doctrine. He also clearly pointed out five witnesses of Tradition as the Magisterium, the Creeds, the writing of the Fathers, the liturgy of the church, and the consensus of theologians. From Feingold's view and presentation, Vatican II did much to preserve and to enhance the development of Tradition.

## Evaluation of the Presentations of Gaillardetz and Feingold on Tradition

A reading of Gaillardetz and Feingold on tradition leaves one with no doubt that Feingold did a better job. This is because he took time to explain issues in such a way that his readers could have a grasp of what was at stake. Although Gaillardetz tried in his shot at this subject, however, he did not sound convincing and confident as to defending the church's view on Tradition in an unequivocal term.

On the historicity of Tradition, Gaillardetz's idea that it was the Protestant Reformation that awakened the consciousness of Tradition in the Catholic Church sounded a bit weird. He sounded as if prior to the Reformation, in the Catholic Church there was no ongoing debate at all on this issue. On the contrary, from both biblical and church documents perspectives, Feingold demonstrated that discourse on Tradition has existed for ages and so did not have to wait, as Gaillardetz inferred, for the Protestant reformation which rejected its authority. The discussion had been an ongoing one even among the Fathers of the Church. One aspect of Feingold's reflection on Tradition that must not be left unmentioned here is his ability to clearly evaluate the relationship between apostolic tradition and the oral Torah. Through this, he buttressed the unity that exists between the Old and New Testaments. Also, contrary to the views of Gaillardetz, he showed the continuity of Tradition.

## Gaillardetz's Presentation of Magisterium

Gaillardetz, notes that "[a]lthough Vatican II made significant contributions, it offered no systematic treatment of the church or church authority. Consequently, the implications of its vision were closely overlooked." Another statement of his, which leaves much to be desired is his comment regarding *Lumen gentium* (22.1). He thinks that "[t]he council also addressed a topic almost 'completely overlooked' by Vatican I, namely the bishop's relationship to one another as a college."

Through his defense of Sullivan's interpretation of Pope Pius XI's 1863 apostolic letter *Tuas libernter*, Gaillardetz affirmed that the consensus of theologians is a condition or criteria for determining the definitiveness of the teaching of the ordinary universal magisterium. However, Welch argued that it could be a sign, but not a condition (Welch 2003, 6001–2). He equally, pointed out the difference between the "use of sign and condition" in this context (Welch 1998, 18–36). Furthermore, by envisioning and comparing the role of the pope to that of a *"notary public,"* Gaillardetz tends to reduce the discussion on the Magisterium to what Livio Melina (1997, 605–15) describes in his critic of Sullivan as "a dry and minimalistic juridical formalism."

Also, Richard Gaillardetz suggested that in the face of controversy, the determination of the authoritative status of any teaching not solemnly defined can only be pursued tentatively. According to Welch, this "leads to rather unsound conclusions and massive problems." (Welch, p. 608). Following his support of Sullivan's interpretation of can 749, S3 that states that "No doctrine is understood to be infallibly defined unless it is clearly established as such," Gaillardetz insists that in the face of doubt regarding the possibility of infallible teaching act, one should presume that the charism of infallibility has not been engaged until it is clearly demonstrated otherwise. Hence, he surmises, "I conclude that on theological grounds, the principle is equally true that no doctrine should be understood as having been infallibly proposed unless this fact is clearly established, whether the doctrine has been defined or taught by the Ordinary Universal Magisterium."

Speaking on the extraordinary magisterium's infallibility, he noted that it derived from the promise of Christ, "I am with you always till the end of the age" (Matt 28, 20) and His promise of the Holy Spirit. Gaillardetz, also observed that right from the early Church Fathers, the doctrine of infallibility, though not technically speaking by employing the term *infallibility*, but through a conviction that the Holy Spirit indeed did perfect the church. He further noted that the ancient intuition reflects a broader and most inclusive understanding of infallibility—that of the "whole church," which Vatican II articulated thus: "The whole body of the faithful who have received an anointing which comes from the holy one cannot be mistaken in belief" (LG, 12). However, on infallibility, he wrote: "Many people believe that that acknowledging the possibility of error in the church's teaching will undermine the authority of the Magisterium. I am inclined to believe that quite the opposite is the case. It is a mistake to think that unless the Church's teaching office is infallible, it cannot possess any real authority."

## Feingold's Presentation of the Magisterium

Feingold began his discourse on Magisterium, just like Gaillardetz, by acknowledging that it is the teaching arm office of the church, but not the third channel of revelation. Rather, employing *Dei verbum* (10), he noted that its task is that of "authentically interpreting the word of God, whether written or handed on." Hence, the magisterium pertains to the prophetic mission of the church, and it stands in the service of the living revealed word.

On infallibility, he affirmed the fittingness and necessity of an infallible teaching office in clear and unequivocal terms: "The church needs an infallible Magisterium as the rock and foundation on which she is built" (p. 242). He employed many scriptural verses and church documents to buttress this fact. Here, Feingold clearly demonstrated his strong and firm belief in the Magisterium. Through his thesis on infallibility, he strongly showed his support for the teaching office of the church as an organ that has to be protected and respected in order to be able to interpret and preserve the divinely revealed truth. Hence, he briefly critiqued the views of theologians like Karl Rahner and Hans Kung on the issue of infallibility in the church (p. 343).

## Evaluation of the Two Author's Presentations on the Magisterium

The major source of difference between both authors lies on their views of the infallibility of the Magisterium. Feingold strongly believes in the fittingness and necessity of an infallible teaching office for the purpose of preserving the revealed truth from God. He writes: "For if God, has revealed his will to man in time and history, he must provide some way of preserving what he has revealed for the men of all times and places" (p. 343). On the contrary, Gaillardetz's many controversial comments, for example, this one that "[i]t is a mistake to think that unless the Church's teaching office is infallible, it cannot possess any real authority" (Gaillardetz, p. 100) and others like it betrays his negative view of the Magisterium.

On the relationship between the theologian and the Magisterium, somehow Gaillardetz attributed an exaggerated role to the theologian. Somehow, he tended to make the case that that theologians could limit the teaching authority of the pope. On the other hand, while believing that theologians have a great role to play in the church, Feingold thinks that instead of being critical of the Magisterium, theologians should collaborate with it by seeking harmonious ways of resolving issues Feingold, p. 274). He concludes his discourse by warning that public and obstinate dissent against nondefinitive teachings of the ordinary magisterium is very harmful

74

to the church. This is especially when it is done by those (supposedly, theologians) who are seen to speak in the name of and for the church.

## Conclusion

In this paper, we examined and evaluated the presentations of Gaillardetz and Feingold on both topics of Tradition and Magisterium in accordance with the ongoing debate. At the end of each presentation, the views of the authors were jointly evaluated. Thus, comparing and contrasting their view on the topics presented Also, we had recourse to the works or contributions of other authors when and wherever it was necessary in order to clarify issues. In light of our evaluation, we conclude that Feingold is more closely aligned to the Catholic Church's teaching in his presentation on Tradition and Magisterium than Gaillardetz.

# WHERE TRADITION MEETS LITURGY: THEIR RELATIONSHIP

*Liturgical and Sacramental Theology*

## Introduction

There are many words or concepts that when taken outside the ecclesiastical context or usage may definitely be misunderstood. Tradition is one such word or concept that has been variously interpreted or understood. For some, especially, some non-Catholics or some members of other Christian denominations, the word *tradition* sounds archaic and pagan. Yves Congar (2004, 1) recounted how a Russian interpreter unacquainted with ecclesiastical terminology spontaneously translated the word "tradition" by the expression "ancient customs." Even the word *liturgy* does not seem to make much meaning to them, even though, like "the unknown God" worshipped by the Athenians (Acts 17:23), liturgy defines and sustains their daily and entire existence. Yet, these two words or concepts for most of them are the Roman Catholic's inventions and must be eschewed.

It is quite interesting to know that like Siamese twins, tradition and liturgy go together or cannot be separated. While tradition helps in the development, preservation, and transmission of liturgy, liturgy on its part practically keeps alive what is transmitted by tradition. It is "the living" of what is transmitted. Ecclesiastically speaking, we rely heavily on rituals communicated through signs and symbols. Some of these have been practiced over decades and even right from the foundation of Christianity. Others have emerged or evolved through the process of inculturation. This is to say, that even if they appear to be new, there is "something unchanging" (their essence) in them which belongs to the past and still subsists.

So it is obvious that this part or "something unchanging" from the past in them is what makes the rituals or liturgy in general what they are. These did not get to us through the blues or from nothing. They started somewhere in the past and came to us through the tradition which faithfully preserved and transmitted them to us. Liturgy has been handed on from one generation to the other up to this point in time. Hence, symbolic acts communicate and transfer in a powerful and condensed way "the living faith of the dead, and not the dead faith of the living" (Vosloo 2004: *NGTT* 45 (3&4):936–55). The good functioning of one's whole life and that of a faith community depends on its liturgy and rituals, just as it depends on tradition. Liturgy and tradition, along with other aspects of our lives, constitute who we are, and who we are becoming. In other words, they constitute our identity (Wepener 2008). "So, Liturgy is Tradition itself at its highest degree of power and solemnity. No finer expression of the truth could be found (Congar, p. 134).

This brief paper, therefore, will explore these words briefly by trying to find their roots or origin, what they stand for and mean to the church. At the center of this paper will be the relationship between these two important parts of our Christian life. Here, we shall use both the capital "T" or small "t" in talking about tradition in its totality. However, we shall briefly explain for clarity sake what each represents strictly and technically speaking. Although we are very much aware of the fact there are different uses of the word "tradition" in various aspects of life, our focus here is on its ecclesiastical meaning and use.

## What is Tradition?

I have decided to cast the theme of this section and the next following it in the form of a question in order to help us understand what the concepts we are dealing with really mean, that is, both generally and ecclesiastically speaking. For many, tradition is simply a collection of time-honored customs, accepted, not on critical grounds but merely because things have always been so, because "it has always been done." Any attempt to innovation is opposed in the name of tradition, which is considered first and foremost as a conservative force in society and a safeguard against a dangerous liking for novelty, or even against any suggestion of a wider outlook. Tradition is favored because it prevents change (Congar, p. 1). However, there is more to it than this.

In her opening essay to the wonderful catalog of the exhibition "Memory and Imagination: The Legacy of Maidu Indian Artist Frank Day," Rebecca Dobkins (1997, 1) asks the almost impossible question "What are the meanings of 'tradition'?" Etymologically speaking, the word "tradition" comes from the Latin *traditio*, the noun of the verb *tradere,* which literally means "to transmit or to deliver" (Odendal 1991, 1163). On a more general and basic level, the word *tradition* refers to a general "handing over" of knowledge and practices "from generation to generation" (Wepener 2008). Tradition was the name given to those cultural features which, in situations of change, were to be continued to be handed on, thought about, preserved, and not lost. Originally, the concept of tradition, which also literally means "something handed over," in slowly changing societies was almost equivalent to inheritance. Tradition was both the means of making a living and the symbols, stories, and memories which gave one both identity and status. (Nelson H. H. Graburn, 24(2/3):6).

Ecclesiastically speaking, the Church views and holds tradition in a very high esteem. In other words, tradition means more than mere conservativism because something deeper is involved, namely the continual presence of the spirit and of a moral attitude, and the community of ethos. It has to do with the transmission of divine revelation, faith, good news, that is, both the oral and written. Hence, we can speak of the oral and written tradition. The sacred tradition fosters continuity. Tradition is an offering by which the Father's gift is communicated to a great number of people throughout the world and down to successive generations. It is the sharing of a treasure, which itself remains unchanging. It represents a victory over time and its transience, over space and the separation caused by distance (Congar, p. 12). So, strictly speaking, tradition transmits or communicates or delivers the whole of revelation and faith, while excluding nothing.

## The Two Senses of Tradition

It suffices to note at this juncture that tradition with a capital "T" refers to the deposit of revelation that has been entrusted to the church. It is the apostolic tradition. However, there are also the venerable ecclesiastical traditions that do not necessarily form part of the deposit of revelation, even though they have great importance in the life the Church. These ecclesiastical traditions are not a matter of doctrine. Although they do not directly transmit a truth, yet they determine a particular way of acting or worshipping. They are disciplinary, and therefore, they can change to a certain degree. Tradition, then, assumes a second meaning or second quality. It was first the pure and simple transmission of the sacred deposit. It is also the explanation of this deposit, elaborated through its being lived, defended, and explained generation after generation by the people of God (Congar, p. 125).

There is yet another way in which tradition has been spoken of. This has been majorly driven by the context of the debate on the dichotomy between scripture and tradition by the proponents of the hermeneutics of continuity and discontinuity. As Richard R. Gaillardetz observed, in the decades prior to Vatican II, many theologians began to challenge the dominant understanding of tradition at the time. They recognized that the schematization of scripture and tradition as two sources was foreign to the Christian heritage of the first thousand years. Indeed, they insisted that while the late medieval and baroque theologians would speak of "traditions" in the plural, there was a more ancient insight reflected in the use of "tradition" in the singular as a way of naming the whole of the Christian faith passed on from generation to generation (Lawrence, p. 43). We shall not bother about this argument here.

## What is Liturgy?

Joseph Ratzinger (2000, 13) began the first chapter of his famous work *The Spirit of the Liturgy* with these important questions: What is liturgy? What happens during liturgy? What kind of reality do we encounter here? Well, we may not go all the way to treat each of these questions holistically; however, we shall attempt to explain and understand what liturgy is, what it does for us, and what we do in liturgy. First, a very short answer to the first and most important question that forms the theme of this section is that liturgy is life! As brief as this may seem, yet it speaks volumes. To say this is simply to say that liturgy communicates life in its entirety to its receiver. "When we celebrate the liturgy, we participate in an intense and unique way in the totality of our life, in its adorable Lord, in all the men who achieve a new existence in the communion of the Father, in the world that has been reconciled and in time that has been set free" (Jean 2005, 199).

Liturgy is also most popularly defined as the public worship of the people of God. Liturgy (*leitourgia*) is a Greek composite word`, meaning originally a public duty, a service to the state undertaken by a citizen. Its elements are (from *leos*, *laos*, people) meaning public, and ergo, to do. From this, we have *leitourgos*, "a man who performs a public duty," "a public servant," often used as equivalent to the Roman lictor, then *leitourgeo*, "to do such a duty," *leitourgema*, its performance, and *leitourgia*, the public duty itself. In liturgy, both God and man are involved together in one single action. Man looking up to God, and God responding to man. It is also God's work and man's response to God. The reality that liturgy communicates, therefore, is life in its fulness. In Christian use, liturgy meant the public official service of the Church that corresponded to the official service of the temple in the Old Law (Fortescue Adrian, *The Catholic*

*Encyclopedia*, vol. 9). The Catechism of the Catholic Church (1069, 1070) says:

> The word "liturgy" originally meant a "public work" or a "service in the name of/on behalf of the people. "In Christian tradition it means the participation of the People of God in "the work of God" (Jn 17:4). Through the liturgy Christ, our redeemer and high priest, continues the work of our redemption in, with, and through his Church. As the work of Christ, liturgy is also an action of his *Church*. It makes the Church present and manifests her as the visible sign of the communion in Christ between God and men. It engages the faithful in the new life of the community and involves the "conscious, active, and fruitful participation" of everyone.

## The Two Senses of Liturgy

There are two senses in which the word liturgy is used. It must be admitted that these two senses often lead to confusion. First, liturgy often means the whole complex of official services, all the rites, ceremonies, prayers, and sacraments of the Church, as opposed to private devotions. In this sense, we speak of the arrangement of all these services in certain set forms used officially by any local church. So liturgy also means rite. For example, the Byzantine rite or liturgy and the Roman rite or liturgy. In the same sense, one can talk of what differentiates one official service from others by referring to them as "liturgical." For instance, in the Catholic Church, compline is a liturgical service, the Rosary is not (Fortescue Adrian, *The Catholic Encyclopedia*, vol. 9).

The second sense of the word liturgy is the common one in all Eastern Churches, which restricts it to the chief official service. That is, the sacrifice of the Holy Eucharist, which the Roman rite calls the Mass. For example, when a Greek speaks of the "Holy Liturgy," he means only the Eucharistic service. From this sense, the Constitution of the Sacred Liturgy (*Sacrosanctum concilium*, 7 § 2–3) teaches that

> The liturgy then, is rightly seen as an exercise of the priestly office of Jesus Christ. It involves the presentation of man's sanctification under the guise of signs perceptible by the senses, and its accomplishment in ways appropriate to each of these signs. In it, is full public worship is performed by the Mystical Body of Jesus Christ. That is, by the head and his members. From this, it follows that every liturgical celebration, because it is an action of Christ the priest and of his Body which is the Church, is a sacred action surpassing all others. No other action of the Church can equal its efficacy by the same title and to the same degree.

## Where Tradition Meets Liturgy?

We now turn to the last but most important section of this brief paper. Here we hope to take a closer look at the relationship between tradition and liturgy. To help us do this, we shall return to Ratzinger's third question: "What kind of reality do we encounter here?" (Ratzinger 2000, 13). Through this, we shall find out that what tradition transmits and communicates or hands over from generation to generation are concrete realities. If liturgy is life, then tradition transmits life in its entirety and concreteness. The relationship between tradition and liturgy rests mostly on the fact that, in addition to transmitting liturgy, tradition also regulates liturgy. This is especially when we speak of liturgical practices and how liturgy is realized or should be practiced.

What kind of reality then do we find in the liturgy? Certain realities may have been criticized, opposed, or forgotten; their meaning may have been lost, but through tradition, they were preserved by the rite. In spite of this, and, seen under a new light, in happier surroundings, they could be rediscovered intact in their unchanging and somewhat "old-fashioned" setting. Some of the realities we encounter in liturgy that tradition transmits include among many others, divine revelation, prayer, sacraments, and of course, the reality of God. The man who puts to one side any consideration of the reality of God is a realist only in appearance. He is abstracting himself from the One in whom we "live and move and have our being" (Acts 17:28). Through this, Joseph Ratzinger (p. 136) insists that it is only when man's relationship with God is right that all his relationships with his fellowmen, and his dealings with the rest of creation, can be in good order.

A very important aspect of liturgy is divine revelation, which is God himself coming to man. It is a way through which God is visibly present to men. The progression follows from his spoken Word to the same Word which incarnated both in the scriptures (Jn 1:1–14) and in the womb of the Blessed Virgin Mary. In liturgy, we adore both the Word made flesh and the Word made scripture as one and the same. Tradition, no doubt, has helped to preserve, transmit, and communicate divine revelation from age to age. Thus, making it possible for God's people to continue to experience and understand who He is, and how best to approach or worship Him. So "sacred tradition and sacred scripture, then are bound closely and together, and communicate one with the other. For both of them, flowing out from the same divine well spring, come together in some fashion to form one thing, and move as toward one goal" (Bertoldi 1990, 92).

Tradition also transmits liturgy through the great reality of the sacraments, prayers, and feasts. The greatest and most important being, the Eucharistic celebration or feast through which the people encounter God. This is not only taught to us, or merely brought to our notice; it is celebrated, realized, rendered, communicated and present, not simply as a doctrine and truth, but as a lived reality and experience. Whatever the feast we celebrate in the church today, it is always the celebration of the Covenant, whose sacrament is the Mass, the heart of all the feasts, which is also the memorial of the Lord's Pasch (Congar, p. 139).

This celebration of life has been transmitted from one generation to the other. Surely, its form or method of celebration has evolved through inculturations, yet, through the help of tradition, it has retained its uniqueness. Both tradition and liturgy belong together because they both communicate. So as action, an actual celebration, and ritual, the liturgy has an exceptional richness and comprehensiveness. With the help of tradition, the liturgy celebrates the Eucharist and other sacraments. It offers us the means by which we may prepare ourselves to approach it. Together, they bring us into communication with it and envelops it in a whole cult and worship, which radiates naturally from it.

## Conclusion

Contrary to the misguided notion of sola scriptura, it is very obvious that the Scriptures do not express everything entrusted by Christ to the Church for us to live by. So liturgy, together with Tradition, provide us the contact with the whole of these realities themselves, even though this contact is not as immediate as that resulting from a total experience. One point is certain here, and that is the fact that through tradition, these realities have been preserved and transmitted to us through various liturgical activities. Whether they have been transformed or remained the same over the ages makes no much difference, in as much as their essence still subsists and still communicates life to the people of God. Tradition, therefore, is the preserver of liturgy, while liturgy is the lived experience of what tradition preserves. In this, and through this, one cannot but conclude that there is a very realistic and formidable relationship between tradition and liturgy.

# THE BIBLICAL FOUNDATION
# AND THE FUNDAMENTALITY
# OF SACRAMENTS

*Sacraments in General*

## Introduction

Where is it in the Bible? Is it found in the Bible? Unless you show
me where it is in the Bible, I will not believe you, and lots more
like these are questions and arguments that some Christians pose in
order to authenticate what they are saying or must believe. Perhaps,
the genesis of this type of argument could be traced back to Luther
(1445–1546), whose Reformation came with the dictum *sola scriptura* (only the scripture). Fortunately, the event of the ages past and
the Church in her wisdom, under the guidance of the Holy Spirit,
have proved that the Bible (Scripture) is only but one mode of God's
revelation of himself and the mysteries of life to his people.

Tradition is yet another mode through which God continues
to reveal Himself to humanity. Paul writes to the Thessalonians: "So
then, brothers and sisters, stand firm and hold fast to the traditions
that you were taught by us, either by word of mouth or by our letter" (Thessalonians 2:15). Also, the author of the fourth gospel had
a foreknowledge of this problem and, thus, was quick to inform

the church that "there are also many other things that Jesus did; if every one of them were written down, I suppose that the world itself could not contain the books that would be written" (Jn 21, 25). It is, therefore, important to note that although some things many not be stated verbatim or directly in the Bible, but as human beings whom God has endowed with reason and wisdom, it is left for us to read in-between the lines through the ever-bright and illuminative help of the Holy Spirit in other to unravel the hidden mysteries that our lord Jesus Christ left for us his Church.

Sacrament is one Christian doctrine or teaching which needs closer examination as to the credibility of its foundation in the Holy Scriptures. There are seven of them. While some are explicitly mentioned in the Bible, others are only but implicitly mentioned or instituted. However, the word *sacrament* itself is not found anywhere in the Bible. Once the questions of what sacraments are, and their biblical foundations are surmounted, the question of what sacraments in general are presents itself. We shall attempt these questions in this paper.

## Sacrament: Meaning and Etymology

As already pointed out above, as a term or word, *sacrament* is nowhere used in the Bible. Kevin W. Irwin (2006, 910) writes that:

> The word "Sacrament" translates the Latin *sacramentum,* and Greek *mysterion* signifying one of the seven central liturgical rites of the church through which participants experience the paschal mystery of Christ, are formed into the body of Christ and grow in the life of grace. *Mysterion* is found in the scriptures, but its meaning is much broader than the seven rites." In the Old Testament one finds mystery in the following places; Wis 6:22; Dan 2:28.47. In the Synoptic *mysterion* refers to the secret of the kingdom of heaven (Mt 13:11; Mk 4:11; Lk 8:10). In Pauline

writings *mysterion* often refers to Christ (1Cor 1: 7–10; Rom 16: 25–26; Col 1: 26–27; 4:3; Eph 1: 9–10; Tim 3:6). While the rites of baptism and Eucharist are known in the NT era, neither of them is called a sacrament at this time.

The Catechism of the Catholic Church (262) defines sacrament as "an outward sign which confers an in-ward grace." A more elaborate definition is that: "a Sacrament is a sensible sign instituted by Christ to signify and cause justification and sanctification" (Pazhayampallil 2006, 11). Hence, the Church teaches that they are instituted by Christ. Sacraments describe the manifold sanctifying actions of God's Spirit in man. Each of the seven sacraments that the Church celebrates liturgically relates closely to the challenge within human beings to be fully alive in Christ who comes that we may have abundant life. It is of utmost importance to note here that "institution by Christ" means that those actions we call sacraments are specifications and applications of the power that Jesus gave to the Church in and through the apostles during his ministry and after his resurrection. That is, a power containing what was necessary to make God's rule or kingdom triumph over evil by sanctifying the lives of his people from birth to death. Therefore, the sacraments are not inventions of the church but are part of Christ's plan. On the question of whether Christ instituted the sacraments, Raymond Brown (1990, 11) responds thus: "Therefore, in discussing the institution of the sacraments, the norm is not simply what Jesus said in the 20s in Palestine but the evidence for those sacraments in the whole New Testament." Hence, based on this, one can conveniently talk of the biblical roots of the sacraments.

## Biblical Foundations of the Seven Sacraments

*Baptism*

Baptism is the basis or the foundation for the whole Christian life, the gateway to life in the Spirit (*vitae spirtaualis ianua*) and the door which gives access to the other sacraments. Through baptism, we are freed from sin and reborn as sons of God; we become members of Christ. Baptism is the sacrament of regeneration through water in the word (The Catechism of the Catholic Church, 1213). We have the word of Christ: "Very truly, I tell you, no one can enter the kingdom of God without being born of water and Spirit" (John 3:5). Also, "Go therefore and make disciples of all nations, baptizing them in the name of the Father and of the Son and of the Holy Spirit" (Mt 28:19). Jesus' own baptism (Is 42:1–4; Lc 3:15–16, 21–22), and the baptism of the entire household of Cornelius (Acts 10) are few biblical roots of this sacrament.

## Confirmation

This sacrament helps the baptized to be more perfectly bound to the Church and enriches him/her with a special strength of the Holy Spirit. To become "a soldier of Christ," as our ancient understanding would have it, means more precisely to join with others in the struggle of Jesus to build the Father's kingdom of justice, love, and peace (CCC, 1323). Confirmation has its biblical support from the practice of the apostles who imposed their hands on the baptized and conferred on them the gift of the Holy Spirit (cf. Act 8, 14–17; 19, 5–6).

## Eucharist

"The Holy Eucharist completes Christian initiation. It is the source and summit of the Christian life" (CCC, 1324) The Eucharist does not only constitute not a moment in our history. It is also a continually enduring reality. It constantly and prayerfully confirms the hope and expectation that we can remain one with Christ and each other. We will not die nor let others die. We find the institution of the Eucharist in the synoptic Gospels (Mt 26, 26–28; Mk 14, 22–25; Luke 22, 19–20), and Paul recalls that Jesus said, "This is my body that is for you… This cup is the new covenant in my blood. Do this, in remembrance of me." (1 Cor. 11:23–25).

*Penance*

This consecrates the Christian sinner's personal and ecclesial steps of conversion and satisfaction. Though humanly tempted to say no, the Christian community answers by celebrating Christ's pardon which continually reaccepts us into the community against which we have sinned. We admit, celebrate, and are challenged by our proclamations with Jesus that no love progresses without death and resurrection, without sin and reintegration. Jesus empowered his disciples thus: "If you forgive the sins of any, they are forgiven them; if you retain the sins of any, they are retained" (John 20, 23; James 5:6).

*Matrimony*

In marriage, the community celebrates with two people who proclaim the truth that deep lasting love, that mirrors God's love for his people which endures despite all the forces of death that deny or try to kill it. The Bible begins with the creation of man and woman in the image and likeness of God (Gen 2:21–24), and concludes with a vision of the "wedding feast of the Lamb" (Rev 19, 9). Paul also refers to the union of a family as a "great mystery" (Eph. 5:22–23). Christ himself attended a wedding feast (Jn 2:1–12).

*Holy Orders*

This is the sacrament through which the mission entrusted by Christ to his apostles continues to be exercised in the church until the end of time. Thus, it is the sacrament of the apostolic ministry. The institution of the priesthood is contained in the words: "Do this in memory of me" (Luke 22, 19). By these words, according to the Council of Trent, Jesus conferred this priesthood on his apostles and the ordained: "Do this." Christ the Lord not only says "Announce this" or Recount this," but he says: "Do." This word is of critical importance. The priesthood is a sacrament of action (Pope John Paul II, 1984).

*Anointing of the Sick*

Imminent death provides an obvious moment of crisis, especially because at that moment, we cannot help asking what the passive suffering person can do that indicates life. The community comes together again to celebrate, signify, sacramentalize, and prayerfully assent that the person is still important. We have the promulgation of this sacrament when Jesus said to his disciples: "Cure the sick, raise the dead, cleanse the lepers, cast out demons" (Mt 10:7–8), and in the letter of James: "Are any among you sick? The prayer of faith will save the sick, and the Lord will raise them up" (James 5:14–15).

## Sacraments in General and God's Salvific Plan for the World

The theology of the sacraments, which began in the scripture and has been constantly developed in the course of history, is not confined to the understanding of the individual (seven) sacraments only. It is also concerned with the common elements which characterizes all of them intrinsically. The notion of sacrament, when rightly understood, participates in the special character of that life. Life is an eminently concrete notion but at the same time one which is "universal." Life unfolds in a number of individual acts, which must be grasped individually before one can understand and say precisely what life is. So too, it is with the vital action of the Church in the sacraments.

Originally, this symbolic reality of salvific church life bestowed by God's grace, to be known and accepted by man in faith, unfolds in various actions which are individually perceptible. These, along with other means of mediation of salvation are the sacraments, through which the Church and her members shares today and at all times in the triumphant eschatological salvation promised by God through Christ and his Word and wrought by God and Mediator (Schulte 1975, 1477). It suffices to note, therefore, that apart from the seven sacraments that the Church celebrates liturgically, there are other ways the Church views sacraments. John McDermott (1999, 7) captures it in the following way:

> From the beginning salvation has been historically mediated through the humanity of Jesus Christ and after the Resurrection, through the Eucharist and through the community of believers, the ecclesial body of Christ, created by the Eucharist and assembled to celebrate and proclaim Jesus eucharistically present in their midst. God's plane for salvation is sacramental, i.e., he renders himself present in a finite figure, e.g., Jesus' humanity, the Church's sacramental signs, to call for man's total response to love and upon man's response depends on his eternal salvation or damnation.

In light of this, anything through which Jesus comes to us in a tangible, sensible, and visible way has a sacramental character and so lies within the domain of "sacraments in general."

Through history, God has and continues to reveal himself by communicating through signs, symbols, or mediators. In this regard, one can say that God's salvific plan for the world has always been communicated and achieved through mediations. There is nothing like unmediated communication of God or his grace because grace par excellence is Jesus Christ mediated. It suffices, therefore, to note that all those symbols and signs (which includes creation, the Israelite nation, the Church, of course, Jesus Christ himself, etcetera.), through which God had revealed himself, are all sacraments and bear sacramental character. This is because they are both visible and invisible concrete participations which lead to encounter with God.

Also, they all make present the reality, which is God, that they signify. The Church, the body of Christ, is (or ought to be) a sacrament, a sacred sign, and a holy people (1 Pt 2:9). In, through, and with the people of God, the community of believers who profess the same conviction that Jesus is the Lord, we encounter and deepen our relationship with that Lord. Katherine D. and Patrick C. (1970, 31) submit that: "The Church comprises not merely people who receive sacraments, but also people who become sacraments, sacred signs, vehicles for God's love to the Church itself and to the whole world."

## Conclusion

One can emphatically say that sacraments in general are fundamental to God's salvific plan for the world because through them, God continues and succeeds in his "business" and endeavor of saving his people. "Just as everything is prayer, so everything is (or can be) sacramental, a thing made holy. God is totally present in our lives and experiences. The whole world is sacramental, or can become so in the eyes of the believer. Just as everything can become prayer, so everything can become a channel of grace. That is, a means of meeting Jesus" (Katherine and Patrick, p. 17). Any means of meeting Jesus certainly leads to salvation and God. If we are to take this as true, then it means that God can choose who or whatever he wills, as he singlehandedly elected Israel, the Church, and other figures in history for the communication of his love and salvific mission to the entire world.

# THE BIBLICAL ROOT OF THE DIVINE SONSHIP OF THE *TOTUS CHRISTOS*

*Christology and Soteriology*

## Introduction

The divine sonship of Christ and that of all believers has been a widely discussed and debated theme for centuries, and in fact continues till date. Undoubtedly, it was part of the early Christian kerygma broadly attested by different authors and genres (Peppard 2011, 92–110). In what sense is Christ Son of God? How did Christians come to become sons (children) of God with Christ? How come even Christ who was born of a woman like every one of us came to be the only natural Son of God? What is that relationship between Christ's sonship and ours? These are all Christological questions which not only bother on the nature of Christ, but importantly, on our relationship to Christ and God our Father.

This paper seeks to answer some of these questions. In doing this, we hope to clearly prove that Christ is the only natural Son of God. Whereas believers share in the sonship of Christ through adoption. This was made possible by Christ who through his sacrificial death opened the way to the Father for all believers. In the move from proclamation to narration, early Christians had to make a decision about how to portray the metaphor of divine sonship. Is it begotten or adopted? By the fourth century, it became mostly clear: the divine sonship of Christ was by begetting, and that of everyone else was by adoption.

In light of this, we shall explore the scriptures, the Old and the New Testaments, in order to discover how all these became possible. We shall, therefore, begin from the Old Testament in order to see the development of sonship. How did Israel become the beloved or the "first son" (Ex 4, 22) of God among all the nations? This will see us through great Old Testament biblical figures and players like Adam, Noah, Abraham, Moses, and David. Of course, what this means is that we shall do this having one basic thing in mind. This is the fact of God's covenant with them which was the basis of His fraternal or familial bond with Israel. Then we shall walk through the Gospels in order to see what they said about sonship, both of Christ and of the entire believers. Our next port of call shall be to the Pauline epistles, of course not forgetting or neglecting to search for evidences elsewhere in the other epistles and books of the New Testament. In other words, as a paper in biblical theology, it promises to be an adventure into the world of scriptures in other to demonstrate that the divine sonship of Christ is natural, as well as that the divine sonship of all believers (*Totus Christus*) is by adoption. At the end, we shall summarize and draw a brief conclusion based on our findings. The term *natural* as employed here is not to be confused with the term *biological*.

## Divine Sonship in the OT: Israel's Sonship

An important biblical theme often overlooked by Christians is the sonship of Israel. When we hear the expressions "Son of God," "Sonship," or "Divine Sonship," we think of Jesus and possibly of believers. However, we forget that the first son of God mentioned in scripture is the nation of Israel. This oversight, though, is not without reason. The genealogy of sonship is not as simple as it might appear. This is because while one might find it explicitly indicated as in Ex 4:22; in most cases, it is only implied in the Old Testament. So one would be left to discern what exactly this means where it is implied, though without unnecessarily overreading into the particular biblical passage. It may be important to note that the term "Son of God" simply means one who is a righteous person in terms of his character and faith in God. The idea of a "son" in first-century Christian writings was different than it is today. The term *son* simply signified that he came from God and bore His image (Douglas 2013). The title "son of God" is frequent in the Old Testament. The word *son* was employed among the Semites to signify not only filiation but other close connection or intimate relationship. The leaders of the people, kings, princes, judges, as holding authority from God, were called sons of God (Aherne 1912).

Beginning with creation of the world in Genesis 1 and 2, one of the greatest, striking, and significant moment was the moment of the creation of humanity represented by Adam and Eve. After creating the cosmos and every other thing there is in it then, covenantly (though implicitly indicated), "God said, let us make man in our image, after our likeness; and let them have dominion over the fish of the sea, and over the birds of the air…and over every creeping thing that creeps upon the earth. So, God created man in his own image, in the image of God he created him; male and female he created them" (Gen 1:26–27).

It is important to note the emphasis here: "So, God created man in his own image, in the image of God he created him." This underscores the fact that a special bond was established which God could not have established with other created things. As others have noted, while Adam is not specifically identified as the "son of God" in Genesis, his status as such seems to be implied in the Pentateuch. In Genesis 1, God creates Adam in his image and likeness (Gen 1:26–27), terms latter used in reference to Adam and Seth's relationship (Gen 5:3). In light of this, it is no wonder that Adam is identified as the son of God in the gospel of Luke 3: 38 (Kincaid and Barber 2015, 35–64).

Furthermore, this is buttressed by the fact of the dominion God gave man after creating him: "And God blessed them, and God said to them, be fruitful and multiply, and fill the earth and subdue it; and have dominion over the fish of the sea and over the birds of the air and over every living thing that moves upon the earth" (Gen 1:28). The tone and extent of this dominion is what only a Father could extend to his son. As already indicated, sonship might not have been explicitly mentioned here, but the acts and deed of God toward Adam and his wife really indicated that there was something unique in their relationship. At least, one fact is clear: God favored man over other created beings.

If we move further to Noah, where there is a unanimous agreement among scholars that there is a covenant (Gen 9), we find that God favored Noah because he "was a righteous man, blameless in his generation; Noah walked with God" (Gen 6: 9). For this reason, God personally "adopted" Noah and his household and used them to preserve creation during the flood (Gen 7–8). Here, we find again "choosing and favoring" one man and his family over and above others and endowing him with much blessings that only a father could give to a son. This was sealed with a covenant: "Then God said to Noah and to his sons with him, Behold, I establish my covenant with you and your descendants after you…that never again shall all flesh be cut off by the waters of a flood, and never again shall there be a flood to destroy the earth" (Gen 9: 8–10).

Abraham is another figure "adopted" in a dramatic fashion by God as his personal friend. He was also chosen out of many, and his call was strongly tied to his obedience and faith in God. A unique and familial bond was also established between God and the entire humanity through a unique covenant with Abraham. This is a covenant of faith by which God is unconditionally bound to make Abraham and his descendants, the Israelites, a great and blessed nation. "I will make you a great nation; I will bless you and make your name great; And you shall be a blessing. I will bless those who bless you, And I will curse him who curses you; And in you all the families of the earth shall be blessed" (Gen 12:2–3). Here also, we find that although "adoption" or "sonship" were not explicitly mentioned, yet it is obvious this covenant did establish that type of relationship. In this particular case, extending it to all nations rather than to Israel alone. Thus, gradually, we see the scope of this implicit adoption or sonship widening from one man and one family to many.

Moses was another very important figure and player in the Old Testament. Again, in spite of his controversial beginning, God favored him and used him as an instrument of liberation from the political prowess and oppression of Pharaoh the king of Egypt. Given the religious and cultural context of the ancient near eastern world and Israel's adoptive sonship, it is significant that God ordered Moses to go to Pharaoh and inform him that Israel is His *firstborn* son (see Exodus 4:22). This declaration to Pharaoh was followed by Moses's warning that God would kill Pharaoh's *firstborn* son if he refused to let Israel go (Ex 4:23).

This is why this is significant: God treated His adopted son, Israel, as if he were the *firstborn* son. In other words, God did not treat Israel as if Israel's sonship were inferior. The implicit message of Exodus 4:22–23 is that Israel was the same to God as Pharaoh's firstborn son was to him. It is clear from Moses's words to Pharaoh that it was God's great pleasure to give His adopted son all the rights and privileges enjoyed by a firstborn son. God demonstrated His Father-son love for Israel not only through His deliverance of them from their affliction in Egypt (cf. James 1:27), but also through His unfailing care for them in the wilderness. The subsequent history of Israel as God continued to deliver and guide them providentially was a display of God's deep love for His son.

Finally, we come to David, and the Davidic covenant, where we find God also making explicit mention of the term "my Son" in his covenant with David:

> When your days are complete and you lie down with your fathers, I will raise up your descendant after you, who will come forth from you, and I will establish his kingdom. He shall build a house for My name, and I will establish the throne of his kingdom forever. I will be a father to him and he *will be a son to Me*; when he commits iniquity, I will correct him with the rod of men and the strokes of the sons of men. (2 Sam 7:8–17)

From this and many other passages (Ps 2:7; 89: 27: 2Q252 5:3–4; 4Q174 I 1:2:21:2; 1Q28a 2:11–12; 4Q369), we find that divine sonship language is also famously used in connection to the Davidic (Kincaid and Barber, p. 35–64). Although, this oracle was partially fulfilled in Solomon (physically and materially), it was completely fulfilled in Christ in all its ramifications. However, in Solomon's case, his sonship which was made possible through the covenant promise to his father David was at the level of adoption. The pattern continues here as we have seen in the previous figures we have discussed, who were "adopted" by God for their faithfulness or obedience, or out of his own will. In the case of Christ, as we shall see, he was natural. So as soon as a Davidite (Christ) fully accedes to the throne, then God says, in effect, "today I have begotten you. Today you are my son" (Ps 2:7). And again, it is not talking about new birth. It is not talking about ontology. This is said with respect to Solomon, for example (2 Sam 7:14). Yet, so far as ruling is concerned, the Davidic king is to be seen to belong to God's family, to rule like God, to be godlike in that particular respect, just as the person who makes peace is like God along another axis, the peace axis (Ps 82:6).

What can we conclude from this brief exposition of sonship (Israel's) in the Old Testament? Simple! As God's chosen nation, Israel was made God's son, a son by God's sovereign choice, not by genetic connection or some inherent quality of Israel's Jewishness, might, or worth (cf. Deut. 7:7–8, 9:5–6; Isa. 63:8, 16; Jer. 31:9b; Hos. 11:1) (Garner 2016, 145–47). God demonstrated His Father-son love for Israel not only through His deliverance of them from their affliction in Egypt (cf. James 1:27), but also through His unfailing care for them in the wilderness. The subsequent history of Israel, as God continued to deliver and guide them providentially, was a display of God's deep love for His son.

## Divine Sonship in the Synoptic Gospels

In this section, we shall attempt to find out in what ways the gospel presented or viewed Christ as only natural Son of God. Equally important would be how believers are presented as children of God.

Or better put, in what way believers are children of God? Thus, like in the previous section (Old Testament), we shall search for this in each of the four gospels. However, we shall begin with the synoptic gospels and then take the Johannine literature as a whole.

The central theological motif of the gospel of Matthew ("In the person of his Son Jesus, God has come to dwell with his people") is expressed through a chiasm involving 1:23 and 28:20. These verses enclose the entire Gospel with the thought that God is with us and will remain with us forever through Jesus. Both of the passages that comprise this chiasm present Jesus as the Son of God. The context for 1:23 is the virginal conception of Jesus; the context for 28:20 is Jesus' commission to his disciples to baptize "in the name of the Father, Son, and Holy Spirit." Matthew uses the formula "from that time Jesus began" (4:17, 16:21) to organize his Gospel into three parts. The first part (1:1–4:16) contains material that answers the question "Who is Jesus?" and the answer that this material provides to that question is invariably "the Son of God" (see 1:16, 18; 2:15; 3:17; 4:3, 6). Thus, the divine sonship of Jesus is emphasized in that section of this Gospel specifically devoted to establishing his identity.

It is clear that of all the characters in Matthew's narrative, God is the one whose point of view is normative: God's opinion counts more than the opinion of anyone else. Yet, God speaks only twice in the narrative, and both times it is in reference to the identity of Jesus (3:17, 17:5). The only time that God ever enters Matthew's narrative as a character in the story is to declare that Jesus is God's Son. The climax of Matthew's story of Jesus comes in the passion narrative; this is the point to which the entire Gospel builds. The passion in Matthew is organized around the motif of Jesus' divine sonship. First, Jesus claims that the reason his enemies want to kill him is that he is the Son of God (21:33–46). Second, Jesus is sentenced to death for claiming to be the Son of God (26:63–64). Third, Jesus' enemies claim that his crucifixion proves that he is not the Son of God (27:40, 43). Fourth, ironically, Jesus' death actually convinces people that he is the Son of God (27:54). Finally, a subplot in Matthew's Gospel concerns the disciples of Jesus and their relationship to him.

The climax to this "story within the story" comes in 16:13–20, when God reveals to Peter that Jesus is the Son of God (Powell 2009).

In Mark, at the baptism of Jesus, God proclaims him "my Son," and at the cross, when all the mocking of Jesus as the king of the Jews was said and done (15:32), Mark's Roman soldier, a Gentile, recognizes Jesus for who he was, God's self-giving and self-sacrificing king. What irony! Whereas the disciples appear obtuse throughout the entire Gospel, wondering what kind of Christ Jesus is, the Roman centurion grasped it. Thus, Mark's explicit portrayal of Jesus through the synonymous titles "the Christ" and "the Son of God" is that Jesus is "the Christ." He is not merely a wonderworking Christ as portrayed and misunderstood by his disciples (1:14–8:21 with Peter's confession in 8:29), but rather he is a suffering Christ as understood by the Roman centurion as he stood by and watched Jesus suffering a torturous death on the cross (13:1–16:8 with the centurion's confession in 15:39). The true meaning of Jesus as "the Christ" occurs at the foot of the cross. In both life and death, Jesus is "the Christ" (Bateman 2007, 537–59). Thus, the explicit and plain meaning of the phrase "Son of God" in Mark means first and foremost "the Christ."

During the Second Temple period, it was thought that the restoration of a community involved suffering, and thereby this would be part of God's way in which he would restore national Israel. They specifically believed a person or persons who suffered at the hands of the wicked, or the pagans, would suffice for bringing about the restoration of the kingdom (2 Macc 7:36–38; 2 Macc 6:27–29, 9:23–24, 17:20–22, 18:3–4). Jesus was that person (cf. 10:45). Thus, Mark 1:15, 6:4 tells the story of Jesus as the story of a Galilean prophet, announcing the kingdom of Israel's God, summoning Israel to change her direction, that is, to repent" (Wright 1992, 395). Mark, however, takes the concept defining the titles *Christ* and *Son of God* a step further and extends serving and suffering to all those who dare to follow Jesus (Bateman 2007, 537–59).

Jesus is the Son of God in Luke, the angel tells Mary that her child "will be called holy, the Son of God" (1:35). God speaks from heaven at Jesus' baptism, addressing Jesus as "Son" (3:22). God speaks from heaven at Jesus' transfiguration, identifying Jesus as "Son" (9:35). The high priest asks Jesus, "Are you the Son of God?" and Jesus responds, "You have said it. I am" (22:70). In the gospel of Luke, the title "Son of God" emphasizes Jesus' uniqueness and oneness with God, but in this Gospel, the essential ingredient of divine sonship seems to be Jesus' absolute obedience to the will of his Father. Also, in Luke, we find that Satan tempts Jesus as the Son of God, but Jesus refuses to go against God's will (4:1–13). Also, Luke replaces the "cry of dereliction" ("My God, my God, why have you forsaken me?") in Mark's gospel with this: "Father, into thy hands, I commit my spirit" (23:46).

In Luke, Jesus is both the Son and Servant of God: Jesus, the obedient *pais* (2:43), says, "I must be in my Father's house." The Greek word *pais* used in this passage can mean either "son" or "servant." English Bibles regularly translate the term as "son," but the ambiguity in Greek may be intentional (2:49). Jesus describes his mission as the fulfillment of Isaianic prophecy: he has been anointed with the Spirit to do what Isaiah says the "Servant of the Lord" will do (4:16–22; cf. Isa. 61:2). People respond by wondering if he is the "son of Joseph." Of course, the reader knows that he is only "the son, as it was supposed, of Joseph" (3:23), and that actually he is the Son of God (1:35).

The final composite text of Luke-Acts remains before us: Jesus is God's son at conception, baptism, and resurrection. What we might find to be mutually exclusive because of our Nicene emphasis on the when of divine sonship, Luke seems to have found mutually reinforcing. Luke may have had a rhetorical reason for his mixed images of divine sonship, namely, his concern for, and masterful skill with, presenting the history of nascent Christianity to a broad audience with diverse social practices and cultural ideologies (Peppard, p. 91). The more sources of legitimacy that Luke could articulate for Jesus, the better. Such an approach is similar to how the divine sonship of the Roman emperors in the Julio-Claudian era was legitimated.

## Sonship in the Johannine Literatures

We now turn to the Johannine literatures which present the closest and ideal types of portraying the divine sonship. In John, what we find is the great image of Christ as the only begotten Son of God (Jn 3:16; 1 Jn 3:1, 8). Although there are fewer references to Jesus as son of God in Johannine literature and more specifically in the gospel of John, the title "Son of God" plays a significant role in John's narrative. For example, at the beginning of the gospel, John testifies that Jesus is the Son of God (1:49). Nathaniel employs Son of God in apposition to king of Israel, his confession is more profound than he realizes (Frank 1999, 231). For the metaphor of begotten divine sonship, one turns undoubtedly to Johannine literature. There the metaphor of begottenness is used to describe both Christians and Christ himself. Due to the prominence of Jesus' dialogue with Nicodemus in Christian popular consciousness (John 3:1–21, esp. w. 1–10), the fact that Christians are "begotten" or "born" from above is widely known. Being "born again" has caught on as shorthand for being Christian in a way that being "adopted" never has (Peppard, p. 102).

In the famous dialogue already mentioned, Christians are clearly portrayed as "begotten" or "born" in a metaphorical way (John 3:3–8). The begetting happens "from above" and/or "again" (ἄνωθεν [3:3]) and is enacted by water and spirit (3:5), or simply "the spirit" (3:6, 8). The double meaning of the spatial-temporal word ἄνωθεν combines with the twin agency of water and spirit in order to generate an image of divine begetting that is both sacramental and sapiential. The sacrament of baptism is implied by the temporal "again" and the substance of "water," while the spatial imagery of a "spirit" birth "from above" perhaps suggests a wisdom tradition.

The result of the begetting is the ability to see the kingdom of God and enter into it, which is distinct from other NT authors' concepts of inheriting and entering the kingdom of God. For John, the begetting assures not only an eschatological inheritance of a father's goods, as does divine sonship for Paul, but a currently accessible revelation of God as father—God's glory, truth, grace, light, and life. This revelation can happen only through his son, Jesus Christ, who has already claimed possession of the kingdom (John 18:36). The begotten relationship between Christians and God is further solidified in the rest of the Gospel and especially in the first epistle. In John 8:39–47, Jesus draws a kind of "dichotomous key" for the human race, dividing people ultimately into children of God and children of the devil.

Also, in the prologue, we find the narrative: Indeed, God did not send the Son into the world to condemn the world, but in order that the world might be saved through him. Those who believe in him are not condemned; but those who do not believe are condemned already, because they have not believed in the name of the only Son of God (Jn 3: 17–18). Further, in John 5: 25 "Son of God" appears in a section that refers to Jesus as the Son (5: 19, 20, 21, 22, 23, 26) (Frank, p. 231). Speaking of the power the Father has given to the Son, Jesus says: "Very truly, I tell you, the hour is coming, and is now here, when the dead will hear the voice of the Son of God, and those who hear will live" (5:25). These words find an immediate fulfilment in the raising of Lazarus from the dead.

## Divine Sonship in Pauline Corpus

Moving over to the Pauline epistles or corpus, one finds that like in John, Paul also presents an ideal type of portraying divine sonship. He is firm in pointing out that Jesus is the Son of God, the Lord and most importantly the only natural son of God. It is in Paul that it becomes however very clear that believers are divine sons of God through adoption. Hence, the theme of adoption reaches its climax and meaning in Paul. It could be said that Paul's gospel is a gospel of sonship and adoption. That is, God's intention is to bring many sons into glory.

In Gal 3:23–4:7, Paul establishes adoption as his master metaphor for Christian divine sonship, and he returns to it again in Rom 8:12–25. Paul envisions a realistic household of both "slaves" and children in which the children are afforded a παιδαγωγός (tutor) throughout their youth. In this household, the sons of the father, and thus his rightful heirs, are not empowered until adulthood, and they can be drawn from either the slaves or the children (Peppard, p. 95).

In his letter to the Romans, the imagery is quite similar and rather cleaner in its exposition (as are other tropes revised from Galatians into Romans). But here, Paul further emphasizes the adult-age, even eschatological-age, time frame of adoption into God's family. The divine family spirit has been given already the spirit of adoption (Rom 8:15). Adoptive sonship is both already and not yet, a fact that Paul expresses through two images familiar to other ancient apocalyptic: the birth pangs of labor and the firstfruits of harvest. "For the yearning of creation is awaiting the revelation of the sons of God," he writes, and "all of creation has been joined in groans and labor pains until now. Not only that, but we ourselves, who have the first fruits of the spirit, we also groan while we wait for adoption, the redemption of our body" (Rom 8:19, 22–23). David B. Garner (2016, 145–7) notes that, having established the vital resurrection/adoption connection in Romans 8:23, the apostle Paul draws Romans 8 to conclusion with the doxological and pastorally poignant question concerning the sons' security in the Son: "Who shall separate us from the love of Christ?" (Rom. 8:35a).

Paul's understanding of Christian divine sonship is continued in other writings in the Pauline tradition. Ephesians (1:3–14) echoes Galatians 3–4 but somewhat collapses the timeline of adoptive sonship articulated in Romans 8. The Father chose those whom he wanted as sons before the foundation of the world and predestined them for adoptive sonship (1:4–5). But the already aspect of this redemptive adoption is emphasized, since the time when the household plan takes effect, gathering up all things under God as Father and Jesus Christ as Lord seems to be now (1:10).

In 3 Corinthians (apocryphal Pauline), Paul also uses the metaphor of adoptive sonship at a crucial juncture when the author is summarizing his version of Christian doctrine. The next of the doctrines to be passed on is that the human being was fashioned by his Father, and thus, he was sought while he was lost so that he might be made alive through adoptive sonship (7–8). This teaching is intended to refute a doctrine that the "Corinthians" claimed they were being taught by others, that the human being was not created by God. But it also serves to combine different Pauline images into one moment: the eschatological adoption foretold in Romans is united with the "making alive" of the dead Adamic body described in 1 Corinthians (15:22).

## The Divine Sonship of All believers

So far, we have been able to establish from Scriptures that Christ is the son of God, was a Jew and a descendant of David, and that his sonship is natural. Likewise, it is important to think how we Christians are sons of God. In one sense, this is the result of the new birth, something working within us. In the climactic revelation of the Bible, in Revelation 21–22, we are told that the overcomer, that is, the believer who perseveres to the end by overcoming will be called God's son (Rev 21:7). Now, in one sense, believers have been called God's children again and again, implicitly referring to their reliance under the old covenant. Certainly, in the New Testament, various sonship words are used. In John's gospel, one word is used for Jesus the Son of God, and other words are used for believers. In Paul, both Jesus and the Christians are called sons of God, the same word, but we are sons of God by adoption in Rom 8:15, 23. Some subtle distinction is made. However, the power of the metaphor itself, "Son of God," is seen in its greatest form applied to Christians in Revelation 21–22.

The best way to view this is simply from the point of view of Christ's sacrifice on the cross. His paschal mystery initiated the new covenant and thus established a new people with a new status. By offering himself, Christ opened for all believers the door to the Father's house. By paying the price of our sins (Rom 5:6–8), he gave us the leeway of becoming sons with him. For Daniel A. Keating (2000, 100), by being conformed to Christ rather than to the world (Rom 12: 2) through our baptism, we ourselves participate in Him and in the Father. Simply put, we became like him and like God by participating in the life of Christ and in that of God. Conformed into the likeness of the son through the Spirit, we become adopted sons of the Father and share in the divine life of God. It is through this *chrstosis, theosis* or deification (taking certain divine qualities) that we become children of God, as Irenaeus summarized it: "He became what we are and we became what he is…the Lord Jesus Christ…did, through his transcendent love become what we are, that he might bring us to become even more like himself (Irenaeus, *Against Heresies,* 5, preface).

Paul in Galatians, as we have already seen above, called believers children of God: "For in Christ Jesus you are all children of God (literarily, 'sons of God') through faith. As many of you as were baptized into Christ have clothed yourselves with Christ" (Gal 3:26–27). In other words, believers become sons or children of God through faith in Christ Jesus. However, this faith is also a free gift (grace) of God. All these became possible through the "energizing power of grace." This energizing power of grace, therefore, is ordered to a specific end, that is, conformity to the divine Son, which entails a life of holiness and virtue and fulfilling the just requirement of the law (Kincaid and Barber, p. 35–64). Also, redemptive grace procures the filial blessing. Consistent with its eschatologically realized form, redemptive sonship never owes to the intrinsic worth of the redeemed son, but to the grace and sovereign initiative of the Father (Garner, p. 145–7). It is through it that believers are justified and made strong in doing good works, like the Son and the Father in whose life they participate. Hence, for believers, the door of sonship to God clearly articulated in Galatians is spiritual adoption through faith in Jesus Christ. As Paul wrote: "But when the fullness of the time came, God sent forth His Son, born of a woman, born under the Law, so that He might redeem those who were under the Law, that we might receive the adoption as sons" (Gal 4:4–5).

So the picture becomes clearer here that first and foremost believers are sons or children of God. Second and most importantly, this sonship is by a means, since biologically speaking, we are not sons of God. So it is evident that the door to sonship can only be opened by God, who is the sovereign Lord of all. By his initiative, he sent forth his only Son, to be born under the law and to die under the law so that the chosen of God may be freely adopted into the kingdom as justified sons of God. Spiritual adoption is received, not acquired. It is part of God's grace at work in believers through the selfless sacrifice of Christ, and through the action of the Holy Spirit at work in believers as the apostle John tells us: "But to all who received him, who believed in his name, he gave power to become children (sons) of God" (John 1:12).

By the power of God, his children are enabled to receive him and are given the right to become children and heirs by believing in his name, and thereby being justified. This new birth does not come by blood inheritance, nor the desire of the flesh and human nature, nor by man's own will to be a son, but rather by the will and plan of God. Through adoption, God promises, "And I will be a father to you, and you shall be sons and daughters to Me, Says the Lord Almighty" (2 Cor 6:18). According to Packer (1973, 205), adoption is the highest privilege offered by God, even higher than justification. This is not a denial that "justification is the primary blessing because it meets our primary spiritual need." Rather, this is to say that justification is not the highest blessing. Adoption is higher because of the richer relationship with God that it involves. Justification, if viewed as forensic, does not of itself imply any intimate or deep relationship with God, the Judge. In theory, you can have the reality of justification without any close fellowship with God. Having said this, however, it is important and behooves us to see that God works through both justification and adoption in order to make us his children. Hence David V. Meconi (2013, 280) quotes Augustine:

> He who justifies is the same who deifies because by justifying he made (human persons) into children of God: he gave them power to become children of God (Jn 1:2). If we are made God's children, we are made gods: but this is through the grace of the one who adopts and not through the nature of the one who begets. For there is only one Son of God: our Lord and Saviour Jesus Christ... The rest who have been made into gods are thus made by his grace and

not born from his own substance, so as to be what he is, but they come to him through (his) generosity and are thus Christ's coheirs.

## Summary and Conclusion

In this brief work, we have been able to trace the development of sonship from the sacred scriptures beginning from Adam to the Davidic king. Most importantly, we showed that Christ fulfilling the Davidic oracle was the only natural Son of God who ushered in the New Covenant. Through this new covenant, he ushered in believers to participate in his sonship. Supernatural participation is not less real than our real participation in being; rather, it is a different order, and indeed, a more elevated and privileged participation in God. It is a personal participation in God. Through grace, we enter into personal communion of love of the Father, Son, and Holy Spirit.

By the grace of God in baptism, and through the faith demonstrated by believers in Christ, they became fully adopted sons of God. The primary statement in the Christian tradition that upholds this difference takes some form of the saying "We became sons and children or God not by nature, but by grace." A chorus of voices attesting to this ancient, medieval, and modern will help us grasps how widespread is the conviction that deification does not compromise divine transcendence, but rather reveals the divine plan for the glorification of human nature in the incarnate son. Therefore, what makes the sonship of believers interesting and unique is the fact that it was only possible through the obedient and sacrificial action of Christ, the only (natural) Son of God (John 3: 16). This was according to the plan and purpose of God the Father, so that both Sons (Christ and his adopted brethren) might have a unique and inseparable bond. For when the natural Son (Christ) remembers that the adopted came forth through his own sacrifice, He loves them more as His own. Likewise, when the adopted sons or children reflect and remember that their sonship was made possible through the sacrifice of the natural Son, they equally love Him more and more with divine sentiments.

In and through this relationship of adoption and participation, there is a kind of "imperfect hypostatic-like union" established because the adopted sons, though not fully divinized like the natural Son and the Father, share to some degree (though imperfectly) in the divinity and life of the natural Son (Christ). This is what Augustine of Hippo meant when he wrote: "It is evident then as He has called men gods (probably referring to Ps 82:6), that they are deified by his grace, not born of his substance...if we have been made sons of God, we have also been made gods; but this is the effect of grace adopting, not of nature generating (Augustine of Hippo, *Ear. Ps.* 49.2).

There is a covenantal bond established because Christ shares in the life of his adopted brothers, and his adopted brother equally share in the life of Christ through their baptism, obedience of faith, suffering, and good works empowered by the Holy Spirit. Hence, the sonship of Christ is natural, and that of all believers by adoption, through Christ's sacrifice.

# THE EUCHARISTIC RELATIONSHIP BETWEEN ECCLESIOLOGY AND ESCHATOLOGY

## Introduction

The Church as God's kingdom on earth is on a journey toward the eternal kingdom. It is a preparation ground for those who persevere for the final movement. Hence, the Eucharist becomes important, first as a uniting factor or the common ground for the gathering of God's people or the people of God (the *ecclesia* or *communio* or *qahal*) together. Second, it is the spiritual nourishment prefigured by the Passover meal for this community (the new exodus of God's people) for this eschatological journey.

In this brief paper, we shall examine the relationship between ecclesiology and eschatology. The focal or converging point of this determination will be the Eucharist. So we hope to achieve this by first taking a brief excursus into the world of ecclesiology. This excursus will lead us through a brief historical perspective of this very important aspect of theology. Second, we shall have a general overview of eschatology. This concept means different things to different scholars. Some like Karl Barth think it strictly belongs only to the future (hope) and has nothing to do with "the now." Others like Joseph Ratzinger, however, think it could be located both in "the now" and as well as in the future. That is, living in the hope that is "Christ now" and also looking forward to the future (Ratzinger 1988, 43–45).

The third part of this work shall focus on how the Eucharist reflects and unites ecclesiology and eschatology, and how both work toward the same goal for our salvation. This is with a view of showing that the Eucharist is the ground for the gathering of God's people and also prepares and nourishes them for the final eschatological banquet. In the end, we shall seek to draw a conclusion that the church's eschatological vision is strongly enhanced and sustained by the member's participation in the Eucharist, "the source and submit of the Christian life" and worship (CCC 1324).

## An Overview of Ecclesiology

In this section, we hope to first take a brief survey of the concept of ecclesiology and to understand how it really developed. Ecclesiology could be simply defined as the theological study of the church. Here the church means two things. The institution with the magisterial authority, and on the other hand, the church as the people of God or the body of Christ.

Congar's ecclesiology was centered on the structure and life of the church. One essential element of his ecclesiological development concerns his dialectic between the structure and life of the church. He sensed the inherent necessity to distinguish between the visible hierarchically constituted church society and the invisible mystery of heavenly life. Hence, (Congar 1957, 27) started off with the word *ecclesia* which he says can be defined as "the assembly, a body of people coming together." Julie M. Pomerleau, commenting on Congar's ecclesiology notes: "However, the term is not limited to the secular sense of people gathering, because the term also connotes a reference to the Old Testament concept of People of God or Israel." This is the concept of the *Qahal Yahweh* (People of God). Thus, the church is composed both of its members, and a social institution established by God. Through this, Congar established a twofold definition of the church. First, structure. That is the visible social institution. Second, communal life. That is the invisible assembly that makes up the spiritual body of Christ (Congar 1939, 75–80).

For Henri de Lubac (1969, 12), whose ecclesiology offers a model for our times, the church is both a paradox and a mystery (Dennis 1999, 60). Hence, De Lubac notes that "the Church is a mystery for all time, out of man's grasp" This is because, qualitatively, it is totally removed from all other objects of man's knowledge that might be mentioned. "Yet, at the same time, it concerns us, touches us, acts in us, reveals us to ourselves." He noted that the nature of the Church as mystery is much deeper and more grounding than the nature of the church as a paradox (Dennis 1999, 212).

Also, the Church is the Mystical Body of Christ. Hence, drawing from Pauline ecclesiology to the Patristics, De La Soujeole, (2014, 131) concludes that the doctrine of the church as the Mystical Body of Christ has great breadth. This is because "its fundamental richness is that it benefits from a very firm basis in scripture and has been handed down to us by an extremely profound tradition that is largely shared without orthodox brethren." He notes again: "As it emerges from the sources, the theme of the Mystical Body expresses the Church along a line that relates to her essence above all else, *in facto esse*: what the church actually has been from the first day, and what she will never cease to be." De La Soujeole also noted the inclusive nature of the Church: "Indeed, the Body of Christ includes the just of the Old Testament, all those who fully awaited Christ. For the Body of Christ was formed progressively. He concludes, "the Church is young under the patriarchs, and attains adulthood with Christ."

Vatican II did not offer a simple definition of the Church, the sort one might have expected from the title of the first draft *De Ecclesia* whose first chapter was in fact entitled "The Nature of the Church." Joseph Komonchak (1999, 763–68) notes carefully: "It is a mistake, I think to expect to find a fully coherent, systematic and comprehensive ecclesiology in the conciliar document…the Council did not produce a treatise." However, having said this, he went on to clarify the ecclesiology of Vatican II under the following questions: "What is the Church? Where is the Church? What is the Church for?" (*Lumen Gentium*, 8). On the nature of the church, Lumen Gentium chapter 8 made a nuanced discussion on the church's relationship to the kingdom and a number of biblical images of the Church. Special attention was paid to the image of the church as the Body of Christ and the Mystical Body of Christ. In chapter 2, it also described the church as the people of God. We shall not go into full details of how Vatican II treated these themes here. However, it suffices to note that "in these two are concentrated the essential theological description of the church" (Komonchak, p. 3).

On the second question: Where is the Church? Joseph Komonchak observed that one may look to the differentiated ranks of the assembly of believers. The doctrinal commission took pains to point out that the term "People of God" refers to all those who belong to the church (through baptism though), clergy and laity alike. Finally, the role of the Church was addressed theologically by *Lumen gentium* in terms of the Church as sacrament: "The Church is the sign and instrument of intimate union with God and unity of the whole human race."

## The Church and the Kingdom

The quest for the relationship between the Church and the kingdom is one which has lots of intrigues. In biblical theology, the identity of the kingdom and the relationship of the kingdom to Christ and to the Church are crucial. This is important, considering the position of Protestant scholars, and of course, the not-so-well-received remark and barbed quip of Alfred Loisy that "Jesus proclaimed the Kingdom, what came was the church." Benedict sees the presumed dialectic of Church and kingdom as another artificial by-product of the erroneous philosophy that underlines the histori-cal-critical method (Hahn 2009, 125).

On a general level, there are different opinions on this relation-ship. Among Catholic scholars, there is a seemingly general opinion that the Church is identifiable with the kingdom. In other words, it is inseparable with the kingdom (Hahn, p.125). Outside the fold, opinions run wide apart. This is especially among Protestants, who have the tendency of separating the Church from the kingdom of

God or the kingdom of heaven. It suffices to note equally that one could talk about the kingdom of God in two senses. That is as the kingdom which Christ preached and which resides fully in "the church as the summit of divine economy written into the pages of the New and Old Testament" (Hahn, p. 126). In another sense, one could talk of the eschatological kingdom, which is the hope to which we all look forward. That is the "heavenly Jerusalem" (Rev 21:21).

In the parables of the kingdom (Mt 5), one sees that Christ fulfils the laws and prophets. The kingdom of heaven, hence, could be entirely of this life by one "being more righteous than the Pharisees." Hence, at this juncture, the Church emerges as the "present kingdom." It is the preparation ground for the future or the eschatological kingdom which Christ would enact at his Parousia. Mt 16 is very decisive because Christ actually promised to build his Church on Peter (the rock). He also appointed Peter the "majordomo" (the prime minister) of the kingdom of heaven. Verse 24 concludes by speaking of "the Son of Man coming in his kingdom." Evidently, Christ is the "true David" who fulfilled the prophecies of the promise of the kingdom. Given this fact, then "it follows that the kingdom proclaimed by Christ 'must in some sense' be understood as the restored and renewed Davidic kingdom."

On the relationship between Church and kingdom, Hahn commenting on Benedict's view wrote: "His response is calm and simple. A historical reading of the texts reveals that the opposition of the kingdom and Church has no factual basis." At times, his language regarding the kingdom is indistinguishable from his language regarding the Church (Hahn, p. 125–6). Thus, he can identify using statistical analyses and word studies, the kingdom as "the true leitmotiv of Jesus' preaching" and as the foundation of the Church, and thus, the realization of Christ's mission. Vatican II (*Lumen gentium* 5) identifies the Church and the kingdom as inseparable. Just as Christ made the kingdom visible ("the kingdom is clearly visible in the very person of Christ"), so also, the Church "becomes on earth the initial budding forth of that kingdom." Furthermore, it most precisely identifies the kingdom and the church in the following words: "The

Church, or, in other words, the kingdom of Christ now present in mystery, grows visibly."

Hence, the Church and the kingdom, the gathering of the eschatological people of God, are in the one person of Christ (Hahn 2009, 136). The Church in her institutional expression is part of this kingdom preparing all who persevere for the eschatological kingdom. Although the Church as the kingdom preached by Christ in her institutional expression may not administer all reality, however, she prepares the way to the eschatological kingdom. She is an image of the eschatological kingdom, a mystery and an icon of the kingdom to come.

## An Overview of Eschatology

In this section, we shall take a brief excursus on the church's understanding of eschatology. Once the term eschatology is mentioned is, what comes to mind are the three last things: death, judgement, and heaven or hell. For centuries, eschatology was content to lead a quiet life as the final chapter of theology where it was dubbed "the doctrine of the last things." However, with the historical process in crisis, eschatology has moved into the very center of the theological stage. Some twenty years ago, Hans Urs von Balthasar called it the *"storm zone"* (Ratzinger 1988, 1).

Hence, the systematic title of "eschatology" is not as ancient as some might initially think. The simplistic division of the word is *logos* of the "last things" which first appeared within Lutheran seventeenth century dogmatism (Frey 2011, 1–32). In 1664, Philipp Heinrich Friedlieb published a work with the *Eschatologia* as part of a book title. In his book, *Eschatologia,* he introduced the collective ideas of death, the resurrection from the dead, the last judgment, the dissolution of the world, eternal death, and eternal life.

It is important to note that during the early parts of the twentieth century, scholarship attempted to crystallize the meaning of eschatology. Bultmann and Barth provided definitions contrary to their contemporary counterparts and thus provided the need to bifurcate subsequent eschatological discussions. Their discussions surrounded two different items of bifurcation; it was time to distinguish future-oriented and present-oriented eschatology. Hence, it was time to distinguish between "prophetic" (within history) and "apocalyptic" elements of eschatological descriptions (Ratzinger 1988, 57–8). Therefore, the expression of eschatological thought now needs various contextual definitions and referent points. Because of the "already and not yet" tension of New Testament eschatology, and the expression of the Kingdom of God, time referents need to be distinguished between present and future eschatology. So eschatology should not exclusively refer to future events but should include present dimensions as well.

It suffices to say that eschatology, the study of the last things, flows directly from ecclesiology, the doctrine of the church (Olson, 2006). According to Catechism of the Catholic Church (CCC 759), "the Church or the family of God" is gradually formed and takes shape during the stages of human history. In fact, already present in figure at the beginning of the world, this Church was prepared in a marvelous fashion in the history of the people of Israel… Established in this last age of the world and made manifest in the outpouring of the Spirit, it will be brought to glorious completion at the end of time. Therefore, the Catholic Church has always understood herself to be the New Israel (Gal 6:16; Eph 2:11–12) and the new People of God (1 Pet 2:9–10). She is the recipient of the New Covenant given through Christ (Heb 8:8–13). The Old Covenant was not abolished or rejected by Christ. Rather, it was fulfilled and taken up into the New Covenant. The Catholic doctrine also teaches that the Church is intimately related to the kingdom of God. The Church is "ultimately one, holy, catholic, and apostolic in her deepest and ultimate identity. This is because, it is in her that 'the Kingdom of heaven, the Reign of God, already exists and will be fulfilled at the end of time" (CCC 865).

The kingdom is not yet complete but began with the incarnation and will be fully realized at the end of time (CCC 567). In its fullness, the kingdom is not an earthly reign but the final triumph of Christ over the power of sin and Satan, culminating in an eternity spent in communion with the Triune God: "The kingdom has come in the person of Christ, and grows mysteriously in the hearts of those incorporated into him, until its full eschatological manifestation" (CCC 865).

## The Eucharistic Relationship between Ecclesiology and Eschatology

We now come to the most important part of this work. Here, we shall try to answer the question (though not directly as one would expect an answer to any objective question in a class quiz). Here, we shall focus on the Eucharist in order to show how as a sacrament, it links ecclesiology and eschatology. We shall not attempt the historicity of the Eucharist or full theology of the Eucharistic. Rather, we shall try to prove that the Eucharist is the sacrament of unity which prepares the people of God, the "now kingdom," for the "future or eschatological kingdom." First, what is the relationship of the Eucharist with each of these two themes?

## The Eucharist and Ecclesiology

This great theological theme, Eucharistic ecclesiology is one of the central points of deeper interest in Orthodox and Roman Catholic, as well as, Anglican ecclesiology. It has engaged the labors of some of the outstanding theologians of our time: Henri de Lubac, Yves Congar, Joseph Ratzinger, Jean Marie Tillard, Walter Kasper, Bruno Forte, on the Catholic side; Nicholas Afanassieff, Jean Meyendorff, J. J. von Allmen, and specially in our time, John D, Zizoulas, among the Orthodox; to name just a few authors (Arevalo 1999, 220–12). Here, an understanding of the Church's sacramentality suffices. First, the Catechism of the Catholic Church teaches that "the Church is the universal sacrament of Salvation" (CCC 776). In De Lubac's *Catholicism* (1988, 82–83), there is a highly developed understanding of the Church as a sacrament: "If Christ is the sacrament of God, the Church is for us the sacrament of Christ; she represents him, in the full and ancient meaning of the term, she really makes him present" Also, he speaks of the "social aspects" of sacraments. "Since the sacraments are means of salvation, they should be understood as instruments of unity. As they make real, renew or strengthen man's union with Christ, union with the Christian community…all sacraments are essentially sacraments of the church." De Lubac calls it "the sacrament which contains the whole mystery of unity: *Sacramentum unitatis ecclessiaticae"* (De Lubac, p. 89).

The Extraordinary Assembly of the Synod of Bishops in 1985 saw in the concept of an "ecclesiology of communion" the central and fundamental idea of the documents of the Second Vatican Council. (*L'Osservatore Romano*, December 1985:7). The Second Vatican Council in many of its texts affirms and reaffirms the binding together of the Eucharist and the Church. *Lumen Gentium* (LG 3, 11, 26), three times at least teaches that "Strengthened through the Body of Christ in the holy celebration of the Eucharist, they then manifest the unity of the people of God, which through this sublime sacrament is powerfully represented [*significatur*], and wonderfully realized [*efficitur*] in a visible way" (LG, 11). Almost identical, even verbally, is the teaching of *Unitatis redintegratio* and *Orientalium ecclesiarum. Sacrosanctum Concilium* tells us that the Eucharist is the summit of all of the Church's action, and toward it, all apostolic labor is oriented (SC 10, 4); *Presbyterorum Ordinis* says that all priestly ministry finds its highpoint in the Eucharist (PO, 6, 52). In its turn, the Catechism of the Catholic Church (CCC) tells us that the Church lives in eucharistic communities: "She exists in local communities and is made real as a liturgical, and above all, a eucharistic assembly" (CCC 752). Thus, the Church fulfills itself, "realizes" itself in the eucharistic celebration.

From Henri de Lubac (1988, 88–92), we have the saying, "The Eucharist makes the Church, and (in turn), the Church makes the Eucharist." *"Eucharistia facit ecclesiam."* In simplest terms, this tells us that in the Lord's Supper, we have the actualization of the Paschal Mystery (memorial of his passion, death, and resurrection of Jesus) in the diversity of times and places throughout history. Hence, the Eucharist renews in each Christian community and in every Christian life the reconciliation and atonement worked by God, poured out into our hearts, *per ipsum et cum ipso et in ipso,* (through Christ Jesus, with him and in him.) According to St. Augustine (PL 35, 1613), the Eucharist is the sacrament of unity and the bond of love. By the power of the Spirit, through the saving realities of the Eucharist, the Church as the Body of Christ and people of God come to be, and Christian brotherhood is quickened, within every community of faith, sacrament, as well as within the interlocking communities (which are the local sacramental assemblies and the local churches) throughout the world, the *communio ecclesarium*, always in living oneness with that church which "presides over the communion in love." (SC 41; LG 21, 22).

Also, it follows from this that the Church also makes the Eucharist, "*Ecclesia facit eucharistiam*" (Henri de Lubac 1988, xxx). If the Word is not proclaimed (cf. Rom. 10:14–15), if there is no one to celebrate the memorial of the Lord's Pasch in sacrament in obedience to the Lord's command, then there is no Eucharist "realized" in time and place. Thus, the Eucharist demands for its realization, the ministerial service of the Church. It is this immateriality which gathers the people, proclaims the Word, and breaks and shares the bread. "The Eucharist is the source, the center and the summit, the of the Christian life" (CCC 13224). It is also the source and summit of the Church's Trinitarian life, the very core of both its communion and its mission. The Eucharist constitutes the community and puts it at the service of the people. As well as making Jesus present in the host, the Eucharist is given to us to make Him present in the world. The work and achieving of Christ's love in this world in all human history is truly one of the fundamental goals of the Eucharist in the life of the Church. The Eucharist is thus constitutive of the Church's being and activity. This is why Christian antiquity used the same words, *Corpus Christi*, to designate Christ's body born of the Virgin Mary, his eucharistic and his ecclesial body.

## The Eucharist and Eschatology

Thus far, one issue that cannot be contested is the fact that the Church is strongly related to the Eucharist, as we have seen from de Lubac's words: "The Eucharist makes the church and the church makes the Eucharist." How then is the Eucharist related to eschatology, or what role does it play for eschatology? This popular word of Pope John Paul II will suffice to begin out reflection in this session. "The Eucharist, as Christ's saving presence in the community of the faithful and its spiritual food, is the most precious possession which the Church can have in her journey through history." These words first tell us that the church, the body of Christ or the people of God, are in a journey and need something to sustain them on this journey. The mere mention of journey directly points to the fact that the people of God are a pilgrim people moving somewhere, the Kingdom of God (which as we have already seen is not separated from the "now kingdom"). The kingdom which the church proclaims, it has not fully entered, the bride without spot or wrinkle has not emerged, and the church not only shares the same destiny as the world and individual, but as both holy and sinful, shares their same condition in the present, for this is what it means to live in the eschatological age. The Eucharist is a gift to men and women on their journey. If it is true that the sacraments are part of the Church's pilgrimage through history toward the full manifestation of the victory of the risen Christ, it is also true that, especially in the liturgy of the Eucharist, they give us a real foretaste of the eschatological fulfilment for which every human being and all creation are destined (*Lumen Gentium*, 48).

Hence, to ease this journey, Christ gave the church the Eucharist as he fed Elijah in the desert (1 Kg 17:6) and the Israelites too in the desert (Ex 16: 35). Furthermore, this spiritual food keeps the hope of the people of God alive and active as they move toward the final Kingdom which Christ will enact at his parousia. In presenting his second coming (Luke 12:35–40) as a new Passover, Jesus invites His followers to direct their attention to the new event of personal liberation. His final coming (to enact the future kingdom) will be the fulfillment of the Passover. A very important eucharistic motive of Luke 12: 35–40 is the eschatological one. Both this meal (that is, the Passover meal), and the Lord's supper are to be seen as an eschatological Passover banquet. A. J. B. Higgins (1952, 48) describes the Last Supper as looking ahead to the eschatological Passover meal: "Jesus looked forward to the great banquet of the kingdom of God, when all Passover promises of the eschatological joy, of redemption, and of the glorious Messianic age should be fulfilled." So just as the Passover meal proclaims the unity of those keeping watch for the Lord's coming, also the Eucharist continues to foster the communion and unity of the body of Christ, the people of God, or the church for the Lord's coming and the future kingdom. Man is created for the true and eternal happiness which only God's love can give. Even though we remain "aliens and exiles" in this world (1 Pet 2:11), through faith we already share in the fullness of risen life. The eucharistic banquet, by disclosing its powerful eschatological dimension, comes to the aid of our freedom as we continue our journey.

## Final Reflection and Conclusion

As we noted, and from the ongoing discussion so far, one point emerges clear. This is the fact that eschatology, "the study of the last things," flows directly from ecclesiology, "the doctrine of the Church." Put in another way, eschatology constitutes the central and primary aspect of ecclesiology, the beginning of the church, the conception which not only gives the church her identity, but also sustains and inspires her existence. Also, the church is eschatological in its nature. Being eschatological means she ever longs for, and in fact is sustained by, the eschatological banquet. Reflecting on this mystery, one can infer that Jesus' coming responded to an expectation present in the people of Israel, in the whole of humanity, and ultimately in creation itself. By His self-gift, He objectively inaugurated the eschatological age. Christ came to gather together the "scattered People of God" (cf. Jn 11:52) and clearly manifested his intention to gather together the community of the covenant in order to bring to fulfilment the promises made by God to the fathers of old (cf. Jer 23:3; Lk 1:55, 70).

So as a pilgrim people of God, Christ leaves her the Eucharist as food for their journey. The Eucharist is at the same time a center of unity for the movement toward the future kingdom. Hence, the sacrament of the Eucharist remains the basic criterion of any structural expression of the church, the only expression of unity of the pilgrim people of God. "Where there is a Eucharistic meeting (of course, properly constituted), their lives Christ too, there is also the church of God in Christ" moving toward the kingdom. Consequently, every eucharistic celebration sacramentally accomplishes the eschatological gathering of the people of God. For us, the eucharistic banquet is a real foretaste of the final banquet foretold by the prophets (cf. Is 25:6–9) and described in the New Testament as "the marriage-feast of the Lamb" (Rev 19:7–9) to be celebrated in the joy of the communion of saints.

In conclusion, from the foregoing, it is quite obvious that there is a unique eucharistic relationship between ecclesiology and eschatology. The following conclusions could therefore be drawn from our reflection so far. First, the Church is the people of God or the body of Christ. Second, the Church as the people of God or the body of Christ is inseparable with the kingdom of God or kingdom of heaven. Yet, she is institutional (for the sake of leading the people of God). Third, the Church is eschatological. That is to say, she is on a journey and thus looking forward to the eternal kingdom which Christ will inaugurate at his parousia. Fourth, through the Eucharist, Christ nourishes His pilgrim church and prepares her for the final or eschatological banquet. Sixth, the Eucharist is also the center of unity of this community—the people of God. The relationship between the Eucharist and *communio or ecclesia* had already been pointed out by John Paul II in his Encyclical *Ecclesia de Eucharistia*.

He spoke of the memorial of Christ as "the supreme sacramental manifestation of communion in the Church." The unity of ecclesial communion is concretely manifested in the Christian communities and is renewed at the celebration of the Eucharist, which unites them and differentiates them in the particular Churches, *"in quibus et ex quibus una et unica Ecclesia catholica exsistit."* It is within the Eucharistic community that the people of God, the new Israel, are prepared for the future kingdom.

# AN ANALYSIS OF THE MOSAIC COVENANT RATIFICATION IN EX 24: 3–10

*Pentateuch*

## Introduction

One of the major themes in the Old Testament, and Pentateuch in particular, is the concept of Covenant. One could find this theme pervading almost every aspect of Pentateuch, from Genesis to Deuteronomy. Hence, it would not be out of place to say that Pentateuch begins and ends with covenants or if it is referred to as the "book of covenants." It suffices to note that in some cases, (in the book of Pentateuch), one might not find the word *covenant* expressly or actually employed. However, as Scott W. Hahn (2009, 10) points out, this does not mean the absence of covenantal ceremony itself. Hence, with regards to Gen 1–2, Bergsma and Pitre (2017, 197) observed that: "Although, the Jewish and Christian traditions have affirmed the existence of such a covenant, the actual word berith, 'covenant', is lacking in Genesis 1–3."

In this paper, we shall briefly examine this very important concept "Covenant" in light of Ex 24:3–10 (the Sinai Covenant). Hence, we shall do a brief commentary and analysis of the text (Ex

24:3–10). This is with a view of identifying the twofold covenant ratification in the text as well as the role of the divine and the human parties involved in the covenant. Of course, the significance of the twofold ratification of this covenant shall be examined with a view of showing what makes the Sinai Covenant binding on the parties involved. Finally, we shall take a brief excursus to some church and magisterial documents. These would help us to show and conclude that the Sinai Covenant in Exodus 24:3–10 of the Old Testament relates to the Last Supper.

## A Brief Overview of Covenant

While a working definition is necessary for the purpose of this analysis, however, it is important to note that "the very definition of the term 'covenant' (bĕrĭt or diathĕkĕ) in the Old Testament is a matter of controversy" (Hahn 2009, 28). This is simply because biblical scholars are divided roughly into two camps on this issue: those who view covenant in a unilateral perspective as synonymous with "obligation" in the legal sense, and those who recognize it as a bilateral process that establishes or renews kingship relationship between two parties. For the purpose of this theological analysis, we shall adopt the bilateral perspective of covenant. Also, since there are different types of covenants (kinship, treaty, and grant) in the Old Testament as we shall see below, for now, we shall give a general definition of this concept without limiting ourselves to one. However, we hope to give a more specific definition of each below.

Covenant could be defined as "a binding agreement between two or more parties." The parties could be individuals or a group of people (for example, Israel as a nation). In this case, there is usually a principal representative or even representatives of the group in the making of the covenant. When we speak of biblical covenants, we are referring to instances where God has entered into an agreement with mankind. This involves both promises and responsibilities for each party. Despite its diverse contents, covenant is much more than a simple anthology. It is tied together by a successive string of major covenants that God made with His people. While there are many covenants and promises found in the Old Testament, there are some that are of great significance to the salvific or redemptive history of God's people. According to Scott W. Hahn (2009, 28), on a general note also, "At times the covenant partners were of equal status and the obligations of the covenant were distributed equally between them; more frequently, the covenant parties consisted of a superior and inferior, and the covenant obligations were unequally distributed."

## Types of Covenants

There are three principal types or classifications of covenants in the Old Testament. Again, scholars have varying opinions about these classifications. Also, in some cases, they also vary in their opinion about terminology, and in which category or type should a covenant be placed. On this, Hahn observes that "the threefold covenant typology is widely recognized in scholarship, although the terminology used to describe the three types varies." However, it is readily admitted that neither this nor any other system of terminology is completely satisfactory. In this work, and without much ado about this, we shall simply stay with Hahn and speak of the three major types or categories of covenant: kinship, treaty, and grant covenant.

*The Kinship Covenant*: In this type of covenant, "the obligations of the covenant are more or less equally distributed between the two parties. In such a covenant, the parties are usually, but not always, themselves of equal status." Thus, this type of relationship is frequently called a "parity" covenant.

*The Treaty Covenant*: The characteristic mark of this covenant is that the obligations of the covenant are imposed on the inferior party by the superior. Scholars have often termed this arrangement a "vassal covenant" or "treaty-type" covenant because the vassal treaties of the seventh-century Assyrian emperor, Esarhaddon have been considered the paradigmatic examples of the form.

*The Grant Covenant*: Here, the obligations of the covenant rest predominantly with the superior party, who freely accepts responsibilities toward the inferior, usually in response to the inferior's faithfulness or other meritorious qualities. The initiative in establishing a covenant of this form also rests with the superior; it is generally granted as a reward to a faithful vassal or servant.

## The Sinai Covenant: Exodus 24:3–10

In this section, it is important to make some general statements about the book of Exodus. This will help us to understand the "species" we are dealing with and to steer our course well in this analysis. "The book of Exodus is not a historical narrative, at least in any modern sense of that phrase. However, the material is profoundly historical in purpose" (Terence 1991). The primary concern of Exodus is to record and transmit the words of God, words given in a historical context. Exodus 24, specifically, is at the beginning of the story of Israel's time at Sinai (Ex 19–40). It is a high point in the narrative of the Mosaic covenantal legislation, represented through a covenant ceremony involving binding vows, blood ritual, and a cultic meal (Hahn and Mitch 2012, 47).

Durham (1987, 56) observes that the ceremony of Sinai combines elements of all the previous covenants. This is especially with Adam and Abraham and adds to them the symbols of the Passover (cf. Ex 12), which became the central celebration of the Jewish faith as both the salvation and judgment of the first-born sons. Childs (1974, 503) advanced this further by asserting that the Exodus covenant, culminating in chapter 24, connects the whole narrative of Genesis to the future events of Leviticus, Numbers, and Deuteronomy. Likewise, the Pentateuch as a whole sets the stage for King David and the prophets of Christ. The Sinai covenant in Exodus 24:3–10 under the periscope of this analysis principally belongs to the kinship type of covenant. This is because of the blood and familial relationship established through it. Hahn and Curtis (p. 48) note that: "The language of the text is purposefully nuptial." However, one could still find in it some elements of the treaty type of covenant.

In verses 1–2 of Exodus (though not included with the scope of this analysis), God extends an invitation to Israel through her representatives: "Come up to the Lord, you (Moses) and Aaron, Nadab, and Abihu, and seventy of the elders of Israel." From these representatives, God picked Moses alone to approach him. In this, we see a suzerain (God), inviting and dictating the conditions of the meeting to his vassal (Israel) to a worship relationship. Verse 3 repeats what was recorded earlier in 19:25: "So, Moses went down to the people and told them" everything about God's invitation and its term. Of course, the people responded: "All the words that the Lord has spoken, we will do" (John 1992, 295). Ex 24:1–11, and verse 3, represents the solemnization ritual that is uniquely Jewish. Thus, the people of Israel participate in a symbolic betrothal to the Lord, having heard the terms of His covenant and responding with their vowed "I do." Here, we see the consent of Israel (the vassal) to the initial covenant proposal of the suzerain (God).

What follows is a very important aspect of the covenantal process, writing down the terms of the contract, and also preparing for the next, final, and most important phase of the covenantal process. Verses 4–5 are only the second time that the Pentateuch mentions burnt offerings and fellowship offering side-by-side, and the other mention in Ex 20:24 provides another evidence to link these passages to the same narrative origin. Also, the prohibition against golden or silver idols in Ex 20:23 establishes a strong literary connection to the golden calf incident in Ex 32:1–6 (Viscichini 2017, 10). The ratification of the covenant which is taking place in these verses of Ex 24 has significant parallels to the covenant violation in Ex 32 as well. Both passages involve the making of an altar (24:4 and 32:5), burnt offerings and fellowship offerings (24:5 and 32:6), and eating and drinking in God's presence (24:11 and 32:6). The covenant ratification in verses 3–11 offers a skillfully constructed finale to the giving of the laws beginning in Ex 21. Nevertheless, popular scholarship has been entirely indecisive in deciding on the authorship of these passages (Alexander 1999, 8).

Within verses 6–8 lies the main act of the covenant and its ratification. Here, it is important to take note of the sequence of events. As a sign of great respect for God (the suzerain, whose divine presence resided in the altar), first, "Moses took half of the blood and put it in basins, and half of the blood he dashed against the altar" (v. 6).

Second, "he took the book of the covenant, and read it in the hearing of the people (v. 7). Here, God has "sworn his oath" (according to his instructions to Moses) through the blood of the animal sprinkled on his altar. Finally, Moses turned to the people. As part of their oath and ratification of the covenant to whose words, conditions, and terms (rights and obligations) they had already assented, He "took the blood and dashed it on the people, and said, 'see the blood of the covenant that the Lord has made with you in accordance with all these words'" (v.8). It suffices to note that for the first time in the whole of our text (Ex 24, 3–10), we see the word *covenant* used.

Verses 9–11 describe the sacred meal which marked the second part of the ratification. "The sacrificial banquet on the flesh of the peace-offerings given by Yahweh as host to his worshippers strengthens the bond between him and them, and ends the ceremony of ratification" (Power 1954). The phrase "and they beheld God" is a metaphor for an interior or prophetic vision because man cannot see God directly in this life (Ex 33:20–23, Jn 1:18, 1 Jn 4:12). It also provides a literal foreshadowing of Eucharistic adoration (Viscichini, p. 10). It is, in the words of Jon Courson (2003), "Christophany" or an Old Testament vision of the incarnate Christ.

## The Significance of Covenant Ratification in Exodus 24:3–10

First, the Sinai covenant ratification signifies the communion of blood and life between God and man represented by Israel. It seals the covenant and gives it a permanent and binding character. A familial bond with God is further established by the mingling of blood on the altar, which represents God (Ex 24:6), and on the people (Ex 24:8), symbolizing that God and Israel have made a bond as strong, or stronger, than genetic biology (Viscichini, p. 11). The blood also represents the curse of death which must accompany any covenant transgression. On a third level, the blood of the young bulls or oxen (24:5) is a direct affront to the idolatry of animals in the Egyptian religion (Scott and Curtis, p.48). The sprinkling of the blood of the slain or sacrificed animals on the people means that their fate would be that of the animals, should they violate the covenant. Through ratification, the covenant is solemnized. That is, actualized or officially established (Hahn 2010, 28). We see this also in Genesis 15:17–20, where the presence of God appears in the form of "a smoking fire and a flaming torch," moving between the pieces and promising Abram the land of Canaan. To move between the pieces while uttering promises was a ceremonial way of stating: "If I do not keep your commandments, may I be slain like these animals" (Bergsma and Pitre 2017, 243–44). Hence, the blood of the covenant ritual has a twofold sense.

Also, there is the ritual banquet at the foot of the mountain (vv. 10–11). After the blood sacrifice is offered at the foot of the mountain, the representatives of the people journey up to the top of the mountain, and indeed, into God's very presence in heaven where "they beheld God, and ate and drank" (Ex. 24:11). This meal, like the Passover meal before it, is the second ratification and what completes the covenant. On this, Bergsma and Pitre (p. 224) observe that this meal points to the liturgical nature of the covenant. It "signifies the familial relationship between God and Israel" (Gen 31:44–54). It is not an ordinary banquet. It is "a theophanic covenant banquet: a sacrificial feast in which God appears and reveals himself to his people."

Here, what comes out clearly are the two complementary consequences of the covenant, atoning for sin and restoring communion. We see these elements in the Sinai covenant ceremony of Exodus 24:1–11 prefigured in the Last Supper. Hence, the twofold ratification of the Sinai covenant, especially with a communal meal foreshadows the Last Supper, where Christ's blood brings about the new and ultimate covenant (Mt 26:28; 1 Cor 11:23–25; CCC, 782).

## The Sinai Covenant and Magisterial Documents

The Sinai Covenant ratification in the Old Testament has much in common with the Last Supper of the New Testament. A perusal at some magisterial documents will reveal this unequivocal relationship between them. John Paul II in his encyclical letter *Ecclesia De Eucharistia* (April 17, 2017) notes that: "By analogy with the

Covenant of Mount Sinai, sealed by sacrifice and the sprinkling of blood, the actions and words of Jesus at the Last Supper laid the foundations of the new messianic community, the People of the New Covenant." In a seemingly direct reference to the Sinai Covenant ceremony, *Evangelium Vitae* (March 25, 1995), notes that it "is fulfilled and comes true in Christ: his is the sprinkled blood which redeems, purifies and saves." Paul VI in *Mysterium Fidei* (September 3, 1965) wrote that, "Just as Moses made the Old Testament sacred with the blood of calves, so too Christ the Lord took the New Testament, of which He is the Mediator, and made it sacred through His own blood, in instituting the mystery of the Eucharist." These words of Mary at the wedding of Cana, "Do whatever He tells you" (Jn 2:5) appeared in *Marialis Cultus* (February 2, 1975) of Paul VI as reechoing the words of Israel at Sinai, "all the words that the Lord has spoken we will do" (Ex 24:3). Of course, earlier church fathers and doctors, including Augustine and Thomas Aquinas, also attested to the significance of this (Viscichini, p. 11).

The Catechism of the Catholic Church declares that "for the Old Covenant has never been revoked," rather, it has been fulfilled. It describes the Old Covenant and Testament as "integral and irreplaceable." This means that Exodus and Passover as its integral parts are adopted into the New Testament. Hence, the Church affirms that the covenant of Exodus 24 is inseparable from the tradition of the Ten Commandments; "the Decalogue is never handed down without first recalling the covenant" (CCC §121–123, 129, 1093, 2060).

## Conclusion

Exodus 24:1–10 describes the Sinai Covenant and its dual ratification. That is, blood sacrifice and sacred meal. The first part of the ratification process consists of erecting a stone altar and twelve pillars, one for each tribe of Jacob, and the sprinkling of blood of a sacrificial animal on the altar, which represents God's oath in the covenant. The firstborn sons, acting as priests, offer a sacrifice of young bulls for burnt offerings as well as meal offerings. The Israelites swear again to obey the commands of God. Another half of the blood is then splashed on the people. The second part of the ratification process involved the literal ascent of Moses, Nadab, Abihu, and the seventy elders up Mount Sinai, and the mystical vision they experienced. Then, an actual meal (which bears a great theological and liturgical significance, and prefigures the Eucharistic meal or adoration), is celebrated to consummate the covenantal union.

Following our analysis of Ex 24:3–10, it is quite easy to conclude that the ratification of the Sinai covenant in Ex 24:3–10 has an enormous relationship with the Last Supper. The Mountain of Sinai is a type of the Tabernacle, the Temple, and the Mystical Body of Christ. It is the place where man can approach God's dwelling in a tangible presence (Viscichini, p. 22). The reading of the "words of God" is an example of common covenantal ritual action and prefigures the Christian Liturgy of the Word. The oath sworn by the Israelites foreshadows the witnesses of later prophets and of the disciples of Christ, who respond with faith to the words directly from the mouth of God. In the New Covenant, Christ himself will act as priest and as the sacrificial lamb. The solemnization of the covenant, by the sprinkling of blood on the altar and on the people, reechoed in John's Gospel when blood and water pour from the side of Christ (John 19, 34). The theophany and mystical experience on Mount Sinai harken forward to the Transfiguration of Christ on Mount Tabor. The sharing of a covenant meal also embodies a type of Holy Communion which will become the source and summit of life in the New Covenant.

# THE DAVIDIC COVENANT (2 SAM 7): LITERARY AND THEOLOGICAL FULFILLMENT

*Historical Books of the Old Testament*

## Introduction

In understanding the promises of a future kingdom given to Israel, one of the major Scriptures is that containing the Davidic covenant in 2 Sam 7 and 1 Ch 17. Though the word *covenant* (*bèrît*) does not occur in 2 Sam 7, that chapter contains in substance the arrangement which has become known as the "Davidic covenant." The purpose of this arrangement was to engraft the emerging dynastic monarchy which was taking shape under David, after Saul's intermediate kingship had been brought to an end, into the framework of the Sinaitic covenantal structure by which Israel's national life was regulated.

In this covenant, the promise of a king and a kingdom is narrowed to David's seed. The biblical expositions of the passage (2 Sam 23:5) makes it clear that it provides the initial delineation of the Davidic covenant. In his covenant with David, Yahweh presents David with two categories of promises (David 1964, 28, 114), those that find realization during David's lifetime (2 Sam 7:8–11) and those that find fulfillment after his death (Michael 1999, 233–50).

In this brief paper, we shall examine the import of the Davidic covenant in light of its remote and proximate content within the Old Testament, and within the book of Samuel. We shall also examine how this oracle or covenant is fulfilled in the New Testament. This would help us appreciate the significance of God's covenant with David for understanding the content and meaning of the New Testament.

## The Biblical Content and Character of the Davidic Covenant: 2 Samuel 7:8–16

In general, when literature on the Hebrew Bible speaks of "covenant" in a theological sense, that is, one between God and a human party, what is meant is that covenant associated with the Sinaitic experience, of which we read in the last four books of the Pentateuch. There are, it must be stressed, other theological covenants, such as those with Abraham (Genesis 15, 17:1–15), with the Levites (e.g., Jer 33:11–22), with Phinehas (Num 25:1–25), and especially that with David, which receives more attention in the Hebrew Bible than any covenant except the Sinaitic (Levenson 1979, 205–6). Two sources speak in detail of this covenant, 2 Samuel 7 and Psalm 89. Here is the relevant excerpt from the first, Nathan's oracle to David:

> *Thus, says the LORD of host, I will make for you a great name, like the name of the great ones of the earth. And I will appoint a place for my people Israel, and will plant them, that they may dwell in their own place, and be disturbed no more; and violent men shall afflict them no more, as formerly, and I will give you rest from all your enemies. Moreover, the LORD declares to you that the LORD will make you a house. When your days are fulfilled and you lie down with your fathers, I will raise up your offspring after you, who shall come forth from your body, and I will establish his kingdom. He shall build a house for my name, and I will establish the throne of his*

*kingdom forever. I will be his father, and he shall be my son… And your house and your kingdom shall be made sure for ever before me; your throne shall be established forever.*

This is a very important passage, and it is through this passage that one has the idea of an eternal and unconditional covenant between God and the house or the dynasty of David. Although the word *covenant* is not explicitly employed here, this is now the fifth covenant that we have met: the Adamic covenant, the Noahic covenant, the Abrahamic covenant, the Sinaitic covenant, and now the Davidic covenant (Hayes, 2017). The Noahic, Abrahamic, Davidic covenants are often called "covenants of promise (Blaising and Bock 2010, 159) or "grant" covenants" (Waltke 1988, 124), whereas the Mosaic covenant is likened to a "suzerain-vassal" treaty (Weinfeld 1970, 185). The familial properties of the covenant are evident, most notably in the emphasis on the divine sonship of David's seed. The basis for the Davidic grant-type covenant is God's oath (Hahn 2009).

The law of Moses and the sacrificial system are critical to the understanding and legitimacy of David's kingdom. But before we can consider the specific character of David's kingdom, we need to begin with some background. God's covenant with David comes as the last in a sequence of covenants found in the Old Testament. These covenants with Adam, Noah, Abraham, Moses, and David form the narrative structure of the Old Testament. Judges marks the point in the biblical narrative where it becomes apparent that the economy of the Mosaic covenant, even in its final Deuteronomic form, is inadequate for the flourishing of God's people. The sacred author begins to turn our attention forward, toward the anticipation of a king who will inaugurate a new covenant (2 Sam 7:1–17) which will not replace but assimilate and even transform the Mosaic covenant. The background to the covenant with David, and the entire story of Israel, is God's three-part promise to Abraham: to give him and his descendants their own land, to make them a great and blessed nation, and to make the children of Abraham the source of divine blessing for all the families of the earth (Gen 12:1–4).

Each of these promises was upgraded to a covenant by God (Gen 15, 17:4–8, 22:15–18). It was for the sake of this covenant with Abraham that the Israelites were brought out of Egypt (Ex 2:24, 6:5). And it was for the sake of this covenant with Abraham that David's kingdom is established. In Nathan's oracle, God repeats three times that He is making this covenant with David "for My people Israel" (2 Sam 7:8, 10, 11). This recalls the language God used to explain His actions in liberating Abraham's children from Egypt (Ex 3:7, 10; Lev 26:12). Later, in the psalmist's reflections, the Davidic monarch is seen fulfilling God's promise to Abraham: "In him shall all the tribes of the earth be blessed, all the nations" (see Psalm 72:17; compare Genesis 12:3, 22:18).

## The Remote Context of the Davidic Covenant

Here, we shall take a close look at the content of this oracle and its remote context within the book of Samuel and the time of David. The primary reason for David's significance within the Old Testament is his reception of an everlasting covenant from God (2 Sam 7:8–16; 2 Sam 23:5; Ps 89:20–37) that bestows upon himself and his heirs the status of son of God and universal high king (Ps 89:27). The sonship that was offered to Israel at Sinai, but rejected in its subsequent history of idolatry, is granted now to the Davidic king. In this way, Israel experiences the blessings of divine filiation, at least indirectly. This Davidic covenant assimilates and integrates many of the promises and blessings of previous covenants and will become the focus of the eschatological hopes of Israel in the prophets (Pitre 2017, 101). Only after the Ark was established does God renew His covenant with Israel through an oracle delivered by the prophet Nathan (2 Sam 7:8–16; 1 Ch 17:7–14).

First, he tells David that "the Lord will establish a house for you." In biblical terms, "house" means royal dynasty. This means that David's kingdom will be a dynasty, one that endures for generations. Next, God promises that David's son will assume his throne: "I will raise up your heir, and make his kingdom firm." The firmness of his kingdom is another indicator that the kingdom will remain. David's son will also, according to the promise, "build a house for my name." In other words, David's son will build a temple as a permanent home for God's presence in the Ark of the Covenant. Of this royal son of David, God further promises: "I will be a Father to him and he shall be a son to Me." This is the language of covenant adoption. The son of David will be adopted as God's own son. This marks the first time in Scripture that the idea of divine sonship is applied to one individual. While God had referred to Israel as His firstborn son, no one as yet in the Bible has been called, in effect, a "son of God." God's promise is unconditional, according to Nathan. The royal son is expected to keep God's law and will be punished for transgressions against the Law. But God will never disown David's heir or dissolve his kingdom. Nathan conveys this message: "If he does wrong, I will correct him with human chastisements, but I will not withdraw my favor from him" (Pitre 2017, 101). Finally, God states the conclusion that all of these promises point to: "Your house and your kingdom shall endure forever." This means that David's dynasty will never end; there will always be an heir of David seated upon his throne.

## The Proximate Context of the Oracle

In this brief section, we hope to examine the relationship between the Davidic covenant and the preceding covenants. However, we shall limit this quest to its relationship to two particular covenants: the Abrahamic and Mosaic covenants. The background to the covenant with David, and indeed the entire story of Israel, is God's threefold promise to Abraham (Gen 12:1–4), as we saw in the last section. The link between the Davidic and Abrahamic covenants is clearly manifest. Walter Kaiser (1974, 298) suggests at least four great moments in biblical history that supply both the impetus for progressive revelation and the glue for its organic and continuous nature. First, the promise given to Abraham in Genesis 12, 15, 17. Second, the promise declared to David in 2 Samuel 7. Third, the promise outlined in the New Covenant of Jeremiah 31, and forth, the day when many of these promises found initial realization in the death and resurrection of Christ. Ronald Youngblood's (1992, 880) understanding is that 2

Samuel 7 is "the center and focus of the Deuteronomic history itself." Walter Brueggemann (1990, 253, 259) regards it as the "dramatic and theological center of the entire Samuel corpus" and as "the most crucial theological statement in the Old Testament." Robert Gordon (1986, 235) called this chapter the "ideological summit in the Old Testament as a whole." John Levenson (1979, 205–6) contended that God's covenant with David "receives more attention in the Hebrew Bible than any covenant except the Sinaitic."

First and foremost, both are grant-type covenants involving a divine oath that is directed at blessing all nations through the promised seed. Second, the Abrahamic covenant involves three promissory elements (land, kingship, and world blessing). All three of these are fulfilled in the Davidic covenant, at least provisionally. Third, Abraham and David are both archetypal father-figures whose faithful obedience caused their sons to receive a covenant grant of blessing by divine oath in connection with Jerusalem. Fourth, from a canonical reading of the OT, Abraham and David are the sole witnesses to the royal priesthood of Melchizedek.

It was for the sake of this covenant with Abraham that the Israelites were brought out of Egypt (Ex 2:24, 6:5). It was for the sake of this covenant with Abraham that David's kingdom is established. In Nathan's oracle, God repeats three times that He is making this covenant with David for "for My people Israel" (2 Sam 7:8, 10, 11). This recalls the language God used to explain His actions in liberating Abraham's children from Egypt (Ex 3:7, 10; Lev 26:12). Later, in the psalmist's reflections, the Davidic monarch is seen fulfilling God's promise to Abraham: "In him shall all the tribes of the earth be blessed, all the nations" (Ps 72:17; Gen 12:3, 22:18).

Comparing the Mosaic or Sinaitic covenant with the Davidic, it is quite easy to see that they appear to represent two distinct covenant types. For another, the canonical treatment of the Davidic and Mosaic covenants varies widely according to the different canonical traditions in which they occur (for example, the Deuteronomistic history and the Psalms). They are characterized by two varying responses by Israel to God and his appointed mediator. As a consequence, the two covenants effect two distinct and dissimilar types of relationship between God and his people, which in turn produced two distinct understandings and experiences of divine sonship. The Davidic covenant appears, prima facie, very different from the Sinaitic Covenant and the Hittite suzerainty treaties, which have so advanced our knowledge of it. In fact, for many years, it seemed as though there were no compelling extrabiblical analogues to the Davidic covenant, whose nature thus remained opaque in comparison with the Sinaitic. This opacity has not prevented theologians and historians of the religion of Israel from commenting upon the most problematic ideational point. That is, the relationship of these two diverse covenants to each other.

The Davidic and Mosaic covenants may be contrasted as contraries since the Davidic grant-type covenant and the Deuteronomic treaty-type covenant both rest on the prior foundation of the Mosaic kinship-type covenant (Ex 19–24). This means that the divine sonship of Israel, as a nation, is ultimately based on, and derived from, the original covenant at Sinai (Levenson 1979, 206). Only after it was violated did covenant vassalage overshadow Israel, taking the form of the Deuteronomic covenant.

## Fulfilment of Oracle in The New Testament

Second, Sam 7:8–16 articulates the Davidic covenant in two parts: promises that find realization during David's life and promises that find realization after David's death. Though grant covenants such as the Davidic are often considered unconditional, conditionality and unconditionality are not mutually exclusive. God's covenant with David had both elements (Michael 1999, 233–50). God's establishment of His covenant with David represents one of the theological high points of the Old Testament Scriptures. This key event builds on the preceding covenants and looks forward to the ultimate establishment of God's reign on the earth. The psalmists and prophets provide additional details concerning the ideal Davidite who will lead God's chosen nation in righteousness. The New Testament applies various Old Testament texts about this Davidite to Jesus Christ (Mat 1:1–17; Acts 13:33–34; Heb 1:5; 5:5).

So one fact that clearly presents itself to any careful reader interested in the fulfilment of the Davidic covenant is that it points toward the New Testament, especially toward the gospel according to Luke and the Acts of the Apostles. These present Jesus as the Christ, the Son of David cum Son of God, whose birthplace, ministry, resurrection, and enthronement are all depicted in terms drawn from the Davidic covenant. In physical terms, the virtual failure of the Davidic line occurred in 586 BC, but in spiritual terms, we cannot but read 2 Sam 7:13 other than finally in terms of New Testament Christology. Hence, the Davidic monarch was the Christ (i.e., the Messiah or Anointed One [William 1980, 40–47]). The anointed status of the Davidic king was so integral to his identity that he is frequently referred to simply as "the anointed one" or "the Lord's anointed."

The books of Samuel recount the antecedent events to David's reception of this covenant and his lived response to it. The story of David brings out all the strengths and weaknesses of the beginnings of the religious institution of the kingdom for the people of God. The kingdom established by David is the closest Old Testament parallel to the New Testament church (Brown 1992, 5–6). If Jesus is the Davidic king, then his kingdom is the Davidic kingdom. That kingdom is present already because it was conferred on the disciples at the Last Supper. Their rulership over Israel is manifested in their rulership over the *ekklēsia (church)*. The *ekklēsia* is the incipient, growing kingdom of David, incorporating Jews, Israelites, and the nations under the reign of Jesus, the Davidic king, which is exercised through his Spirit-empowered apostolic vice regents. The institution narrative in Luke 22 is the key passage for Luke's theology of Davidic covenant restoration in Christ. In it, we have the convergence of two themes of primary importance: the father-son relationship and the role of covenant. This is clearly seen in Jesus' words to His apostles in Luke 22:28–30: "You are those who have continued with me in my trials; and I covenant to you, as my Father covenanted to me, a kingdom, that you may eat and drink at my table in my kingdom, and sit on thrones judging the twelve tribes of Israel" (Hahn 2009, 237).

Hence, for Luke, Jesus' kingdom is the kingdom of David, restored and transformed. This becomes abundantly clear when one examines Luke for evidence of the elements of the Davidic covenant. These will include, for example, Jesus' kingdom is founded on a covenant. Gabriel's description of Jesus to Mary in Lk 1:32–33 is taken point-for-point from the key Davidic covenant text, 2 Samuel 7; Jesus is the natural Son of God (Lk 1:35), and the title is used of him throughout the Gospel; Jesus is the Messiah (Lk 2:11, 4:41), a title only applied to kings in the OT (1 Sam 16:6, 24:6), and He is the "Christ of God" (9:20), a title only applied to David (2 Sam 23:1); Jesus' royal mission is bound up with Jerusalem. So for Luke, it is theologically important that the word of God go forth from Jerusalem to the ends of the earth (Luke 24:47), as it was important for David that the ark goes forth to Jerusalem. Jesus' royal mission is bound up with the Temple (Luke 1:5–23); Jesus' kingship extends over all the nations. Hence, Simeon speaks of Jesus as "a light of revelation to the nations" (2:32), and the last but not the least, the everlasting reign of Christ is presumed in the rest of the Gospel, especially where Jesus is portrayed as the mediator of eternal life (18:18–30).

## Conclusion

From this brief study, one point emerges clear. This is the fact that, as part of the revelation of God's plan for his chosen people, the Davidic Covenant has both immediate and far-reaching implications. Hence, in addition to establishing David's dynasty, this covenant looks forward to a descendant of David (Solomon through to Christ, the definitive figure), who would bring peace and justice to God's people through his reign. Although, there is divided opinion about the fulfillment of the Davidic covenant, given the scriptural evidences, one could without much doubt conclude that the Davidic covenant is fulfilled in Christ, who proceeds from the line of David. This evidence is clear both from the Old, as well as from the New Testament (especially) from the gospel of Luke and Acts of the Apostles.

Hence, given the authenticity and inspiration of the Scriptures, the testimony of the angel to Mary is conclusive on the fulfilment of the Davidic covenant: "And behold, thou shall conceive in thy womb, and bring forth a son, and shall call his name Jesus. He shall be great, and shall be called the Son of the Most High: and the Lord God shall give unto him the throne of his father David: and he shall reign over the house of Jacob forever; and of his kingdom there shall be no end" (Luke 1:31–33). The promise of David's throne, kingdom, and all that is involved, is transferred by this prophecy to Jesus Christ, "the Son of David" (Mat 1:1). The line that began with David has its consummation and eternal fulfillment in Christ.

# Development of Prophecy in Israel: The Relevance of Prophet Amos

## *Old Testament Prophets*

### Introduction

Prophecy and prophetic movement are at the epicenter of virtually all the important polemic in the Hebrew Scriptures. This is because it was the activities of the prophets that sustained the Jewish nation in spite of the many upheavals in their history. The word *prophet* itself is a potential source of confusion as to the nature of the office and movement. This is because the picture of prophecy of Israel presented in the OT is by no means uniform and embraces such different phenomena that seem well-nigh impossible to bring it under a single commentator (Gerhard 1983, 796). So the attempt to write a history of OT prophecy can be only partially successful and leaves many open questions at decisive points (Ceresko 1992, 221).

Focusing on the word can be helpful in gaining some insight into the role and function of a prophet from Israel's past. Various terms from the earlier days of prophecy, for example, *rō'eh* "seer" (1 Sam 9, 9) or *hōzeh,* "discerner" (2 Sam 24, 11; Amos 7, 12), stress the more clairvoyant element of prophecy. But the most common term for prophet in the OT is *nabu*. However, Gerhard observes that "nabu covers only one aspect of what is to be called prophecy in the OT, and it is notably less prominent in most important area, that of the so-called writing prophets." Scholars in general relate nabu to an Akkadian cognate root, meaning "to call," "to commission." The noun in Hebrew thus belongs to vocation terminology and bears the sense of "one called" or "one commissioned." It implies the official standing of the one who carries the title as a spokesperson chosen by God to deliver a message in God's name. Our English word prophet is derived from the Greek προπετές (prophētēs) which the Septuagint translated nabî' (Ceresko 1992, 221). προφετες in Greek means "spokesperson," and accurately, the primary meaning of the Hebrew term.

## Brief History of Prophecy

The Deuteronomic history, the major literary complex following the foundational Torah or Law (Pentateuch) in the Hebrew Bible, goes under the name former prophets and not historical books. In the latter prophets (Isaiah, Jeremiah, Ezekiel, Daniel and book of the twelve), we have the complement to the former prophets in the form of the writings of both the prophets themselves and reflections and redactional activity of their disciples and schools that cherished and handed on their teachings. The term prophet was transferred by tradition to earlier figures. Abraham is given the title in Gen 20:7. The characteristic feature in this case is due to Abraham's power of intercession for his people. Only in the priestly tradition (Ex 7:1) is Aaron called prophet. This takes up the statement in Ex 4:16 that Aaron will speak for Moses as a prophet. Therefore, the prophet for the priestly tradition is one who speaks on the commission of the superior. The observation in Ex 15:20 that Miriam was a prophetess is probably related to the ancient song of the Red Sea in verse 21. Should this be true, cultic dancing and singing are features which give rise to the designation. The expression prophet is frequently used in relation to Moses. Reflection on his position in Num 12:6–8 emphatically places him above other prophets. Another tradition finds in Moses the prophet beyond compare with whom Yahweh deals (Deut 34:10). It is expressly stated that no similar prophet would arise, though Joshua received the spirit from Moses by laying on of hand. In Deut 18:15–19, Moses is regarded as the beginning of a prophet series.

As we have already seen above, the prophets are presented in two parts: the former comprising what we often called the historical books—Joshua through II Kings, and the latter prophets comprising the three major prophets with the twelve minor prophets. According to David P. Reid (1980), prophets are also often spoken of as pre-classical and classical. The distinction being that the words of the preclassical prophets were not handed on in a separate collection. Of course, what we call preclassical, the Hebrew Scriptures, term the "former." We read of these men and women in the historical books, and they play a vital role in the author's interpretation of Israel's history. If we think of the timeline of Israel's history, the period of the so-called classical prophecy is two hundred years plus (750–550 BC), and the preclassical periods could go back three hundred years before that.

Again, we need to distinguish what we can know of their history as the outcome of the word spoken by God and acted through these prophets. This is what makes, for instance, the Elijah-Elisha material (1 Kg 17–2 Kg 10) so very powerful. It was not just what they did, but the stories handed on about them enabled Israel to speak in an expanded yet concrete way about the "way of God" with His people (Wolff 1978, 32). It is true that scholars have tried to impose idealistic theories of historical development upon the data about the prophets using such categories as spirit, cult, and ecstasy. This downgrading of the earlier manifestations of prophecy in favor of later classical forms was aligned with the need to show that Israel's religion reached a zenith of development in the classical prophets, living behind its lower forms of religious expressions originating from Moses.

We can gain insight into the distribution of former and latter prophets by reflecting on the historical data of the eighth century BC. Were there not very different circumstances obtaining then, especially when one remembers that the interrelationships of kings and peoples shift a lot in the period just before the fall of Samaria in 721 BC? Up till that time, the ministry of the prophets was directed primarily to the kings of the North and South. One recalls the court prophets, Gad and Nathan, in the days of King David and the constant consultation of the prophets on the part of northern kings. In a way, one might say that the prophets "went public" when the kings proved very weak (2 King 15–17), and in doing so, made it possible for a wider prophetic ministry to take hold (Reid 1980, 10). This idea of "going public" was a major factor leading to the eventual collections of the sayings of the prophets and their being handed on from generation to generation.

The classical period, which was the crest of the wave and the falling apart of prophecy in the post-exilic period, together with the demise of kingship, was not totally unexpected or lamentable. The prophets lived on in memory. The classical prophecy can be classified or grouped in three stages. The second half of the eighth century (750 BC) saw the menace of the Assyrian power and the prophetic ministry of Amos and Hosea in the North. In the South, Micah and Isaiah offered interpretations of the times too much for the leaders of their day, but happily connected somehow with the reform of the good king, Hezekiah (716–687 BC). The second half of the seventh century witnessed the demise of the Assyrians and the rise of the Babylonians, times interpreted in the ministries of Nahum, Habakkuk, Zephaniah, and immortalized Jeremiah. If the immediacy of the word of God in the ministry of the former prophets began to give way to the challenging mediacy of that word in the latter prophets, that transition found its poignancy in the prophet from Jeremiah. The third grouping of events can be designated the exilic and also the post-exilic prophets: Obadiah, Ezekiel, Haggai, Zechariah Joel, and also, 2 and 3 Isaiah. The historical phenomenon of prophecy has run its course, it was now almost a literary phenomenon, and in fact, two prophetic books, Malachi and Jonah, may represent such final literalization of the prophetic movement.

## Prophet Amos

The book of Amos provides a good example of the way in which our present prophetic books were formed. At its origin lies the eighth-century prophet Amos himself, a towering figure whose life, word, and activity had a profound impact on the people of his day (Ceresko 1992, 241). He launched a new and vigorous movement in Israel that lasted for hundreds of years. We have been given very little biographical information about Amos, but that which we have is quite interesting. Amos 1:1, the editorial introduction to the entire book, tells us the prophet was a shepherd from the region of Judean village of Tekoa, a few miles away from Jerusalem. The order of Jeroboam II, delivered through Amaziah, suggests that Amos's Judean roots were well-known, and it is likely that at the conclusion of his prophetic work, he returned to his native land. At some point in his life, Amos responded to God's call that he becomes a prophet, although he apparently had no previous prophetic connection (7:14). We are ignorant of Amos's formal education, but his words betray an individual who was both knowledgeable of Israel's religious traditions and skilled in the literary and rhetorical forms in which he casts his messages.

## The Time of Amos

Amos's prophetic activities seem to have been of short duration, perhaps only a year. Scholars date the time of the activity at about 760 BC. The book of Amos makes it clear that while the prophet was a southerner (1:1), his work was done in the north (7:10). So, as a literary work, the book of Amos is a historical reflection of what life was like in the eighth century Israel as seen through the eyes and experience of the book's central character, Amos, a herder and a sycamore dresser from Tekoa (1:1) who became a prophet by God's choice. Norman K. Gottwald (1985, 356) notes that the focus of Amos's attack was the upper classes that enjoyed a certain degree of prosperity during the reign of Jeroboam II. He comments: "The greedy upper classes, with governmental and judicial convenience, were systematically expropriating the land of commoners." Doorly W. J. (1989, 24–25) adds that "the people being oppressed in Amos' time were the poor, the needy and even the righteous. Farmers were forced to grow cash crops such as wine and oil, which they did not need for survival."

## Message of Prophet Amos

In Amos's message, which includes a severe judgment on one Amaziah who would set himself against the word of God (7:14–17), we see two dimensions of the ministry of Amos. The first dimension is Amos taking his place among the prophets whom God raises up. "I was not a prophet, but God took me…" The second dimension is being a minister of the word of God (Tucker 1973, 423). Rendtorff (1967) thinks that one effective means by which Amos animates his message is through the messenger speech. He speaks and assumes the role of a herald from the king. The message is that of the sovereign, and the human speaker is merely the vehicle through which the message passes. Typically, this oracle is prefaced by the words, "thus says the Yahweh…" Also, Yahweh is frequently represented in the first person in order to heighten the awareness of the hearers that the message is not that of the prophet, but that of God. Amos's messages are not essays in theology but are communications to the people of God delivered in the heat of prophetic passion. So they are shaped so as to have maximum impact upon Amos's hearers. However, it is impossible to infer something of the overarching concepts about God's will for Israel which drove Amos to respond to the call of the Lord. Amos's message is being based on the following principles.

First, Yahweh, Israel's God, is sovereign over the world. Yahweh the creator of the world "forms the mountains, and divides the winds" (4:1), made the starry constellations, divided the day from the night, and summons the rain (5:8). Because he is the sovereign Lord, the presence of Yahweh is inescapable (Am 9:2, Ps 139:8). Yahweh's power is matched by his holiness and righteousness. The first of these terms implies a quality which one might call transcendence or "otherwise," while the second, that is often linked with the

147

word *justifies*, denotes a moral integrity and predictability on the part of Israel's God. These aspects of God's nature are connected to the burning passion of God that all peoples, especially Israel, should display a similar integrity.

Second, Yahweh has a special relationship with Israel. Nowhere does Amos use the word *covenant*, a term which many other Old Testament writers employ to designate God's election of Israel, the chosen people. Nevertheless, the idea of the covenant is implicit in Amos's thought. "You only have I known of all the families of the earth" (3:2) refers to this special relationship between God and Israel. The choice of Israel as God's people has resulted in repeated acts by God through which Israel has been saved from danger and destruction. There is a twofold sense in which Amos uses the word *Israel*, and in which he views this special relationship between God and Israel. Sometimes he means by Israel the whole Hebrew people who conquered and came into the land of Canaan (2:9–10). On the other hand, Amos's particular concern is with the kingdom and, "Israel" refers to this nation, which he calls "Samaria" (3:9), "Joseph" (5:6), etc.

Third, because Israel has broken this relationship, God will destroy the nation. The history of God's dealing with this people is a long story of God's love and Israel's rejection of that love. Repeatedly, God has chastened the people in order to win them back, but it has been to no avail (4, 6–11). Over and over, God's mercy has been expressed so that while they have been punished for their sins, yet they have not been destroyed (7:1–6). But most of Amos's prophetic messages reflect his despairing belief that the nations will never turn from its evil ways. Some students of Amos have identified the brief oracle in 3:2 as the summary of Amos's preaching concerning God's election of Israel's election and destruction. The North used their prosperity to purchase laziness and indolence (6:4–7). And perhaps the worst of all, they had gained prosperity, in part at least, by dishonesty and fraud (8:4–19).

## Conclusion: Relevance of the Book of Amos

The book of Amos is still very much relevant today because it continues to ring the bell for the need of repentance to all unjust structures: government, rulers, nations, and even people who oppress others, people who capitalize on the weakness of the poor, the needy, children, and even women to oppress them. For those in the modern world, it is a warning that becoming prosperous at the expense of the weak, and that to sustain our wealth by debauchery and through deprivation of the poor will attract the wrath of God. The message of Amos is, therefore, still very much relevant to us today because it is the word of God and, as such, is ever powerful and defiles age and time.

# Evaluating the Messianic Prophecy in the Book of Zecharias

*Prophets*

## Introduction

Messianic prophecy is generally understood as referring to those prophecies or "predictions" in the Old Testament, which in one way or the other alludes to the coming of the Messiah. Some, including both Jewish and Christians scholars, are of the opinion that these prophecies were basically predictions about both a "now" and a "not yet" aspect. These scholar's opinion is based on the hermeneutical principle or concept of an inaugurated eschatology. They often fit contemporary fulfilments of their predictions into the ultimate and final fulfilments of the climatic work of God in the last day (Walter 1995, 137).

On the other hand, there are those whose opinion about messianic prophecies is anchored on the hermeneutical concept of corporate solidarity or collective messianism. A principle where the relationship between the individual and the community is purely reciprocal. In this case, "Israel," for example, could have a variety of meanings, including a political organization, a religious body, and even a spiritually minded group. For example, Adrian M. Leske (2000, 162) is of the opinion that the "king" in Zechariah 9:9 should not be interpreted as a future messianic Davidite. Rather, in terms of Deutero-Isaiah's democratization of kingship in Is 55:3–5, the "king" is God's faithful people who are to present God's gracious rule through their faithfulness to the covenant and their consequent witness to God's blessings before the nations.

The reason for the choice of Zechariah for this paper cannot be overemphasized. Although the major prophets, Isaiah, Jeremiah, Ezekiel, and Daniel, offer much on the doctrine of the messianic prophesies, Zechariah (one of the twelve minor prophets), has a lot to offer too. Zechariah is the longest of the minor prophets. It is also one of the most frequently quoted Old Testament books in the New Testament. One-third of its appearance in the NT could be found in the gospels, and thirty-one references or allusion to Zechariah could be found in the book of Revelation. If this is true, then this brief paper will help see the fulfilment of the messianic prophecies of Zechariah in Christ, the Davidic king.

This brief work will identify the messianic prophecies or themes in the book of Zechariah. These would be analyzed both from the Jewish (OT) and Christian exegetical perspective. Their possible fulfilment in Christ would also be a very important point of interest in this paper. After all, a brief conclusion would be drawn. However, before all these, we shall take a brief excursus of the book of Zechariah. This will help acquaint us with the prophet's life and mission.

## Overview of Zechariah: Life, Context, and Mission

Zechariah lived in the late-sixth to early-fifth centuries BC, long after the fall of Assyria in 612–609 BC (Robert 2010, 561). Though Zechariah was born during the exile of Israel to Babylon, his writing occurred once the Jewish people were back in the land. When Cyrus, the Persian monarch, conquered Babylon (ca. 536 BC), he issued an edict permitting the Israelites to return to their homeland (Is 44:26–45:6). It is estimated that approximately 125,000 Jews came back to Canaan in three campaigns led by Zerubbabel (536 BC), Ezra (457

BC), and Nehemiah (444 BC). Under the leadership of Zerubbabel, some fifty thousand Hebrews returned home. Among these were two prophets of considerable importance, Haggai and Zechariah. The Jews began rebuilding their temple but soon became discouraged, and the work fell idle, and remained so for fourteen years (Garrett 2004, 2). It was Haggai's appointed task to stir up the people to complete the temple project (see Ezra 5:1, 6:14; the book of Haggai). Zechariah, a companion prophet who began his ministry about two months following Haggai, was chosen to motivate the Hebrews to repentance and a deeper level of spiritual dedication (Zech 1:1–6). Jewish tradition maintains that the prophet Zechariah was a man of the great synagogue. That is, the group that is believed to have carefully preserved the Hebrew scriptures and traditions after the exile (Smith, p. 2).

The book of Zechariah falls into two major segments. Chapters 1–8 deal principally with Judah's spiritual restoration. The eight visions of Zechariah 1–8 provide wonderful, restorative words of hope, the dawning of a new era. Zechariah 9–14 paints a markedly different picture. They primarily express a concern about Israel and her Messiah. Reminiscent of the earlier visions against Israel's enemies (Zech 2:1–4, 2:10–17), one initially encounters oracles against Israel's enemies in 9:3–6. Like most prophecies, there is also a sudden switch. Soon one reads, however, of the sparing of some of the Philistines. A major difference between the two sections concerns the future of the people of ancient Israel. While vision 6 (5:1–4) warns against punishment for sinners, 11:4–16 portrays a wayward flock that will be punished. Only a third will remain (David 2000, 488).

## The Messianic Prophecies in Zechariah

While Isaiah is generally characterized as the "messianic prophet," there is a significant messianic emphasis in Zechariah's document as well. In a period of history that was rather dark, it was Zechariah's chore to declare that even though Israel no longer had a king (only a foreign-appointed provincial governor), the messianic torch had not gone out. The glorious day of the coming ruler was on the prophetic horizon. The Judaean tradition that a descendant of David would be on the throne forever, based on 2 Sam 7:12–16, and constantly reinforced in the royal liturgy and the psalms (particularly Psalms 2, 45, 72, 89, 110, and 132), had become the basis of the hope for an ideal king of David's line. Isaiah described such a king as a "shoot" (נצר)from the stump of Jesse (Is 10:33–11:10), Jeremiah as "a righteous branch" (צמח צדוק,) Jer 23:5), Ezekiel as a tender cutting from the lofty top of a cedar (Ez 17:22–25). While some prophets in the period leading up to the exile were alienated by the corruption of the Davidic line and put their hope only in the kingship of Yahweh (Zeph 3:15). According to Sigmund Mowinckel (1954, 155–86), both Jeremiah and Ezekiel continued to express hope in a Davidite who would truly represent Yahweh as a good shepherd (Jer 23:1–6; Ez 34:1–24, 37:15–28).

Many years have passed since C. H. Dodd (1952, 61–110) offered a reconstruction of what he called "the Bible of the Early Church." It deals with the portions of the Old Testament that are preferably used as sources of quotations and allusions in the New Testament. These come under the title "Apocalyptic-eschatological Scriptures." From this series of complex and obscure oracles come such quotations as those on the king riding on a donkey (Zech 9, 9 in Matt 21, 5; John 12, 15), on the thirty pieces of silver thrown into the temple (Zech 11, 13 in Matt 27:9–10), and on looking on the pierced one (Zech 12:10 in Jn 19:37; Rev 1:7). As this brief list already shows, several of these apocalyptic-eschatological prophecies from Zechariah are applied in the NT to Jesus' passion and death: they serve an apocalyptic-eschatological interpretation of the life and death of Jesus (Martinus 1993, 494–511). We shall now examine just five of these "messianic prophecies" in the book of Zechariah.

## Zechariah 3:8–10

The prophet Isaiah had spoken of a "branch" that would come out of the stock of Jesse, father of David (Is 11:1–5), and Jeremiah echoed the happy refrain, telling of the "righteous Branch" who would reign as king (23:5–6). Through Zechariah, the Lord proclaims: "Behold, I will bring forth my servant the Branch" (3:8). The promise is expanded in 6:12–13 where the Branch is identified as: (a) a human person; (b) one who would "grow up" from childhood (cf. Isaiah 53:2; Micah 5:2); (c) he would build the temple of God, a figure for the church (cf. 1 Cor 3:16; 6:19; Eph 2:21–22; 1 Pt 2:5); (d) the Branch would be glorified (cf. Lk 24:26), and (e) then simultaneously serve as a king and priest, with perfect harmony prevailing between these offices, a refrain echoed in the book of Heb 1:1–4.

## Zechariah 9:9

The last part of the book and prophecy of Zechariah 9–14 has often been referred to as the most difficult section in the prophetic corpus. Much has been written on various problems and issues in these chapters, with great diversity of interpretation. However, one matter on which there has been majority consensus has been the identity of the king entering Jerusalem in Zechariah 9:9. He is usually described as a future messianic king, a descendant of David. How strange, therefore, that the greatest ruler who ever claimed the hearts of men, the King of kings, should make his final entry into Jerusalem on the back of a donkey. Especially, one that never had been ridden. In the midst of an excited crowd, "an unbroken animal remains calm under the hand of the Messiah who controls nature (Matt 8:23–27; 14:22–32)." The entrance into the city was intended to be symbolic (Carson 1984, 438).

"Rejoice greatly, O daughter Zion! Shout aloud, O daughter Jerusalem!" (v. 9) is Yahweh's announcement. It draws on a number of prophetic pronouncements in which a herald announces the coming of a king, but particularly on Zeph 3:14 (echoed in Zech 2:14). As noted earlier, Leske Adrian argues in favor of cooperate or collective messianism. Hence, for him, "if one accepts the influence of Isaiah 53 on Zech 9:9, one should expect that 'your king' in Zech 9:9 is the servant, that is, God's faithful people." He pins it specifically as referring to Judah as a nation without seeing any reason for its future fulfilment in the Davidic king, or particularly in Christ. "It is the people of Judah, therefore, who are depicted in Zech 9:9 as the instruments of God's reign, to be joined by all the tribes of Israel (9:10, 13; 10:6–12) as they were prior to the monarchy." Although, Leske Adrian is not the only one with this opinion (due to reasons which bear some amount of concreteness), however, the allusions to this prophecy and its fulfilment in the New Testament writings cannot but suggest otherwise.

A key term in the passage is *meek*. The Greek words *praus* (an adjective) and *prautes* (a noun) were employed in a variety of senses in antiquity. Meekness has both a vertical and horizontal dimension. This superb quality finds its ultimate expression in the great king who entered Jerusalem en route to the cross. Meekness reflects a submissive attitude of the soul toward God. It beautifully pictures the sacrifice of the Lord Jesus in leaving heaven and through obedience becoming a servant on our behalf (Phil 2:5–8). It accurately describes the faithfulness of Christ during the third of a century he was on earth (Jn 8:29). The term denotes the benevolent demeanor of him who invites all men to "learn of" him, for he is "meek and lowly in heart" and offers "rest" (Mt 11:29) for the weary soul (Findlay 1990).

## Zechariah 11:12–13

Zechariah 11 is an ominous chapter in that it deals with a projected "slaughter" of God's "flock," designated as the "flock of slaughter" (vv. 4, 7). Most scholars are convinced that this is a prophetic preview of the Roman invasion of the Jewish people in AD 70. The reason for the prophesied devastation lies in Israel's rejection of God's true Shepherd, Jesus Christ. In Zechariah 11:10–13, we see that the first covenant with Moses and the Jews will be revoked when Jesus is killed, and a new covenant is established. Then the exact price for which Jesus was betrayed by Judas, thirty pieces of silver is mentioned. After this, the fact that Judas threw the money back into the temple, also that it was used to buy a potter's field was mentioned. This is a prophecy with such great specificity that it is hard to imagine how a skeptic of the inspiration of the Bible can possibly deny what is going on here when he said to them. "'If it is good in your sight, give me my wages; but if not, never mind!' So they weighed out thirty shekels of silver as my wages. Then the Lord said to me, "throw it to the potter, that magnificent price at which I was valued by them. So, I took the thirty shekels of silver and threw them to the potter in the house of the Lord." The prophecy prefigures Mt 24: 14–15: "Then one of the twelve, named Judas Iscariot, went to the chief priests and said, 'What are you willing to give me to betray Him to you?' And they weighed out thirty pieces of silver to him."

## Zechariah 12:10

The prophet speaks of a coming "day" when there would be great "mourning" in Jerusalem. This is not a mourning over Jerusalem's fall (Zech 11:1), but a mourning on the part of many Jews because of the realization that they had crucified their Messiah. They were not to despair in hopelessness. The Lord would "pour out" (signifying abundance) a "spirit of grace and supplication." This is a grace that will awaken guilty persons to cry out in supplication for pardon (Walter 1995, 223). Also, a dominant feature of this grace or compassion from our Lord is a grace that forgives sin. In fact, it is a grace that can forgive even the piercing of the Messiah. The term *grace* points to the generous gift of Jesus as the atoning sacrifice for the sins of the world. That is, for those who access God's favor by means of obedience to Christ (Rom 3:24–26, 5:1–2, Eph 2:8–9, Titus 3:4–7, and Heb 5:8–9).

This prophecy that Israel will see someone whom they "pierced" is amazing because it is God Himself speaking. The Lord is the one who is "pierced." Is 53:5 also predicts that the Messiah would be pierced: "But he was pierced for our transgressions." This fits later descriptions of Jesus Christ's suffering. Indeed, the New Testament specifies that this prophecy is truly Messianic. This verse indicates a future time when the Jewish people will plead for the mercy of God. Zechariah's verse is mentioned in John 19:36–37 when Jesus, hanging on the cross, was pierced with a spear. In addition to the idea of a "pierced" God is the concept of the "only child." Zechariah's mention of a "firstborn son" bears an unmistakable connection to Jesus as God's Son. The Hebrew word *bekor* was translated in the Septuagint as *prototokos*, the same term used for Jesus in Col 1:15: "He is the image of the invisible God, the firstborn (*prototokos*) of all creation." (Menken, p.13). Of course, there is Jn 3: 16, which includes a reference to Jesus as God's "one and only Son."

## Zechariah 13:7

This prophecies of Zech 13:7 is also cited by the Markan Jesus at the beginning of the passion narrative when he announces the defection of his disciples: "I will strike the shepherd, and the sheep will be scattered" (Mk 14:27). The prophecy returns in Matthew (26:31), in John (16:32), in the epistle of Barnabas (5:12), and in Justin's dialogue with Trypho (53:6). At the end of his farewell discourse, the Johannine Jesus says to his disciples: "The hour is coming, and it has come, that you will be scattered (σκορπισθῆτε), each one to his home, and you will leave me alone" (John 16:32). Apparently, we have here an allusion to Zech 13:7. It is true that the allusion is not very close to the biblical text. However, it is in any case closer to the Hebrew text than to the LXX, where "to be scattered" is missing. However, John's wording resembles the marked quotation from Zech 13:7 in Mark 14:27, where we find δια σκορπισθήσονται, "they (the sheep) will be scattered."

It is also relevant that the synoptic quotation and the Johannine allusion occur at approximately the same point in the gospel narrative and have the same function. That is to show that the near defection of the disciples had been foreseen in Scripture. Moreover, the word σκορπισθῆτε creates within John's gospel an intertextual relationship with the shepherd discourse in John 10 (Ben-Porat 1976, 105–28). The Johannine Jesus says there that the wolf "scatters" (σκορπί-ζει) the sheep in the absence of "the good shepherd" who "lays down his life for the sheep" (10, 12, cf. v. 11). Through the intratextual relation the shepherd (Jesus) and the sheep (the disciples) of Zech 13:7 are indirectly present in John 16:32.

## Conclusion

The book of Zechariah is punctuated with a variety of marvelous symbols, taken mostly from Old Testament images. The messianic prophecies in the book of Zechariah is a source of great encouragement and hope when interpreted and understood correctly. By being interpreted correctly, I mean, when the right hermeneutical tools which appreciate the unity of the Bible, and reads or approaches it with faith is employed. In other words, both hermeneutical principles, inaugurated eschatology and corporate or collective solidarity, are important here, and each will play its role in doing justice to these prophecies. Read in this fashion, one cannot but conclude that the messianic prophecies of Zechariah have a lot to tell about Jesus Christ, who is from the line of David, a Davidic king.

It is important to conclude this brief paper by saying that though partly fulfilled in Jesus Christ of Nazareth who came through the line of David, yet some of these prophecies await their eschatological fulfilment on the "day of the Lord" or "on that day" (Zech 9:9; 12:10; 14:2; Mt 24:43–44; Rom 2:6; 1 Thes 5:2–3). Jesus has been "pierced," but there will still be a future time when all of Jerusalem (a symbol of humanity) will see Him and mourn their ill treatment of Him. At that time, we shall cry out to God for mercy, and He will answer us by saving us from our enemies: "On that day, the Lord will shield those who live in Jerusalem… I will set out to destroy all the nations that attack Jerusalem" (Zech 12:8–9).

# WISDOM LITERATURE IN THE CANON OF THE OLD TESTAMENT

*Hebrew Poetry*

## Introduction

In one of his articles, David J. A. Clines (1980: No. 2. Vol. xxxiv) remarked that: "The distinction between the Bible as literature and the Bible as scripture is largely artificial. The Church can properly hear its Bible as scripture only when it reads it as literature." This is only by way of stressing the importance of the study of Hebrew poetry and the wisdom literatures in particular as "literature." Looking at the structures of most of the Old Testament writings, one cannot but accept the fact that the writers or composers of most of the books have the flair for poetry, even if some of them were not professionally minded poets. It thus becomes important that to understand these writings, one has to carefully study their literary nature while keeping in mind the fact that they are also sacred writings. In this regard, Luther's encouragement, therefore, becomes necessary for one wishing to study Hebrew poetry and the wisdom literatures in particular. He encourages thus:

> Certainly, it is my desire that there shall
> be as many poets and rhetoricians as possible,

because I see that these studies as by no other means, people are wonderfully fitted for the grasping of sacred truth and for handling it skillfully and happily. Therefore, I beg of you that at my request you will urge your people to be diligent in the study of poetry and rhetoric. (Smith and Jacobs 1918, II, 176)

The aim of this paper is to briefly explore wisdom literature in the canon of the Old Testament and wisdom in the Old Testament, and what writers, composers, and the entire people of the Old Testament period mean when they employ the term *wisdom*. To do this, we shall start from the latter (i.e., wisdom in the Old Testament before exploring the wisdom literatures in the canon of the Old Testament). The fact that the word wisdom constitutes an integral part of the phrase "Wisdom Literatures" necessitated this twist in order of presentation. This is because once the meaning and usage of the term wisdom in the OT is grasped, then one needs little effort to understand the wisdom literatures.

## Wisdom in the Old Testament

The literary genre of wisdom is found in the whole of Old Testament, but especially in a section of the third part of the Hebrew Bible, the Wisdom Literature. The word wisdom (Hebrew, *Hokmāh*; Greek, *Sophia*) is a term that can be used to indicate or designate certain books which dealt particularly with biblical wisdom. Or it can refer to a certain movement in the ancient world associated with "teacher" or sages. It can also suggest a particular understanding of reality which presents some contrast with other biblical books. Wisdom has a fairly wide range of meaning, which includes the following: the ability or gift of divination/magic as in the case of the wise men from Egypt (Gen 41:8; Ex. 7, 11). It is also applied to skill (i.e., artisan) such as metalwork (Ex 36:2, 8), carpentry, and weaving. Sometimes it is applied to being clever or cunning (Prov 30:24–28). Wisdom, which in most cases is oriented to proper action, is fundamental and as such more practical than theoretical. Most wisdom sayings are filled with valued judgments that urge a given course of action. Further understanding of wisdom can be supplemented by the broad semantic range of terms associated with understand, advice, reprove, etc., as well as by opposites, fool etc. (Murphy 1992, 920–31).

According to Eugen Biser (1987, 1817–21), the biblical notion of wisdom in the Old Testament went through development outside the Bible, though in the reverse direction. According to the original use of the word, the basic notion was that of experience and skill gained in active contact with men and things. Hence, in the earlier books, especially Proverbs, wisdom is the fruit of experience, and its origin in practical realities is reflected by the form it takes—maxims often couched in paradoxical terms and strung together without much logical sequence. "Wisdom can therefore be taught with the help of explanations drawing on a variety of sources, but it was more easily to be attained from the contemplation of models like Joseph and Solomon. Therefore, Old Testament wisdom made increasing use of metaphors to explain and bring home its message. Biblical wisdom connotes a search for 'order.' Israel experienced the mystery of God more radically in the area of wisdom than in the traditions of its own history."

## Wisdom Literature

The need for the study of wisdom books of the Scripture as literatures cannot in any way be overflogged because even the Dogmatic Constitution on Divine Revelation of Vatican II (III.12) accords on this need when it points out that "those who search the intention of sacred writers must...have regard for "literary forms." For truth is proposed and expressed in a variety of ways, depending on whether a text is history of one kind or another, or whether its form is that of prophecy, poetry, or some other type of speech... For the correct understanding of what the sacred writer wanted to assert, due attention must be paid to the customary and characteristic styles of perceiving, speaking, and narrating which prevailed at the time of the sacred writer.

Wisdom literature takes up a fairly large part of the canonical Old Testament. Proverb, Job, Ecclesiastes, Ecclesiasticus, Wisdom of Solomon belong entirely to this type, and many sections from other books must also be reckoned to it (e.g., the warning in Tobit 4). These books belong as they stand to the post-exilic period. They show, therefore, how much the artistic wisdom sayings were loved at that time in Judaism. The Hebrew term for wisdom occurs in one form or another 318 times in the Old Testament, and over half of these (183) are found in Proverbs, Job, and Ecclesiastes. Hence, these three books along with Sirach and Wisdom of Solomon have come to represent Israel's "Wisdom Literatures (Eissfeldt 1974, 81–82).

The origin of wisdom literatures has been pretty difficult to pinpoint or determine. However, there are two schools of thought that has tried resolving the question of this origin. These are the tribal and scribal schools. Both of their proposals are quite worthy of consideration. The tribal school holds that wisdom literatures originated in families and the tribes of Israel. Before the tribal confederation period, clan and family wisdom (popular wisdom) had flourished for centuries among the various peoples who made up early Israel. So the family and clan or tribe was believed to be the first context for transmitting popular wisdom, the type that is found in Prov. 4:1–5. This popular Israelite wisdom bears the mark of Israel's religious culture. A religion characterized especially by their worship of Yahweh, the God who stands by the poor and frees the oppressed. The scribal school holds that it originated from the court of Jerusalem (i.e., from the royal class.) They hold that this is so because of the similarities that the literatures presented with Egyptian wisdom. This new dimension was added to Israelite wisdom with the establishment of the monarchy around 1000 BC. This new dimension is marked by its connection with writing and the concerns of the royal court and temple (Murphy, p. 920–31). David had scribes and bureaucrats in his administration (2 Sam. 20:23–25), and Solomon consolidated more toward statehood (1 Kg 1:3–11). Scribal schools were established as a vital part of the administrative structure of the palace and temple in Jerusalem.

On authorship and dating of wisdom literatures, it suffices to note that Solomonic authorship is explicitly claimed for three wisdom books: Proverbs, Ecclesiastes, and Wisdom of Solomon (the wise man par excellence). This authorship might be better understood as patronage, as in the case of Davidic authorship of Psalms. Only portions of Proverb (especially 10–31) can be considered as coming from pre-exilic period, and it is not possible to date these, although Proverb 25:1 mentions the "the men of (king) Hezekiah" as being engaged in some kind of scribal activity. Whereas Ecclesiastes was agreed by scholars to have been written in the post-exilic period, possibly in the third century, Ecclesiasticus (Ben Sirac) can be securely dated to the first part of the second century, probably 200–180 BC. Although a majority opinion considers Job as post-exilic in date, a pre-exilic origin cannot be excluded. The Wisdom of Solomon is generally assigned to the last half of the first century BC. Judging from the foregoing, it could be succinctly capitulated that the wisdom literature is largely a post-exilic phenomenon, even if its origins are the pre-exilic period.

Among the common themes in wisdom literatures include human experience, which is a source for knowledge and insight. This experience comes from reflection on one's life and provides an important criterion for the determination of behavior. Therefore, one cannot describe the biblical wisdom literature without trying to understand the experience that lies behind it. The sayings or the "wisdom teachings" are the encoding of a lived experience, and only facets of encounter with reality can be captured in words. It is the encounter which generated into the world and human beings. Another theme like the centrality of God, which one only becomes aware of only through conscious reflection and attention to the writings also feature in the wisdom literatures. Also, one finds the "wisdom of woman." This usually occurs in the image of personified wisdom.

## Conclusion

Although a literary approach to the Old Testament might appear to lower our expectation for clear messages and general truths or for proof to equip arsenals for theological warfare, it heightens our sensitivities to being moved, amused, elated, angered, and persuaded. When a literature provokes in us these kinds of reactions, then it has the capacity to create. What more could one ask of a Scripture? Nothing, I say!

# 17

# The Sapiential Literatures: Exploring the Book of Proverbs

*Wisdom Literatures*

## Introduction

In general, the term *wisdom* (sapiential) designates a mentality pre-occupied with the practical. The books of the Bible which are classified as sapiential are but a part of the abundant sapiential literatures found especially in the orient. They must be situated in that context in order that their province or originality is better understood.

The term "Wisdom Literature" or "Sapiential Book" designates three books in the canonical Old Testament (Job, Proverbs, and Ecclesiastes), two books in the Apocrypha (Ecclesiasticus or Sirach and the Wisdom of Solomon), and sometimes other portions of the Old Testament. There is much in the wisdom books that is puzzling and even astonishing. They are in some ways quite "unbiblical." For instance, the book of Job tells of a man who is made to suffer horribly as a result of a causal wager between Yahweh and Satan, and it tells how the hero, ignorant of the wager but very much aware he does not deserve his suffering, hurls questions and challenges at the Almighty that verge on blasphemy.

Wisdom writers in both Mesopotamia and Egypt dealt with similar questions: the sufferings of the innocent and justice of the gods. Ecclesiastes goes beyond Job's questioning of God's justice. It presents the bleak prospect that humans can understand almost nothing about this world and about their place in it except that they will come to the same end that animals do, and that the best way to occupy themselves in view of that end is merely to eat and drink and be merry.

## Proverbs

The book of Proverbs is a work of wisdom. The best starting point in any consideration of the wisdom material is the book of Proverbs, which contains some of the oldest wisdom maxims collected by the sages of Israel. No one would deny that Proverbs contains wisdom genres and is to be classified as wisdom literature. It is, therefore, a good point to start when trying to define wisdom (Dell 2000, 14). According to Whybary (1994, 3), to call Proverbs a book of wisdom is fully justified. The word wisdom (*hokmāh* in Hebrew) occurs thirty-nine times, and the adjective wise (*hākām*) forty-seven times in the thirty-one chapters of the book of Proverbs. Furthermore, the basic form of wisdom is the proverb of which the book chiefly consists. If we characterize the forms, content, and context so far as it can be known of the book of Proverbs and then compare other books to it, we shall be well on the way to defining the nature of wisdom as a genre, and it will have a starting point from which to clarify the extent of the wisdom literature.

The word of God, as it has come to us through the experiences of the people of God, expresses all the emotions of the life of faith, and it deals with many areas of experience that might seem mundane. This is nowhere most true than in the poetic and wisdom literatures. The book of Proverbs is one among the sapiential books of the Hebrew scripture or the canon of the Old Testament. It not only examines moral issues, but it also helps us deal with the ordinary matters of life, such as indebtedness and work habit. In a nutshell, it is a collection of wise counsel for living well. Shepherd's Notes (2000,

9) writes that: "In Proverbs, wisdom begins with God; His central-ity is assumed throughout. Wise people are those who know God, trust Him, and behave toward others according to God's principles." Attitudes and actions have consequences, and these are spelled out in short, pithy, unforgettable sayings.

Although Proverb is not negative in spirit when compared to the other two wisdom literatures (Job and Ecclesiastes), and although it cheerfully advises that the first principle of wisdom is to have a proper respect for God, nevertheless it seems remarkably this-worldly in its advice on how to conduct one's life. Certainly, it pays scanty attention to the proper form of religious worship or to the ecstasy and despair of a soul communing with God or to the great facts of Israel's relationship to her deity, Yahweh.

## Meaning and Etymology

The Hebrew word translated Proverb has a broader meaning than does the English word. This word probably means "to rule" or "to be like." A proverb is a snapshot from life that shows us what life is like (Crenshaw 1992, 515–17). Proverbs is an anthology of admonitions and isolated sayings concerning wisdom and wise conducts. Commenting on the meaning of Proverb, James Hasting (1963, 812) writes: "In the Bible there is no essential difference between the proverbs and the parables. The Hebrew *Māshal* and the Greek *parabolĕ*, meaning 'resemblance,' were applied indiscriminately to both." The value arising from this likeness was twofold. In the first place, as the moral truth seemed to emerge from the observed habits of animals, objects in nature, familiar utensils, or occurrences in the daily life, such juxtaposition gave to the ethical precepts or fact of conduct the surprise and challenge of discovery.

The Hebrew title of Proverbs *Misle Selomoh*, according to James L. Crenshaw (1992, 515–17), derives from the superscription in 10:1. Variants of this title are *Sĕpĕr hokmāh* and *mislot*. The Septuagint title is *Paromiae*, and the vulgate has *Proverbia*, from which comes the English title Proverbs. In the Hebrew Bible, Masal designates a wide range of literary types—taunt, allegory, lament, simile, and so on. But its etymology implies likeness and, in the view of some interpreters, authoritative word. The fundamental feature of the sayings within the book, therefore, seems to be "comparism." Brief proverbial sayings set one image over against another making an explicit or implicit comparison. Not every isolated saying compares two things, however, and some sayings extend considerably beyond a single distich, in the process multiplying the number of likeness under consideration.

## Authorship and Date

From the very different character of the various collections of which the book is composed, it is apparent that the book must have been formed gradually. According to the common opinion, the oldest collection is 10:1–22. Although certain features of the book associate the name "Solomon" with discrete units, other names also occur in connection with specific section of the book. The book takes the form of an anthology, its individual components coming from various periods in Israel's history. At least two and probably three short sections stem from non-Israelite sources, making the anthology truly international. A satisfactory explanation has not surfaced for the prominence of Solomon's name in the book of Proverbs or for the implicit attribution of Ecclesiastes to him and implicit mention of him as author in Song of Songs and Wisdom of Solomon (Driver 1961, 404–05).

At what date this collection (i.e., first oldest collection—Prov 10:1–22.16) was formed cannot be determined with precision, but from the general picture of society which the Proverbs seem to reflect, and especially from the manner in which the king is uniformly alluded to, it is generally referred to the golden days of the monarchy; Delitzsch Franz (1880) thinks of the reign of Jehoshaphat; Ewald assigns it to the beginning of eighth century. From the ongoing therefore, one finds that like most biblical wisdom, Proverbs is notoriously difficult to date, largely because of the timeless quality of its teaching. Sages endeavored to communicate insights that transcend space and time (Driver, p. 404–05). Their teachings are aimed at universal assent by any intelligent individual, Israelite or non-Israelite. Assigning relative chronology to the various collections in the book of Proverbs must therefore be done with considerable reservation and caution. Commenting on this, Thomas P. McCreesh (2007, 453) observes that a date for the present book is hard to determine. Two stages can be inferred. First was the family or clan collection of proverbs. Then under Solomon and other kings (25:1), the collection and editing of the traditional wisdom was fostered. The book itself represents a special redaction of some of these earlier materials. A probable date for the book is the late sixth or early fifth century. The proverbs dealing with the king would also seem to indicate a time not far removed from the monarchy.

## Canonicity and Liturgical Use

Commenting on the canonicity of the book of Proverbs, Robert A. and Feuillt A (1970, 81) described the book of Proverbs as proto-canonical. According to them:

> The rabbinical discussions about it were terminated at the council of Jamnia. It is not certain that Theodore of Mopsuestia formally denied its inspiration, but he certainly underestimated this work by stressing that it could be explained by human wisdom alone. To be noted however, is the fact that the biblical opinion of Theodore of Mopsuestia were discussed at the council of Constantinople, as is generally the case, that they were the object of a formal condemnation.

The book of Proverbs is frequently cited in the New Testament. It was nevertheless scarcely commented on by the Fathers of the Church. Besides, the passage applied to the Blessed Virgin, the liturgy uses the poem of the valiant wife (Common of Holy Women and Feast of St Anne).

## Content/Structure

During the earliest phases of Israelite society, power rested in elders who perpetuated their singular authority only through legal status and traditional sayings. Apodictic law compelled assent in so far as it voiced the will of respected figures whose wide experience, fairness, and good judgment set them apart from ordinary citizens as custodians of valuable lore. Similarly, proverbial sayings carried the weight of cumulative experiences, hence embodied a way of life that was binding on anyone or persons who questioned the fundamental basis of society. These two, law and traditional saying, constitute ancient Israel's attempt to establish and maintain order in complex human relationship.

Many indications of internal criticism/attribution to different authors, the variety of subjects treated, and the diversity of literary forms enable us to distinguish eight sections in the book of Proverbs. The introduction is one of a more recent date: 1:8–9 (invitation to acquire wisdom); 10:1–22, 16 (rule and conduct), "Solomon"; 22:17–24, 34 (duties toward neighbor, rules of temperance, concerning idleness); 25–29, (various maxims) "sages"," Solomon" and Scribes of Ezekias; 30:1–4 (divine wisdom)—Agur; 30:15–33 (numerical mesalim), anonymous; 31:1–9 (counsel for kings)—"Lemuel"; 31:10–31 (praise of the valiant wife), anonymous (Robert and Feuillt 1970, 80).

Furthermore, the book of Proverbs is made up of a number of collections, the oldest of which is Proverbs 10:1–22; sixteen consists of mainly proverbial sayings. Proverbs 22:17–24, 22 is generally dated fairly early and marked off as a separate section on the grounds of similarity with the Egyptian Instruction of Amenemope. Other collections are Proverbs 25–9, described as having been copied by the "men of Hezekiah" (25:1), a seventeenth-century king of Israel, and Proverbs 30 and 31 which are separate shorter pieces, each with its own attribution. Finally, there is Proverbs 1–9, which is often considered the latest part of the book but which may well contain earlier material. This is the more theologically developed part, and Katharine Dell (2000, 14) suggests that it "may have been placed at the beginning of the final book as a kind of preface to the whole."

So the book represents several centuries of thought on the part of the sage. Developments of doctrine are discernable in it. In the two primitive collections, the dominant tone is that of human and worldly wisdom, disconcerting to the Christian reader, though even here one proverb in every seven is religious in theme. This religious teaching is not speculative but practical: God rewards truth, chastity, purity of heart, humility and punishes their contrary vices. The opening chapters offer the same principles of human and sacred wisdom; they emphasize vices, of which the earlier sages do not speak, such as adultery (Prov 2:16ff; 5:2ff). The epilogue too bears witness to a greater respect for women. More important still, the prologue offers the first example of a logically ordered doctrine of wisdom, its worth and its function as guide and controller of behavior. The speaker is wisdom herself; she sings her own praise and explains her relationship with God, in whom she has been from all eternity and whom she assisted when He made the world (Prov 8:22–31).

## Literary and Poetic Feature of Proverbs

The proverbial genre is paradoxical, simple, mundane and at the same time profound, abstract, and transcendent. The nature of the proverbial material is one factor in the shifting views of scholars on contextual matters. It was supposed that much of the material was literary from the start, and the oral stage was not perceived to be as significant as it was once thought to be by older scholars, and as it was, there was a development from simple to more complicated forms of proverbs, from one-limbed sayings to multilimbed ones, and from proverbial forms to instruction forms (McKane, 1970). Unlike the book of Job which takes the form of a prose story interrupted in the middle by a poetic dialogue, Proverbs and the other wisdom literatures take the form of something like a classroom lecture in which the instructors in wisdom undertake three tasks. First, to describe what they observed in life (experiential wisdom). Second, to advise their audience how to live. And third, to praise wisdom as a quality. Therefore, as a literary device, the author of Proverbs employed the characteristic parallelism of Hebrew poetry. The parallel structure of

Hebrew poetry makes it a particularly suitable literary vehicle for a society that depended on memory for the transmission of tradition and for the moralizing that the wise men engaged in. One must add here quickly that although there is great advancement in the method of transmission of tradition this time around due to the development of science and technology, the book of Proverbs is still very much relevant to us today, as we shall see shortly in the section below.

So literary forms were developing well beyond the simple proverb to become a complex literary exercise, and the book of Proverbs was thought to provide evidence of that development. Narrative texts were included in this development, Joseph narrative, with Joseph as the exemplar of the wise counselor at Pharaoh's court, and the Succession Narrative, telling of the succession to the throne, for example, were seen as products of the Solomonic enlightenment, the work of courtiers who were close to the events described. It was also held that J (Yahwistic) source of the Pentateuch may have found its context here as a celebration of the nation's history, reflecting the confidence of the national pride generated by this age of prosperity, written to preserve tribal stories that were in danger of being lost. However, many would take issues with this supposition nowadays. For example, in his book *The Composition of the Book of Proverbs*, Whybray (1994) has found much uncertainty in the attempt to locate and date literary developments such as those from one-limbed to multilimbed sayings and prefers to see different genres such as "instructions" and "maxims" as different strands of the Tradition.

One related problem encountered in the study of Proverbs is that we do not know precisely when the transition from oral to literary transmission took place, nor do we know that it was in fact a strict line of development from one to the other. Archeological discoveries of inscriptions suggest that writing became more widespread in the eighth century BC, and we have the evidence in Proverb 25:1 that the officials of Hezekiah copied that particular collection from Proverbs 25–9, at least. We have evidence of literary activity at the time of Josiah with the finding of the book of the law in the temple (2 Kings 22:8–10).

## Types of Proverbs

This simply concerns the manner of stating the proverbs. This is divided into two major forms: admonitions and sayings. There are, however, other specific types of proverbs, and these include the following: instructions (Prov 4:1), numerical sayings (Prov 30:18–19), better than saying (Prov 28:6), comparative saying (Prov 30:33), admonition saying (Prov 15:8), beatitude (Prov 14:21), paradoxical saying (Prov 26:4–5), acrostic (Prov 31:10–31), popular/folk saying and pairs (Prov 10:1–22, 17, 25–29).

Scholars usually distinguish between a saying and a proverb masal, as these are found in the Old Testament. The saying has no particular rhythm or parallelism, in contrast to the Proverb which is an art form, the result of literary artifice. A typical saying is (1 Sam 10:12) "Is Saul among the prophets?" This is to be compared with (Jer 23, 38), "What has straw to do with wheat?" (25:5–8). Although 1 Sam 10:12 is explicitly called a masal, these sayings do not have the literary expression found in the popular proverb which are usually marked by a play on word, or contrast, or by some literary device: "Let not him who girding on his weapon boast himself as he who is ungirding" (1 Kg 20, 11); "As is the share of him who goes down into the battle, even so is his portion who remains with the baggage, they shall share alike" (1 Sam 29:24). It is not possible to determine the extent to which the proverbs in Old Testament wisdom literature have their origins in popular wisdom; probably many do. But they seem to owe their final literary expressions and their preservation to the sages who used them for instructions (Murphy 1952, 6–8). The directness and sharpness of Proverb is best expressed by the parallelism of a couplet: *The door turns on its hinges; the sluggard, on his bed* (Pr 26, 14). The book of Proverbs is most likely a collection of such two-line sayings. In many instances, however, the proverb may become more prosaic, as when a reason is added to the saying.

The primary form in the book of Proverb is, unsurprisingly, the proverb—a single- or double-line sentence, its content usually characterized by comments about human relationships in everyday attempt not only to further understanding, but also to master life by noting regular patterns. For example, "Like clouds and wind without rain is one who boasts of a gift never given" (Prov 25:14). The repetition of experience as Katharine Dell (2000, 14) views it led to the establishment of a principle, so that patterns could be found that represented truth, not cold facts but truths based on repeated observation. That is, truths about human beings in relationship with each other and with the natural world around them. Different areas of life were closely examined, and patterns were found which allowed a picture of the world gradually to emerge within which individuals could make sense of their own lives.

There is a variety of different form in which we find the basic proverb. Sometimes proverbs consist simply of statements of fact with no comparative element, for example, Pr 20: 14, "Bad, bad, says the buyer, then goes away and boasts." There are proverbs in which the consequence of an action is pointed out in exhortatory tone: "My child, fear the Lord and the king, and do not disobey either of them; for disaster comes from them suddenly and who knows the ruins that both can bring?" (Pr 24:21–22). There are some proverbs which are condemnations, often using repetition: "The evil has no future; the lamp of the wicked will go out" (Pr 24:20). There are some which make a contrast (or are paradoxical), and are known as antithetical comparisons: "The wicked earn no real gain, but those who sow righteousness get a true reward" (Pr 11:18). There are commands: "Leave the presence of a fool, for there you do not find words of knowledge" (Pr. 14:7), and there are antithetical commands: "Lay aside immaturity, and live, and walk in the way of insight" (Pr 9:6). There are many similes which can be spotted by the use of "like" or "as," for example Pr 26:14: "As a door turns on its hinges, so does a lazy person in bed."

There are also metaphors, for example Pr 15:19 where the metaphor of thorns is used: "The way of the lazy is overgrown with thorns, but the path of the upright is a level highway." We also find numerical proverbs, an activity related to a liking for lists, for example Pr 30:18–19, "Three things are too wonderful for me; four I do not understand: the way of an eagle in the sky, the way of a snake on a rock, the way of a ship on the high seas, and the way of a man with a girl." Numerical proverb is a distinct type which appears sophisticated but may, on the contrary, belong to early stages of proverb making. It takes the form of a culminating numerical progression as we have already seen above. The explanation of the idiom which occurs (also in Ugaritic poetry) lies in the fact that it is found in synonymous parallels; yet, since a whole number cannot have a synonym, it is paired with the number next below it (Roth 1962, 300).

It suffices to note that the book of Proverbs does not only contain proverbs. It also contains longer "instructions," often though to parallel instructions from Egypt. Up to ten instructions could be found in Proverbs 1–9 which according to Whybray (p. 15–16) take the form of addresses from father to son(s) about moral issues, particularly to avoid evil company and to beware of loose women (1:8–19; 2:1–22; 3:1–12; 3:21–35; 4:1–9; 4:0–19; 4,:20–27; 5:1–23; 6:20–35; 7:1–27). Whybray argues that "It is unlikely that these are ten sections of one instruction since they lack structure, a group and are rather repetitive. Rather, they are separate pieces of instruction, representing Israelite attempts to establish an instruction genre along Egyptian lines."

Finally, we also find in Proverbs some pockets of autobiographical narrative where we read the author's experience, for example in the description of loose women in Pr 7:6–9, "For at the window of my house I looked out through my lattice, and I saw among the simple ones, I observed among the youths, a young man without sense, passing along the street near her corner, taking the road to her house in the twilight, in the evening, at the time of night and darkness;" and in Pr 24:30–4 in a cautionary tale about laziness. Another form found chiefly in Proverbs 1–9 is the hymnic description of wisdom personified as a woman and the creative principle alongside God, as Pr 1:20–33 and Pr 8. At first, she is portrayed as a woman speaking to passersby in public places, calling to them to accept the gifts she has to offer. She is clearly here a counterpart to loose woman, described above in Pr 7:6–9. However, in Proverbs 8, notably in verses 22–31, she takes on a new dimension as it becomes clear that she is alongside God, the first of his creative acts and present during the creation of the world. Thus, wisdom is linked to the order of the world; it is a fundamental part of its structure and the way it is governed: "The Lord created me at the beginning of his work, the first of his acts of long ago. Ages ago I was set up, at the first, before the beginning of the earth" (8, 22).

## The Message of Proverbs

Basically, the teaching of Proverbs follows a concept that is wide enough to include the practical, moral, and religious aspects of life, and in Proverbs as it is in foreign models, these are not sharply distinguished one from the other. The Israelite's conviction that everything in heaven and earth was under the control of his God enabled him in the end to see more clearly than his neighbors and true relationship between wisdom and religious faith. This insight is not apparent in every part of Proverbs, but in its final form, which represents the full maturity of Israelite thought on this subject. The book teaches that wisdom is first and foremost the possession of God himself completely expressed in Pr 2:3–8 (Ackroyd P.R. et al, 1972, 9). In other passages (1:20–33; 8:1–6), the same thought is expressed in vivid symbolism. Wisdom is there represented as personally being related to God, who offers divine instruction to men.

This teaching which provides a counterbalance to the tendency of some strands of Israelite thought to regard wisdom as essentially human arrogance leading to rebellion against God eventually came to make important contribution not only to Jewish faith but to Christian teaching as well. Since the book represents several centuries of thought on the part of the sages, developments of doctrine are discernable in it. In the two primitive collections, the dominant tone is that of human worldly wisdom disconcerting to the Christian reader. Though even here, one proverb in every seven is religious in theme. This religious teaching is not speculative but practical; God rewards truth, charity, purity of heart, humility, and punishes their contrary vices. The source and the sum of all these virtues is wisdom, that is to say the fear of Yahweh (15, 16, 33; 16:6; 22:4), who alone is worthy of trust (20:22; 29:25).

It however suffices to note that the teaching or the message of the book of Proverbs has been far transcended by Christ, the wisdom of God; even so, several maxims anticipate the moral teaching of the gospel. It should also be remembered that true religion can develop only on the foundations of human decency.

## The Relevance of Message to Modern Man

In order to appreciate the relevance of Proverbs to modern man and society at large, it is worthy of note that Proverb has a universal framework and character. This is to say, that it is true and conveys meaning to all peoples of the world. Even today, its universality, rather than diminishes, continues to increase, and there is no other time that Proverbs is needed more than in our modern world. They are "short sentences drawn from long experiences." They present themselves as ancient wisdom, yet are amazingly contemporary and very much relevant to modern man as much as they were to the ancient world.

Therefore, there is one respect in which Proverbs, like the other wisdom books of the Old Testament, has completely preserved the character of the international wisdom tradition. This is its complete silence about natural concerns. Apart from the reference to Solomon, Hezekiah, and Yahweh, there is nothing to make the reader aware that this is part of the literature of Israel. This remarkable fact marks out the wisdom books of the Old Testament (and most specifically Proverbs) and puts them in a class of their own. Elsewhere in the Old Testament, there is hardly a page where there is not some reference to Israel, its history, its special relationship with Yahweh, its sense of being guided by him and of obligation to him, and its rejection of all other gods.

In Proverbs, there is nothing of this sort. God is frequently mentioned as ruler of the universe, an arbiter of man's destiny, and is known by his name Yahweh. Proverbs appears be addressed not to a particular nation or a particular age, but to the individual, whoever he may be and in whatever age he may live in. Hence, it tactically bears the signature or address: "To whom it may concern." Its observations and advice are applicable to anyone. So this makes the message of Proverb to appear "eternal" and relevant to and for all generations. This is one of the great merits of Proverbs. Whereas elsewhere in the Old Testament, the emphasis is on the people of God and worshiping community, Proverbs takes account of humankind's (irrespective of his era or epoch) individual life and his problems, calling him away as an individual from folly and evil and urging them to embrace wisdom and righteousness. So as wisdom knows no period and age, so Proverbs being itself laden with wisdom is very much relevant to modern man.

However, it is important to point out by way of criticism that the literary form in which the teachings in Proverbs are expressed may be unfamiliar to modern readers. So there is little to be gained from attempting to read straight through it without a break. Ackroyd et al (1972, 9) feels that Proverbs cannot be used in its entirety either as a moral handbook or as a guide to spirituality. This, he feels, is due to the fact that it lacks the passion and moral exactness of the prophets. Although this may be true to some degree, yet Proverbs shows us a people wrestling with a problem which faces us all today in the modern world. That is, how to live and work in the world and keep one's feet firmly on the ground, while at the same time acknowledging the claims of God and trusting in his guidance of the world. Like the other books of the Old Testament, Proverbs is in one sense a very human book, but it is also rooted in a confident religious faith.

Finally, on the relevance of Proverbs, the book is a veritable compendium of choices and advice to aid the would-be wise person to tread carefully the path of wisdom. Love is better than hatred, kindness and generosity rather than pride, and hope better than despair. The modern world, more than ever in history, need these virtues now, thus making the book of Proverbs very relevant to the modern man. Some proverbs draw comparisons from the natural world to illuminate human behavior: "Better to meet a she-bear robbed of its cubs than to confront a fool immersed in folly" (Pr 17:12) and "A continual dripping of a rainy day and a contentious wife are alike: to restrain her is to restrain the wind or to grasp oil in the right hand" (Pr 27:16). These comparisons are not in any way outdated or obsolete because they feet in well to the same situations we find today in our world.

## The Relationship of the Book of Proverbs to My Culture

A popular Igbo adage says that *"Ilu bu mmanu ndi Igbo ji esulu ji."* Literally translated as "Proverb is the palm oil with which the Igbos eat yam (Onwudufor 2008, V). This underscores the importance of proverbs ("ilu"), which is compared to the palm oil which is a very important (food ingredient) in the life of the Igbos. The universality of Proverbs makes it relevant to my culture. One can find most of the contents of Proverbs in operation in the way the Igbos admonish, command, and make choices. Also, one finds parallels of the content of the book of Proverbs in Igbo proverbs. Example: "Entrust all you do to Yahweh and your plans will be realized" (Pr 16:4). In Igbo, we have *"Onye bu chi ya uzo ogba gbue onwe ya na oso"* (if one neglects or moves faster than his God, he will get exhausted). These two proverbs are similar in the sense that both of them are warning the reader of the need to depend or commit his or her way to God by letting Him lead the way.

*"Ana eji ehihe achu ewu ojii"* (It is good to look for the black goat in the day light) is an Igbo proverb which is like that which says: "make hay while the sun shines." Among the Igbos, this instruction is given for a lot of reasons, especially to young people. They are advised through it to do the right thing at the right time and stage of life, else, when they miss the mark, it will be difficult for them to make up their losses. So through it, hard work is equally encouraged. So the center of "Igbo moral theology" is decrement: To do the right things at the right time. One finds in the book of Proverbs half a dozen terms which are in tune or related to Igbo culture with regards to morals, and try to explain what this entails. Decrement is insight and wisdom; it is intuition; it is understanding, subtlety, prudence (Pr 1:2–3). It can also be described as a path. Also, an Igbo proverb captures this: *"Eliwe uzo liwe ehi, agam a toro uzo hapu ehi."* This simply means that I will prefer to follow the right path instead of accepting a gift of cow. Here, one finds that both the path of life and

cow are valued in my culture, but wisdom through the instrumentality of decrement will help one to make the right judgment and take the right and timely decision. This has to do with making the right choice. So if we believe that we can make choices that have no consequences, we are choosing the path of death (Pr 2:18). We should instead choose the path of life (Pr 10:17; 7:6–11).

*"Oji oso agbakwuru ogu amaghi na ogu bu onwu"* is also an Igbo proverb which simply says that one who rushes to engage in a fight, war or in fact any act of violence is ignorant of the fact that it could lead to his own death. Just as the book of Proverbs points out numerously that human relations and community-building depends on love (*agbara obi agbara uto*—when your hearts are united, you enjoy a happy relationship). Through the instrumentality of proverbs like these, the Igbos abhor violence because it is contrary to love, destructive and distorts the fraternal balance of the entire community. In Pr 1:10–19, we have a perfect description of violence. It is unprovoked, sets traps for the honest and innocent, and it is a tendency to personal gain. Most importantly, it lacks wisdom because its activities are irrational and spontaneous. Violence, therefore, for the Igbos is a trap that leads to death, *"oji oso agbakwuru ogu"*—"one who irrationally rushes to war (violence)" will definitely end up in death. Those who hate wisdom love death (Pr 8:6). So wisdom and discernment make us slow to anger (4:17; 15:18; 19:11), while every fool is quick to start off a quarrel (a fight or a war) (Pr 20:3). Another Igbo proverb which is related to all these says that *"Onye ujo ji ndu ya na nke onye ike."* That is, one who "fears" (not being timid though), safeguards his life, as well as that of the strong or irascible man. Fear here, rather than being viewed pejoratively, is a sign of strength, because it represents prudence and discernment. Such a person will hardly give in to violence.

Justice *(sĕdāqāh)* is the basic category of the book of Proverbs. This is equally related to the Igbo culture. Pr 29:7 says that "the wicked do not acknowledge the rights of the poor." In Igbo language, this is understood as *"Egbe belu, Ugo belu, nke si ibe ya e bela, nku kpwaa ya."* Literally translated, this means let the Eagle as well as the Dove perch, which ever refuses the other to perch, let its wing break.

This also means "Live and let live" *("biri kam biri")*. This is justice for the Igbos. The book of Proverbs has a good number of related proverbs or "sayings" which decry oppression of the poor and encourages the just man. "The recompense of the just leads to life" (Pr 10:16); the wicked, on the other hand, "increase their wealth by opposing the poor (Pr 22:16); "They trust in their riches (11.7.28). Hence, the Igbos will ask: *"Omegbu nnwa ogbenye, oji nke ya ala mmuo?"* (will he who oppresses or cheats the poor go with his own wealth to the land of the dead?) So the book of Proverb is strongly related to the Igbo concept of justice, equity and fairness, or fair dealings with others, especially, the weak.

The book of Proverbs closes (in chapter 31) with the figure of woman-wisdom in two senses. The first is that of the mother and the counselor of kings, and the second, that of the capable woman who administers and maintains a household and all those who dwell in it. In this, we find that the character of the woman is exposed. The Igbos pay special attention to the character of a woman. Several commentators have seen in this poem the instruction of a mother given to her daughter. The young woman learns the alphabet, and at the same time is taught how to be responsible in a patriarchal society (Farmer 1998, 860). This is exactly the case among the Igbos. The mother has a great responsibility toward instructing and teaching her daughters how to live well, especially in marriage. Hence, the Igbo proverb says, *"O na bu nne ewu n'ata, nwa ya ana ele ya anya na onu"* (as the mother-goat chews, its siblings observe it closely in order to learn). So if a young lady fails to live up to expectation in her matrimonial home or society at large, the Igbos asks, *"Azu kwara gi asu?"* (Were you trained or instructed at all?) Hence, much emphasis is placed on the fact that the lady was not properly trained or schooled by her mother or parents.

Furthermore, the Igbos have the following proverbs: *"Agwa bu mma nwanyi"* (the character of a woman is her beauty, or the beauty of a woman lies in the strength of her character) and *"Nwanyi mara obi di ya, odi ka ojiri ogwu jide ya"* (a woman who masters her husband appears to the people as though she charmed him). So, for the Igbos, the virtues or the attributes enumerated by Ps 31:10 (virtuous or worthy or noble or perfect or valiant) are actually what makes a good and beautiful woman. It is equally these that will make her a good wife and mother. Till date, this text still plays a very important role in the marriage in the entire Igbo worldview. The large household that a strong woman administers includes an extended family and servants. She goes to market, buys the household items, takes care of the children, and manages the home. A woman in Igbo culture who succeeds in managing her home and bringing up all her children without any flaws is revered and admired. In recent times and most especially for Catholics, titles like *"Nneoma"* (Good Mother), *"Nne ora"* (Mother of all), *"Ezinne"* (Good Mother) etc., are given to such accomplished women in recognition of their virtues, bravery, and exemplary life in their family and the entire community. So proverbs in this regard becomes an available tool or paradigm for the Igbo in either choosing a wife, or determining the kind of wife a woman is or will become. Also, they believe strongly that a good wife is a product of good home, where the mother has done her work of instructing or schooling her daughters well. Hence, if a lady misbehaves, they will attribute it to her mother. All these put together revolves round the ability of the woman to display some level of wisdom. So just as woman-wisdom represents the housewife ideal for the post-exilic Judah, and as an ideal for all human beings, so it presents her as an ideal for the Igbo culture. A good and a beautiful Igbo lady or woman or wife is the one who is free, capable, wise, loving, an axis and security of the typical Igbo large household. These shows that the woman is important in the culture of the Igbos, as the book of Proverbs portrays.

## Conclusion

From the study and exposition of the book of Proverbs and Wisdom at large, one fact emerges. This is the fact that wisdom begins with experience, human experience of the world and of God the creator and sustainer of the world. Wisdom as presented in Proverbs has both a practical and theological dimension. It represents the cumulative experience of many generations. It offers advice, exhortation, and warning on everyday matters, yet its contribution is both profoundly theological and practical. This is the simple reason why the book of Proverbs remains relevant to the modern man and to diverse cultures, like the Igbo culture used as a point of reference here in this study.

Finally, every language, people, and culture have its own proverbs and "sayings" which enrich and animates ordinary speech. Ancient Israel was no exception. Proverbs represent the accumulated experience of a people and express it in a brief and memorable form. Among the educated people, especially in a modern world like the one in which we live in today, they function as a rough and ready philosophy, and a set of practical rules, and are handed down from one generation to the next. Also, because of their "universal strength," they remain relevant to people of all ages and culture. Although Proverbs cannot be used in its entirety either as a moral handbook or as a guide to spirituality because it lacks the passion and moral exactness of the prophets, yet it shows us (even in our modern world) a people wrestling with a problem which faces us all today. It shows us how to live and work in the world and keep one's feet firmly on the ground, while at the same time acknowledging the claims of God and trusting in his guidance of the world.

# AN OVERVIEW OF THE
# BOOK OF THE PSALMS

*The Book of the Psalms*

**Introduction**

The book of Psalms or the psalter is the hymnal of Israel worship and the Bible's book of personal devotions. In it, we not only find expression of all the emotions of life but also some of the most profound teachings in the entire Scripture. The Psalms express every emotion the believer encounters in life, be it praise and love for God, anger at those who practice violence and deceit, personal grief and confusion, or appreciation for God's truths. Traditionally, scholars speak of Psalms and Song of Solomon as being the books of biblical poetry. The book of Psalms gives us the best example of biblical hymns and reflections that are read Shepherd's Note 2000, 50. Be that as it may, Clinton McCann (1980, 117) is quick to point out that:

> It is not customary to think of the Psalms as "instructions" but rather as liturgical materials, primarily hymns and prayers from ancient Israel and Judah. The interpretation of the book of Psalms in the twentieth century has been dominated by the form-critical and cult-functional

method. This new interest in editorial activity clearly is related to the current trend in biblical studies toward unitary, literary, and canonical readings of the Bible. Although the Psalms may have originated primarily within the liturgical life of ancient Israel and Judah, they were nonetheless appropriated, preserved, and transmitted as instruction for the faithful. The condition of the Church and culture in the late twentieth century reinforces the need to recover the book of Psalms for what they can teach us.

The Psalter (Greek, *psalterion*, the stringed instrument used for the accompaniment of such songs or psalms) is a collection of 150 psalms. The Hebrew name for the psalter is *tehillim*, hymns, but this designation fits only a certain number of psalms. Among the "inspirations" at the head of most of the psalms, the word "hymn of praise" is in fact used only once (Ps 145). The usual inscription is *mizmor*, which implies musical accompaniment. Some of these psalms are also entitled "Songs," and this term, standing alone, is found in the inspiration of every psalm in the collection known as the "Songs of Ascents" (Ps 120–134). Other designations are less frequent and sometimes difficult to explain. Finally, the psalter exhibits a complex literary structure that not only determines its shapes but provides the reader with interpretive clues for reading both the whole and its parts.

## Authorship and Date

The psalter was not complete until late in Israelite history (in the post-exilic era). However, it contains hymns written over a period of hundreds of years. A primary source of information regarding the date and authority of individual psalms are the superscriptions found above many psalms. The inscriptions relate seventy-three to David, twelve to Asaph, eleven to sons of Korah, one each to Heman, Ethan (or Jeduthum), Moses, and Solomon. The inscriptions in the Greek version do not always correspond with the Hebrew text and credit David with eighty-two psalms. The Syriac version shows still greater divergence. Other psalms, including some of the psalms of Ascent (Ps 120–134) and Hallelujah Psalms (Ps 146–150) are anonymous. These superscriptions, if taken at face value, would date many of the psalms to the early tenth century (Psalms of David), and at least one to the fifteenth century (Ps 90). Many scholars have asserted that David did not write the psalms attributed to him. But there are no historical reasons why David could not have authored those psalms. David had a reputation as a singer and as a devoted servant of the Lord, and nothing in his life is incompatible with his being a psalmist. One difficulty that has been raised is that some of the psalms of David seem to refer to the Temple (for example, 27:4), which did not exist in his day. But terms like "house of the Lord," "holy place," and "house of God" are regularly used of the tent of meeting, and need not be taken as references to Solomon's Temple.

Earlier critics dated many of the psalms late in Israel's history, some as late as the Maccabean period. For two reasons, however, this is no longer possible. First, the Ugaritic songs and hymns show parallels to many of the psalms. The grammar and poetic forms are similar. The Ugaritic tradition of hymn-writing is ancient (before the twelfth century BC) and implies that many of the psalms may be ancient. Second, a fragmentary, second-century BC copy of the biblical collection of psalms was found in the Dead Sea Scrolls (Shepherd's Note, p. 1–10). This proves beyond doubt that Psalms was composed well before the second century BC, since it must have taken a long time for the written psalms to be recognized as Scripture and for the psalm to be organized. There is no reason, therefore, to date all the psalms late. Generally speaking, they can be dated to three broad periods: (1) Pre-exilic. This would include those psalms that are very much like the Ugaritic songs, "the royal psalms" and those that mention the Northern Kingdom. (2) Exilic. This would include the dirge songs that lament the fall of Jerusalem and call for vengeance on the Edomites and others. (3) Postexilic. This would include psalms that emphasize the written law, such as Ps 119.

## Poetry and Types of Psalms

Modern understanding has been considerably enriched in recent years by the study of ancient Near Eastern literature. This is with regards to the following literary indices: (a) Vocabulary: Poetry tends to make use of words uncommon in the day to day language. Thus, the meaning of a number of terms was forgotten even in antiquity. Their translation has been aided by investigating cognate terms in related languages. The identification of parallel word pairs common to Hebrew and other ancient Near Eastern literatures has also proved helpful in clarifying obscure terms. (b) Literary level: Recent studies have shown a tendency to eschew large scale alteration of Hebrew text. Rather, the emphasis has been on the analysis of the individual psalms as they come down to us. Particular attention has been paid to the structure and literary devices (chiasm, merism, inclusion, etc.). (c) Imagery: Students of Hebrew poetry have long noted the use of "stock" images and concepts that reappears in a number of compositions. In many cases, these images are part of the wider conceptual world of the ancient Near East.

The classification of psalms is not exhaustive since there are secondary forms which are exceptional and composite, or does it always correspond to a grouping of the psalms by subject matter or purpose. However, a more satisfying classification is obtained by the study of the various literary types of which there are, broadly speaking, three of them: (a) Hymns (Ps 8, 19, 145–150, etc.). Typical psalms consists basically of three parts: the introduction, the body, and the conclusion. Their structure is fairly uniform, and each opens with an invitation to praise God. The body of the hymn indicates motives for praise, the wonders of God as shown in nature particularly, in his work of creation, and as shown in human history, particularly in his saving work for his people. The conclusion either repeats the introductory formula or expresses a prayer (John and Michael 2007, 525). (b) Entireties of laments (e.g., Ps 7, 12, 13, etc.): These comprise the largest category, including about forty individual laments and at least a dozen national or communal laments. The standard format of these psalms includes the following elements: the invocation of God's name; a description of present need; prayer for help and deliverance, frequently with an imperative ("hear,"); reason why God should help the one praying; vow to offer praise or sacrifice when the petition is heard; and grateful praise to God. A prominent feature of the lament is the abrupt shift from the lament's proper elements to the concluding confession of praise for divine aid. (c) Thanksgiving (e.g., 18, 21, 30, 33, 34, etc.): The psalms of entreaty may end with gratitude to God for granting the request. In thanksgiving psalms, this gratitude becomes the main theme. These are relatively few in number. Some are collective, and others are individual. In the collective, the community thanks God for danger averted, a successful harvest, divine favor shown to the king. The individual, having recalled past distress and God's answer to his prayer, expresses his gratitude and exhorts all the devout to join him in praising God. The literary structure of the thanksgiving psalms resembles that of the hymns.

Some authors have expanded the types of psalms. However, they are basically referring to the same thing. For example, John S. K and Michael L. B. (p. 525), in addition to the types discussed above, included the following: Wisdom Psalms (by their form and content, these show connection with the Old Testament literatures. E.g., 1, 34, 37, etc); Liturgical Psalms (these are psalms which are believed to have derived from the cultic life of Israel, such as entrance liturgies. E.g., Ps 15 and 24, 3–6); Historical Psalms (these are psalms containing narratives concern God's great works throughout the history of Israel). Under this heading may be listed Ps 78; 105–6; 135–36.

## Theological Themes in the Psalm

The psalms help today's believers to understand God, themselves, and their relationship to God. The psalms picture God as the Creator, who is worthy and capable of using His creative might to rescue His people from the Just Judge of the entire world who rewards the righteous and opposes the wicked. This picture of God presented in the psalter is not radically different from what we find elsewhere in OT, as John and Michael (2007) asserts that

A number of Psalms emphasize God's role as Creator. Several contain brief "creation account (Ps 74:12–17; 89:10–13; 104:3–10; 136:5–9) describing Yahweh's victory over the powers of chaos, the ordering of the cosmos etc. The psalms also share with other Hebrew literatures, especially poetry, a number of epithets for the God of Israel. The ordinary word for God is Elohim. Some of Yahweh's titles and epithets are drawn from the larger world of Canaanite religion and mythology.

The psalm has been called the "songbook" of the *Temple*. It is not surprising then to note the importance of the Temple in the theology of the psalms. The Temple was the "deity's palace." From this palace (*hekal*), God reigned on earth, bestowing salvation and blessing (Ps 18, 7; 20, 2, 7; 36, 10) and judging humankind (Ps 9, 8–9; 11, 4–6, etc.). The Israelite went to the Temple, where he hoped to "see" God, as a subject of a king went to the palace. Also, themes pertaining to afterlife (sheol) are visible in the psalms. The Israelites had no clear belief in afterlife until the end of the OT period; yet, they believed in a shadowy existence of after-death in "sheol" or the "netherworld." Hence, psalmist's suffering from some illness occasionally refer to themselves as going down to sheol (Ps 22:30; 28:1; 115:17; 143:7). In the psalms, one also finds that the enemies of the psalmists receive a good deal of attention. The identification of these figures is controversial. Some scholars believe that to a certain extent, the problem is connected with the identity of the psalmist. If the majority of the psalms are compositions by private individuals, the enemies may simply be personal foes. Several attributes of God or the psalmist are highlighted. "Justice" or righteousness in the Israelite view, is essentially a relational concept. One is righteous when acting in accordance with the obligations that flow from certain relationships. Thus, Yahweh, Creator, or Savior of his people, and the covenant God of Israel manifests His righteousness by maintaining the world in order and saving his people from harm.

## Conclusion

The spiritual value of the psalms needs no commendation. The Psalms were the prayers of the OT. In it, God inspired the feeling that His children ought to have toward Him and His words. They ought to use His word when speaking to Him. They were recited by Jesus himself, by the Virgin Mary, the apostles and early martyrs. The Christian church has adopted them unchanged for her official prayer. In light of this, therefore, it is pertinent to say that the list of teachings we gain from the psalms has no end. Its 150 songs call us to pray, to praise, to confess, and to testify. The prayer path to God is open at all times for all people in all situations. At times, we should take our feelings to God. He hears and accepts us. In his own way, He answers and brings us salvation. If we seek and call on Him through the Psalms, we will find Him, and He will answer us.

# PSALM 149: THE SONG OF THE REDEEMED AND THE NEW PEOPLE OF GOD

*The Fifth Book of the Psalms*

## Introduction

While I was a seminarian, one of the psalms that I longed to sing and hear at the Lauds of every Sunday of Psalter Week 1 is Psalm 149. This was probably because of the way and the tune with which we sang this psalm to the point that I mastered singing it without any script or by heart. The rhythm was so great! Many years after, that tune and rhythm still resonates in me. It still remains as new as the call of the psalmist: "Sing a new to the Lord." Unfortunately, much as this psalm resonates in me, I have not taken time to explore it. During my first encounter with the course on Psalms and Wisdom Literatures, I actually wrote my term paper on Proverbs, another interesting part of this course. Thanks goodness, I have another opportunity to explore this rich psalm.

Therefore, this paper seeks to explore psalm 149 with the aim of showing that it is a call to the redeemed and new people to constantly praise God. This new people of God represent the Church, whose head is Christ the Redeemer or the new Davidic king. The people of

God are called to sing and rejoice for what their Lord and king has done for them.

## Authorship and Date

Psalm 149 belongs to the fifth psalter of the psalms. It has an anonymous author (Hassel 2001, 71). Quite naturally, many scholars assign this psalm to a particular historical event, like the Maccabean warrior Nehemiah's triumph over hostile neighbors (Van Gemeren, Willem 2017, 1–880). Anthony Ceresko (1986, 177–94) goes even further back to argue that the psalm in its entirety clearly alludes to the Exodus and the conquest of Canaan. Erhard S Gerstenberger (1991) also acknowledges that allusions to the exodus experience are subconsciously present. Yet, there is no consensus as to what event it refers to because the psalm, as usual, has been disassociated from its original historical setting. As a result, the psalm's allusions may fit into almost any age, including that of the Maccabees (Kilnam 2006, 89).

That the language of the psalm undoubtedly betrays the pre-exilic and perhaps even pre-monarchic period is apparent, but the language does not help date the psalm, or to propose its possible *sitz im leben*. Some view this psalm to be eschatological, in that it refers to the final redemption of Israel or the final judgment of Yahweh. Others suggest the Maccabean period as the most probable setting, since the coupling of praise with battle readiness also betrays a Maccabean tone. Ceresko also argues that the psalm celebrates a victory that had already been accomplished. He points out that the psalm as a whole alludes to the language of the Exodus and possession of Canaan. For example, he suggests that verses 6–9 allude to the narratives of Israel's possession of Canaan.

When one takes into consideration the possibility that the first stanza also alludes to the narratives of the Exodus, Ceresko's suggestion becomes more convincing than other suggestions. Commenting on the date of the compilation of the fifth psalter to which psalm 149 belongs, Bullock Hassel (p. 71) concludes that a compelling evidence that the psalter was completed by the third century BC is to be found in the fact that the Septuagint, translated by 250 and 150 BC, included the Psalms in the order and form of the Hebrew canonical version.

## Psalm 149: The Text

Praise the Lord. [a] Sing to the Lord a new song, his praise in the assembly of his faithful people [2]Let Israel rejoice in their Maker; let the people of Zion be glad in their King.[3]Let them praise his name with dancing and make music to him with timbrel and harp. [4]For the Lord takes delight in his people; he crowns the humble with victory.[5]Let his faithful people rejoice in this honor and sing for joy on their beds. [6]May the praise of God be in their mouths and a double-edged sword in their hands, [7] to inflict vengeance on the nations and punishment on the peoples, [8] to bind their kings with fetters, their nobles with shackles of iron, [9] to carry out the sentence written against them. This is the glory of all his faithful people. Praise the Lord!

## Form, Structure, and Setting of Psalm 149

Psalm 149 is the fourth hymn of the quintuplet Hallelujah psalms that conclude the psalter. The communal character of the psalm is evident in its call (v. 1). As usual, the now-familiar call to praise frames the psalm. This Hallelujah frame forms a threefold inclusion (Kilnam, p. 89). Two sets of summons to praise (vv. 1–3 and 5–6), and two aspects of praise (public praise in v. 1 and private praise in v. 5) support the twofold literary structure of the psalm. Second, with the strategic placement of יַעְלְזוּ in the beginning, middle, and ending of the psalm, verse 5 functions as a pivot point. Third, יַעְלְזוּ in verse 5 is the only grammatical subject for the entire second stanza (vv. 5–9), implying that verse 5 fits better with the subsequent verses than the preceding ones (Gerstenberger S. Erhard S. Psalms 1994, 454).

The role of the preposition "B" throughout the psalm also supports the twofold structure. As Allen points out, that its occurrence in the nine verses reveals a definite pattern (1/2/2/2/1/2/2/2/1), which does not support the threefold pattern (Leslie 1983, 398). Thus, when we take these four elements into consideration, the two-fold structure explains the psalm better (Kilnam, p. 100).

Psalm 149 has a chiastic structure. It consists of two stanzas, vv. 1–4 and 5–9. The first stanza begins with a typical summons to praise, and it calls for praise of YHWH, the maker and king of Israel, in public. The call is extended to verse 3. Then, as usual, a motive clause follows in verse 4. The second stanza renews the summons to praise now in private (v. 5). A motive clause, however, is lacking in the second stanza. Since verse 5 functions as a pivot or hinge, the second stanza shares the motive clause of the first (Nashville: Abingdon, 2003:73–150, 315). The uniqueness of Psalm 149 has given rise to various proposals for its Sitz im Leben. The psalm seems to refer to some specific historical event in ancient Israel. Perhaps, a war against Israel's enemies (vv. 6–9) may have been its original setting in life (Kilnam, p. 100).

## Psalm 149: A Call to Praise

Sing to Yahweh a new song, His praises in the congregation of the faithful. The psalm opens with a customary summons to people to praise Yahweh: "Sing to Yahweh a new song." They are to sing a new song in the assembly of the faithful because Yahweh continually renews them. That is to say, each new deliverance or saving act of God becomes an occasion for His faithful to compose and celebrate with a new song. In other words, praise proceeds from real life experiences, and as such, praise is an appropriate response for God's deliverance. Psalm 149 typifies a communal character as a hymn. Most of all, one is to express gratitude to God by praising Him, but it must be done in the presence of others, the faithful in particular. Thus, praise consists of two central facets, giving honor to God and testimony to other human beings. Praise, then, is both the language to God and about God (Patrick 1986, 64, 69). When one praises God, in return it evokes praises in others. In v. 2, the idea that God is the "Maker" of His covenant people is fairly common.

Psalm 149 also calls to be ready to fight, with swords sharpened on both sides in their hands. This has been interpreted differently by commentators. Commenting on the ending of Psalm 149, Augustine of Hippo wrote that the phrase of the sword has a "mystical meaning," dividing temporal and eternal things. James L. Mays (p. 446–49) comments: "There is an eschatological, almost apocalyptic, dimension to the psalm's anticipation of a warfare of the faithful that will settle the conflict of the kingdoms of this world and the kingdom of God." At last, the people of Israel had turned to their sovereign Lord and left vengeance in his hands (Dt 32:35). At last, they had come to David's conclusion: "Some trust in chariots and some in horses, but we trust in the name of the Lord our God" (20:7).

## Canonical Use of Psalm 149

Canonically speaking, Psalm 149 is a regular part of both Jewish and Christian liturgies. Friedman Rachel (2014, 211–12) wrote that Psalm 149 is recited in its entirety in the *Pesukei D'Zimra* ("Verses of Praise") section of Jewish daily morning prayer. It is traditionally grouped with Psalms 146, 147, and 150, the five concluding chapters of the book of Psalms, which are all recited in their entirety during *Pesukei D'Zimra*, under the classification of "*Halleluyah*" psalms which express praise of God. Brauner Reuven (2013, 51) notes that Psalm 149:2 is recited by the creeping creatures in Perek Shira, and verse 5 is recited after saying Mishnavos for the departed.

Psalm 149 shares the first line with Psalm 98, known as *Cantate Domino*. Both Psalms 149 and 98 are a call to praise God in music and dance because he has chosen his people and helped them to victory. The exodus and conquest are the defining acts of Israel. The people must be ready to do again those acts in the future at the divine command (Ps 149:6–9). In Catholic tradition and liturgy, Psalm 149 is one of the laudate or hymn psalms. With Psalms 148 and 150, it was recited or sung daily during the solemn service of the morning prayer or Lauds according to the Rule of St Benedict (AD 530), (Règle de saint Benoît 2007, 40–41). In the Liturgy of the Hours, Psalm 149 is used for Sunday Lauds. It is also used for feasts and solemnities. In the Eucharistic liturgy, it is used on the Saturday after the Epiphany or before January 7 and at Easter, on the Monday of the sixth week.

## The Church, the New and Redeemed Israel Called to Sing

The historical background of Psalm 149 which places its date of composition with the post-exilic era supports both its classification as a song of praise or halleluiah song. It is a call for all those who have either returned from exile, or at least are free (even if they freely chose to remain in their former land of captivity as was the case in some instances, especially where they have already established a strong bond or raised a family there). This was the contest of Psalm 149. Israel of the Old covenant or testament was called to "Sing to Yahweh a new song." According to Athanasius, "Psalms 105, 107, 113, 117, 135, and 146 to 150 not only show the reasons God should be praised, but tell you how to do it" (Grepp 1980, 101–29). So Psalm 149 insists that the song must be "a new song." This is because of their liberation from slavery and exile. "His faithful people" were not only called to praise Yahweh with a new song; the psalmist equally tells them how to do it: "Let his faithful people rejoice in this honor and sing for joy on their beds. May the praise of God be in their mouths…" (vv. 5–6).

Israel freed from exile or redeemed from slavery prefigures the redeemed and new faithful people of God, the church redeemed by the New Covenant that Christ sealed with his blood. "For this reason, Christ is the mediator of a new covenant, that those who are called may receive the promised eternal inheritance, now that he has died as a ransom to set them free from the sins committed under the first covenant" (Heb 9:14). Commenting on Psalm 149, Augustine reechoes its call: "Let us praise the Lord both in voice, and in understanding, and in good works; and, as this Psalm exhorts, let us sing unto Him a new song." Augustine describes this new faithful people (the church) as the "new man and the church of the saints" who must sing a new song appropriate to his newness: "The old man has an old song, the new man a new song. The Old Testament is an old song, the New Testament a new song. In the Old Testament are temporal and earthly promises."

Arguing against heretics, Augustine insists that "the Church then of the Saints is the Catholic Church. The Church of the Saints is not the Church of Heretics. The Church of the saints is that which God first prefigured before it was seen, and then set forth that it might be seen. His praise is in the children of the kingdom, that is, the Church of the saints." Commenting on the mission of the saints in Psalm 149, Cardinal Bellarmine (2008, 1087), wrote: "The prophet (Psalmist) now explains clearly why he said 'to execute vengeance,' and 'to bind kings in fetters.'" That the saints who on earth have suffered unjust persecution may now "execute the judgment" that was long since "written" like a decree or a resolution, deeply engraved on a pillar, one that could not be changed or erased. "This glory is to all his saints," the glory of sitting with Christ on the clouds and judging the world; and its ruler will be the peculiar privilege of the saints, as St. Paul has it, "Know you not that the saints shall judge this world. And if the world shall be judged by you, are you unworthy to judge the smallest matters?" Truly, therefore, "is this glory to all his saints" (1 Cor 6:2).

## Conclusion

Psalm 149 is a very interesting psalm that calls all those who have been redeemed by the sacrifice of Christ to praise God. This praise is an appreciation of what God had done for his people. So it has to be a "new song." It must be a joyful and heartfelt song. Most importantly, Psalm 149 reminds us that the church is the new faithful people of God which the old prefigures.

# THE WOMEN'S POST-RESURRECTION VISIT: DISCREPANCIES IN THE SYNOPTIC GOSPELS?

*The Synoptic Gospels and Acts*

## Introduction

Many scholars have already written volumes on the Resurrection of Christ and this very important visit of the women which has served as one of the most authentic evidence and eyewitness account of the event. The synoptic problem here has revolved around the following apparent discrepancies: What time of the day did they visit? Who were they and how many were they? In all three Synoptic (Mt 28:1, Mk 16:1–2, Lk 24:1–10) accounts of this visit, there is a slight difference in both the timing and the number of women that visited. However, one general agreement among the three of them is that Mary Magdalen was present, and the visit took place on the first day of the week which is Sunday. Even the fourth gospel agreed to this (Jn 20:1). Although there are other apparent discrepancies surrounding the post-resurrection visit, however, we shall limit ourselves to the ones already highlighted here.

While many have written in support of the resurrection as a true historical event citing the visit and testimony of the women as proof of validity, others, picking holes in the apparent discrepancies in the three accounts of the synoptic gospels, tend to deny the historicity of the resurrection and thus undermine a core Christian belief. Hence, the purpose of this brief paper is first and foremost to contribute to the ongoing debate. Furthermore, to reevaluate the accounts with a bid to showing that the apparent discrepancies do not necessarily limit the credible witness of the women and that the Resurrection of Christ was a true historical event, given the testimony of these women. Here, I am using the word "apparent" as an important description or qualification of the discrepancies in the resurrection accounts of the synoptic gospels. The word "apparent" is important because some who wish to cast doubts and aspersions on the historicity of the resurrection often wish to make more of these differences than necessary. Also, by using the title "the women's visit" supposes that there were more than one involved in the visit, as all the synoptics agreed. The question is how many were they?

## Discrepancies Versus Contradiction

Before proceeding further, I consider it of utmost importance to clarify that discrepancy does not necessarily mean or connote contradiction. This would help us best situate the context of this brief paper and to understand the problem in question here. Skeptics of Christ's resurrection oftentimes claim that the various gospel accounts of Christ's resurrection in the New Testament contradict each other. One of the proponents of what I would like to tag the "contradiction hypothesis" against the gospel's resurrection accounts was a New Testament scholar Bart Ehrman, who unfortunately now seems agnostic. He argues that we cannot trust the Gospel's reports about Jesus' resurrection. In his opening remark at the 2006 debate with William Lane Craig, he affirmed: "I used to believe absolutely everything that Bill (William Lane Craig) just presented. After years of studying, I finally came to the conclusion that everything I had previously thought about the historical evidence of the resurrection was absolutely wrong." (William Lane Craig vs. Bart D. Ehrman debate, March 2006). His basic argument is that the Gospels are "hopelessly contradictory."

During the debate, Bart Ehrman enumerated about five or more discrepancies that he thinks support his claim that the evangelists' resurrection accounts were contradictory. The discrepancies include: (i) How many women were at the tomb? (ii) Did they see the stone rolled away? (iii) Men or angels, and how many? (iv) Did they see Jesus in Jerusalem or later? and (v) Did the women talk? Bart summarized his opening remark thus:

> To sum up, the sources we have (the gospels) are not as good as we would like. They are written many decades after the fact by people who were not there to see these things happen, who have inherited stories that have been changed in the process of transmission. These accounts that we have of Jesus' resurrection are not internally consistent; they are full of discrepancies, including the account of his death and his resurrection.

A superficial reading of the synoptic gospel's account of the women's visit, their time of visit and number does tend to lead to the conclusion that a lot of mistakes were made which resulted to apparent or alleged discrepancies. So while discrepancies in (not only of the gospel writers account) is inevitable in literary and historical accounts, they do not always necessarily amount to contradictions. A contradiction is a difference or disagreement between two things both of which cannot be true. A contradiction does not exist if a plausible explanation can be provided which shows that both things can be true. Unfortunately, it is often the case that when people read seemingly contradictory accounts of the same event, they rarely ask themselves (as they should) whether it is the account that is truly contradictory, or whether the same information is being presented from a different perspective (Hahn and Mitch 2010).

In other words, it is possible that both accounts are accurate, but each of the witnesses are, for whatever reason, simply recording different portions or even different perspectives of the same event? Hence, it is not a contradiction if person A tells us part of the story, and person B relates another portion of the same story. Much to the contrary, the information given by one person actually complements or completes the information given by another (Gosewehr 2016).

## The Resurrection Accounts of the Synoptic Gospels

The Christian faith stands or falls with the truth of the testimony that Christ is risen from the dead. If it were taken away, it would still be possible to piece together from the Christian tradition a series of interesting ideas about God and men, about man's being and his obligations, a kind of religious worldview; but the Christian faith itself would be dead (Ratzinger 2007, 24). Here, we shall do a textual presentation and criticism of each of the synoptic gospel's accounts of the women's post-resurrection visit to the tomb. We shall put them side by side in both their Greek (Westcott and Hart, 188) and English (Ignatius Catholic Study Bible: New Testament, ICSB: NT) translations.

## Mt 28:1

Ὀψὲ δὲ σαββάτων, τῇ ἐπιφωσκούσῃ εἰς μίαν σαββάτων, ἦλθεν Μαρία ἡ Μαγδαληνὴ καὶ ἡ ἄλλη Μαρία θεωρῆσαι τὸν τάφον.

Now after the sabbath, towards the dawn of the first day of the week, Mary Magdalene and the other Mary went to see the tomb.

## Mk 16:1–2

Καὶ διαγενομένου τοῦ σαββάτου ἡ Μαρία ἡ Μαγδαληνὴ καὶ Μαρία ἡ τοῦ Ἰακώβου καὶ Σαλώμη ἠγόρασαν ἀρώματα ἵνα ἐλθοῦσαι ἀλείψωσιν αὐτόν. καὶ λίαν πρωὶ τῇ μιᾷ τῶν σαββάτων ἔρχονται ἐπὶ τὸ μνημεῖον ἀνατείλαντος τοῦ ἡλίου.

And when the sabbath was past, Mary Magdalene, and Mary the mother of James and Salome, bought spices so that they might go and anoint him. ²And very early on the first day of the week they went to the tomb when the sun has risen.

## Lk 24:1–10

τῇ δὲ μιᾷ τῶν σαββάτων ὄρθρου βαθέως ἐπὶ τὸ μνῆμα ἦλθαν φέρουσαι ἃ ἡτοίμασαν ἀρώματα. ¹⁰ ἦσαν δὲ ἡ Μαγδαληνὴ Μαρία καὶ Ἰωάνα καὶ Μαρία ἡ Ἰακώβου· καὶ αἱ λοιπαὶ σὺν αὐταῖς ἔλεγον πρὸς τοὺς ἀποστόλους ταῦτα.

But on the first day of the week, at early dawn, they went to the tomb taking spices which they had prepared… ¹⁰Now it was Mary Magdalene and Joana and Mary the mother of James and other women with them who told this to the apóstoles.

From the verses above, the following are observable. In Mathew's account, the visit took place toward evening, "towards the dawn of the first day (Sunday)." Also, the visiting women were only Mary Magdalene and "the other Mary" (unclearly identified). In Mark's account, the visit took place just after sun rise, "very early on the first day of the week." Mary Magdalene, and Mary the mother of James, and Salome were the visiting women. In Luke's account, the visitors came while it was still dark on the first day of the week, "at early dawn, they went to the tomb." In addition to Mary Magdalene, several other women, including Joana and Mary the mother of James, made the visit to the tomb. Luke alone names Joana in his account, as he alone had named her before as following our Lord in Galilee

(Lk 7:2). It is not an unreasonable inference from this that she was probably his chief informant (Ellicott 1954). Also, Mark alone mentioned Salome in his account.

## What Time did they visit the Tomb?

One of the apparent discrepancies in the synoptic gospel's records of the woman's post-resurrection visit to the tomb has to do with the time of their visit. One issue at stake is that skeptics and critics often accuse the evangelists of not even knowing when the women came to the tomb. The critics really make a mountain out of a mole hill. "There is nothing easier (than to reconcile these accounts) unless one is held up by indifferent minutiae, and if one bears in mind the manner in which each gospel was composed" (Lagrange 1932, 382). Matthew says at break of day; Mark, very early when the sun had just risen; Luke, very early. It should be noted that all three evangelists agree on the day: it was Sunday. Matthew's record is peculiar; he alone mentions the visits of the women "in the evening" at the time of His resurrection, and that the time is accurately fixed by the two Greek words, ὀψὲ and ἐπιφωσκοάτρ. Interestingly, just as Matthew does not mention any morning visits, so none of the other writers mention this evening visit (Hailey 1908, 107–19).

It is important to note that the supposed discrepancy has a lot to do with Mark, who is believed to have said the women came to the tomb "when the sun had risen" (Brooks, 18). However, Mark uses that often-troublesome aorist tense that does not necessarily mean past time. "An aorist participle may express any time (past, present, or rarely future) relative to the main verb." In fact, Young's literal translation, published in 1862, renders this verse as "and early in the morning of the first of the sabbaths, they came unto the sepulchre, at the rising of the sun" (Mark 16:2 YLT). Also, it is entirely possible that the women began their journey while it was still dark, but by the time they arrived at the tomb, the sun was beginning to appear over the horizon. It is clear that in Mark's account, the women are delayed by the purchase of spices. We may suppose then that Magdalene, leaving this matter to the other women, went alone and much in advance of the other women to the tomb, even while it was yet dark, and that the other women who had stopped to purchase ointments and did not reach the sepulchre until the sun had risen.

Although our focus is on the synoptic gospels, here it would not be completely out of place to invoke the fourth gospel in order to buttress the point already made above. Hence, we may say that when John says Magdalene, "ἄρχεται πρωΐ σκοτίας en οὔσης" which may be translated "is on her way before daylight," he has the beginning of the journey in mind, and that when Mark says, ἀνατείλαντος τοῦ ἡλίου (translated "when the sun had risen"), he is referring to the terminus of the journey, the sun having risen while the women were en route to the sepulchre. It is quite plausible to say that Mark spoke loosely, meaning by his words, that that the first light of the aurora was visible from beyond the eastern horizon (Simon-Prado, Praelectiones Biblicae, N. T. I4, p. 612).

## Who Were These Women, and How Many Were They?

Matthew says: Mary Magdalene and the other Mary (Mt. 28:1); Mark: Mary Magdalene, Mary the mother of James, and Salome (Mk. 16:1); Luke: Mary Magdalene, Mary, the mother of James, Joanna, and the other women who were with them (Lk. 24:10). As already mentioned, Matthew does not introduce details which are not strictly necessary, and since according to the Mosaic Law two witnesses were enough to establish a fact (Deut 19:15). He mentions no others, although he does not deny that others shared in the startling discovery of the empty tomb. According to Matthew: "Now after the Sabbath, as it began to dawn toward the first day of the week, Mary Magdalene and the other Mary came to look at the grave" (28:1) (Joseph 1940, 98–111).

While the idea that what each of the gospel authors focused on was a matter of individual perspective can be stretched to breaking point, it certainly seems to be true in Matthew's rendering of that morning's events. Although other gospels (John inclusive, Jn. 20:1) only named particular women, they made it clear that other women were also at the tomb. Matthew and Mark both mentioned Mary

Magdalene and another Mary as being there. What is interesting is that they also state that these same two women watched to see where Jesus was buried. Hence, it is quite interesting that when Matthew writes about the women visiting the tomb, he says nothing about them wanting to anoint Jesus' body, but instead, he says they came to "see" the sepulcher (Mt 28:1). In other words, having been witnesses to his burial, the two Marys were now witnesses to the fact that He was no longer where they had laid Him. Mark adds the name of Salome to the group of women who went early Sunday morning to the tomb of Jesus. The reason for Mark's mentioning these three women is probably that he has already told us in Mk 15:40 that they assisted at a distance at the crucifixion of Jesus, and his mention of them at the tomb on Sunday morning is possibly designed to show that their love and devotion were not extinguished by the horrible death of their master on the cross (Joseph 1940, 98–111).

Luke is more elaborate and, perhaps, more complete in his enumeration of the witnesses of the empty tomb. This could be in pursuance of his principle to investigate all things diligently, according to the way an eyewitness had handed them down (Lk. 1:2–3). Since he had not been an eyewitness himself, he would have the word of as many eyewitnesses as possible to the empty tomb (Joseph, p. 106). Luke's words could very well point to the fact that two separate groups of women told the disciples what had happened. When Luke said "*also*," the other women with them were telling these things to the apostles; the word "also" could very well indicate a second telling.

The first group might have included Joanna and the two Marys, with Mary Magdalene as the spokesperson. The second group possibly consisting of the other women who had also been at the tomb. And when Luke wrote that Mary Magdalene, Joanna, and Mary the mother of James returned from the tomb and reported all these things to the eleven, he could have been summarizing the actions of *all* the women. A very important point that must be borne in mind while reading these accounts is the fact that these were never intended to be comprehensive lists of every single woman who went to the sepulcher that morning, as is perfectly evident from Luke's account. While he only names three women, he speaks about "the other women with them." It is important to note also that John collaborates Luke's account. He only names Mary Magdalene but acknowledges the presence of additional women (Jn 20:2). In her report to the disciples, Mary Magdalene uses the plural pronoun "we." "They have taken away the Lord out of the tomb, and we do not know where they have laid Him." (Jn 20:3).

So how many women went to the tomb, and who were they? One solution here is to recall that Matthew did not absolutely deny that three women went to the tomb that day. He simply did not mention three, whereas Mark does. While, as already mentioned, Luke chose to mention more. John especially wishes to focus on Mary Magdalene (who is what all of them have in common) and may have found it unnecessary to mention the others. Additionally, Matthew and Mark's mention of one angel need not be seen as an absolute denial that there were two, as described in Luke and John. So another solution is simply to acknowledge the discrepancies in the accounts but underscore the fact that the number of women and the number of angels is *not* the central point. The point is that the tomb was discovered empty by one or several women, and they were instructed to tell the apostles what they saw and heard (Charles Pope, 2010).

## What is the Aim of the Resurrection Accounts?

Modern readers of the resurrection accounts have constantly asked historical questions of the text rather than evangelical or theological ones about what the gospel writer is challenging us to accept or to deny by means of this particular narrative (Pernn 1976, 6). Rudolf Bultmann raised an objection against resurrection faith by arguing that even if Jesus had come back from the grave, we would have to say that a miraculous natural event such as the resuscitation of a dead man would not help us and would not be essentially relevant (Ratzinger 2012, 243). Norman Perrin (1976) sees Mark's resurrection narrative as primordial myth because, unlike Matthew's and Luke's, it is not concerned with the founding of a Christian community distinct from the Jewish. He reverses the Markan stress on the apocalyptic coming of the Son of Man. In a consistent way he maintains with Jesus' own stress on the kingdom of God as something experienced by each person in his or her own lifetime. (Benjamin 1981, 4–38).

Thus, he summarizes Mark's message as follows: "For me to say 'Jesus is risen' in Markan terms means to say that I experience Jesus as ultimacy in the historicity of my every day, and that that experience transforms my everydayness as Mark expected the coming of Jesus as Son of Man to transform the world" (Norman Pernn, p. 38). The resurrection account in Matthew "makes the story of Jesus the foundation myth of Christian origins." For a generation once removed from Mark's and needing to distinguish itself from nascent rabbinic Judaism. To speak of the resurrection in Matthean terms is to say that Jesus is risen into the church. The resurrection of Jesus makes possible the life of the church, and the life of the church is the validation of the claim that Jesus is risen.

Mark meant to conclude his account at 16:8. Both Mark and Paul knew only of the fact of appearances, not of narratives describing them. Mark's unique contribution was to combine the angel's proclamation of the empty tomb (16:6) with the announcement of the appearance of Jesus to his disciples (16:7). Though acknowledging that scholars disagree about the historicity of the empty tomb story, Ulrich sees it as integral to the whole passion-resurrection account (Benjamin, p. 36). "His tomb is the authentication of his triumph over his foes" who had unjustly executed him. Nevertheless, it is not intended as a proof of the resurrection nor of the bodily reality of the risen Jesus but as a "trophy of the victory over those who set out to murder Jesus and to destroy him" (Wilckens 1978, 134). The evidence of the empty tomb has historical value. The fact that the tomb was empty was never challenged by Jewish leaders (Mt 28:11–15), only the manner of its occurrence (Brown 1973, 113–25). Furthermore, it is likely that "the place where they laid him" (Mk 16. 6) may well have been the location of a cultic commemoration of the resurrection in a way paralleling aetiological cult legends in the Jewish tradition (Wilckens, p. 119).

Clearly, each of the three synoptic gospel writers had a different intention., a different mind focus. They each told of the same historical events, but each put an emphasis on this aspect or that aspect. If they all said the same thing, there would hardly be need of four, one would do. Different witnesses to the same event can see things a little bit differently and tell the story a little bit differently, and yet the variations can still be accurate and true. The same could be true with the Gospel writers. Each witness sees from his own view and emphasizes some things more than others, and the Holy Spirit intends to say something a little different each time as well, in each case sometimes literally, sometimes figuratively. And it does not need to be the case of either/or; the differences are easily explained as each of the seeming "discrepancies" being true. There is no doubt that the Church Fathers noted these apparent discrepancies. However, they did not edit the gospels or try to harmonize them as Tatian did with his Diatessaron. Instead, they left them with way they are with their apparent discrepancies. Rather than as a proof of contradiction, they left them as a proof that they (the Fathers) were not promoting a fanciful lie about the Lord's Resurrection.

## Conclusion

In light of what we have seen so far, when one reads the three synoptic gospels' accounts of the Resurrection, one can easily be perplexed by some apparent discrepancies in the details. However, the good news is that it is quite clear that many, if not most, of the differences or discrepancies can be easily reconciled. It is possible to ultimately weld together a pretty clear and unified account of the resurrection of Christ from the synoptic gospel's perspectives while not reducing both the historical and theological integrity of the Lord's Resurrection.

The different perspectives in the gospel's accounts of Christ's resurrection are indicative of the veracity of the eyewitness statements. Those who have seen something unexpected often report the details in somewhat of a frenetic and seemingly disconnected way, as they attempt to communicate the depth of what they have witnessed even while processing the events for themselves. Were the gospel writers or the disciples lying, they would have presented a uniform story. Then the same critics who try to point out contradictions in the gospels would no doubt accuse them of collusion or intentional effort to impose a false story on others if they found exact verbal parallelism and a singular account of the resurrection.

In the end, the recordings of the resurrection found in the synoptic gospels complement each other and harmonize quite well upon closer examination. So it is more noble and convenient to view and speak of them in terms of complementarity rather than contradiction. Most importantly, they strongly agree on the one key fact that has universal life impact. That is, that Christ is risen from the dead.

# CHRIST'S DEATH AND THE INAUGURATION OF THE NEW TEMPLE THEME IN JOHN'S GOSPEL

*Johannine Literature and Apocalypses*

## Introduction

In the gospel of John chapter 2, Jesus did some; if it were today, some would have described him as been very imprudent. However, many authors have argued that his action was in line with the prophetic style of the time, citing the actions of some prophets like Amos, Ezekiel, Isaiah, Jeremiah, Elijah, Elisha, Hosea, and lots more. Apart from turning over the table of temple merchants and chasing them out from the temple with whip, Christ compared himself to the Temple. In fact, he called himself the Temple, insisting: "Destroy this temple, and I will rebuild it in three days (ἀπεκρίθη Ἰησοῦς καὶ εἶπεν αὐτοῖς Λύσατε τὸν ναὸν τοῦτον καὶ ἐν τρισὶν ἡμέραις ἐγερῶ αὐτόν") (Jn 2:19). To his Jewish adversaries and hearers, this was a bogus and blasphemous claim of a wretched carpenter's son. However, it was not taken lightly by his Jewish hearers and interlocutors in his discourse. They did not understand what he meant because they took his word literally. Of course, the temple with its splendor and elegance was eventually destroyed in AD 70, thirty-seven years after Christ's "scandalous death" (Humphreys and Waddington 1985).

The single most solid fact we have about Jesus' life is his death. Jesus was crucified. Thus, Paul, the gospels, Josephus, Tacitus, and more witnesses attested to this. The evidence does not get any better than this (Josephus 1991, 56–92). However, after his provoking speech, His disciples had to wait till his resurrection before they could unpack the true meaning of his words as John tells us: "But the temple he had spoken of was his body. After he was raised from the dead, his disciples recalled what he had said. Then, they believed the scripture and the words that Jesus had spoken" (Jn 2:21–22). Also, Christ's discourse with the Samaritan woman points to him as the new and eschatological temple where "those who worship God will worship him in Spirit and in truth" (Jn 4:7–26).

In recent years, the notion of Jesus' definition of Himself as the New Temple in the Gospels, and particularly in the fourth gospel, has received significant scholarly attention. Not only did Jesus declare Himself to be the Temple, He also foreshadows the replacement of the Jerusalem Temple as being founded in His own person in an eschatological context (Jn 2:19–21) (González 2016—Vol. XV- No. 2 Artículo). Hence, in keeping with the title of this paper, our focus here would be on the meaning and significance of Jesus' action and his discourse with his Jewish adversaries over the Temple. Most importantly, we shall argue that Christ's death on the cross inaugurated the New Temple, thus bringing to fulfillment his words and prophecy in John 2:19. To achieve this, we shall take a brief look at the development and significance of the Temple as "an institution" in Israel's history. As an institution, it means that the Temple played religious, political, and social role in the life and history of Israel.

## The Development and Significance of the Temple in Israel/Judaism

According to Jewish tradition, the original Jerusalem temple was ordained by Yahweh through the Davidic Covenant: "When your days are fulfilled and you lie down with your ancestors, I will raise up your offspring after you, who shall come forth from your body, and I will establish his kingdom. He shall build a house for my name, and I will establish the throne of his kingdom forever" (2 Samuel 7). The construction of the first Temple and its period marked a transition from nomadic or migrant, to a settled and established lifestyle. The Israelite or Judean community was no longer mobile, and therefore, the portability of the Tabernacle was no longer a priority. The Tabernacle was a portable and ornate tent shrine. It served as the terrestrial home for ancient Israel's deity from its construction at Mount Sinai under the supervision of Moses, until it was replaced by Solomon's Temple (Homan 2006). Not only was the community no longer mobile, but a monarchy was also established, representing a significant transition in the political and socioeconomic way of life. Interestingly enough, within close proximity to the Temple, a palace was established, architecturally symbolizing to the Israelites that Yahweh was working through the king. In a sense, the Temple became the king's "private chapel," presenting the Temple as an elitist form of worship, a concept that was strengthened by the power of the developing priestly class.

The Temple played religious, economic, and political role in Israel, as well as in Judaism. It was the center of worship, with sacrifice playing an important, even crucial, role within ancient Judaism. Laws and obligations were established in order to accommodate sacrificial requirements imposed on the Judean community, both within ancient Palestine and in the Diaspora. Both the book of Exodus and Deuteronomy attest to three mandatory pilgrimages: *Pesach*, *Shavuot*, and *Sukkot* (Deut. 16:16–17; Ex 23:14–17).

Before we proceed, it is important to note that although the Temple is referred to as a single institution, the Jerusalem Temple was rebuilt at least three times in antiquity. The first was erected under Solomon, as is described in great detail in 1 Kings 5–6, approximately during the tenth century BC. The second was built by returning exiles in approximately 515 BC, while the third, and most elaborate, was developed under Herod in approximately 19–9 BC, although it remained under renovations until its final destruction in AD 70 (Murray, 2018). Generally, the Temple established by the returning exiles and Herod's Temple are conflated in scholarship and referred to as simply the "Second Temple" or the "Second Temple period." Although the physical characteristics described will refer to Second Temple evidence, the term "Temple" here will represent all three, as it is the general establishment of the institution that is of interest rather than the architectural differences between all three.

## Jesus and the Temple

Jesus and his disciples were Temple participants (e.g., Jn 2:13; 4:45; 5:1; 7:10, 37; 8:20; 10:22–23; 18:20) (Ken 2010, I). Almost all New Testament scholars concur that Jesus of Nazareth overturned the tables of the money changers in the Temple's court around Passover during the final week of his life; that in so doing, he symbolically announced the Temple's impending destruction (some scholars still contest this point), and that this action triggered the events that led directly to his death (Fredriksen, p.1). Jesus' life from beginning to end was bound to the Temple. When Mary had fulfilled the forty-day ritual of purification after giving birth, she and Joseph took the infant Jesus to the Temple in Jerusalem for the ceremonial redemption of the firstborn (Lk 2:22–24). Twelve years later, Mary and Joseph "found him in the temple, sitting in the midst of the doctors, and they were hearing him, and asking him questions."

Near the commencement of His ministry, "Jesus was taken up into the holy city, and the Spirit sat him on the pinnacle of the temple" (Mt 4:5). There Satan made a vain effort to tempt him. During the three years that followed, Jesus was frequently in the Temple courts and in the various structures or colonnades of the inner Temple (Joseph, 1988). "The blind and the lame came to him in the temple; and he healed them" (Mt 21:14). "During the feast, Jesus went up into the temple and taught" (Jn 7: 14). "And early in the morning he came again into the temple, and all the people came unto him; and he sat down and taught them" (Jn 8:2). "He taught daily in the temple" (Lk 19: 47). "All the people came early in the morning to him in the temple, to hear him" (Lk 21:38). "I spoke openly to the world," he said; "I even taught in the synagogue, and in the temple, where the Jews always gather; and I have said nothing secretly" (Jn 18:20), (Ogden. 1991). In fact, most of Jesus' major speeches and the evangelist's dramatic didactic scenes occurred near or in the capitol, often in the precincts of the Temple. The fourth gospel hardly presents a Galilean mission at all.

## The Tale of Two Temples

The past decade has seen remarkable interest in John's view of the Temple, marked by the publication of several monographs and numerous articles. Many of these have been produced independently of one another and reflect a variety of approaches, but all of them find in the traditions and expectations of the Temple vital background to John's presentation of Jesus. Most of these studies, however, continue to assume that John's Temple theme is primarily a reaction to the fall of Jerusalem in CE 70 and conclude from this that Jesus (or the church) in some sense "replaces" the Temple and its festivals, taking their place as the locus of God's presence (Ken, p. i). So there has been serious debate as to whether Christ's prophecy: "destroy this temple and I will rebuild it in three days (ἀπεκρίθη Ἰησοῦς καὶ εἶπεν αὐτοῖς Λύσατε τὸν ναὸν τοῦτον καὶ ἐν τρισὶν ἡμέραις ἐγερῶ αὐτόν" (Jn 2:19) referred solely to the physical destruction of the temple, or to his death, or to both.

John Meier (2001, 501), famously and meticulously states that: "Mk 11:15–17 and John 2:13–17 narrate versions of the so-called cleansing which most likely is a symbolic, prophetic action by which Jesus foretells and, in a sense, unleashes the imminent end of the present temple." Of course, the same temple with its splendor and elegance was eventually destroyed in 70 AD (Humphreys and Waddington 1985). However, Paula adamantly insists: "I do not think that Jesus predicted the Temple's (physical) destruction. I doubt the authenticity of the action attributed to him in the Temple. But, even if the traditions of Jesus' predicting the Temple's destruction were authentic, this still would not help us to discern and establish the meaning of Jesus' action in the Temple court, even if that too, were authentic." Brown T. Ken equally argued that: "John's many references and allusions to the Temple and its festivals are not to be understood merely as a reaction to 70 A.D, but rather, serve an essential purpose in advancing John's more fundamental christological agenda" (cf. 20:31).

## The Death of Christ and the Inauguration of the New Temple

The New Testament teaches that the death of Christ is to be understood as the termination point of the sacrificial system of the Old Testament (Mt 27:51; John 1:29; Heb 8:1–7, 9:1–24, 10:1–14). What then replaces the Jewish temple in the New Testament? This question is pertinent because there is an apparent tension in the New Testament between the focus on Jesus as the new Temple that is particularly found in the gospel of John, and the focus on the true temple as the heavenly sanctuary that is particularly found in the book of Hebrews. (Eliezer González, p. 40).

The point is that under the terms of the old covenant, the temple was the great meeting place between a holy God and his sinful people. This was the place of sacrifice, the place of atonement for sin. The side of the cross where Jesus by his sacrifice pays for our sin, Jesus himself becomes the great meeting place between a holy God and his sinful people. Thus, he becomes the temple, the meeting place between God and his people. Jesus says, "Destroy this temple, and in three days I will raise it up." It is in Jesus' death, in "his destruction," and in his resurrection three days later that Jesus meets our needs and reconciles us to God, becoming the temple, the supreme meeting place between God and sinners (Carson 2010).

The first group who mocked Christ (Mk 15:29–30) told him: "Save yourself! Exercise your power!" Commenting on this, Joseph Ratzinger (2007, 209) says: "They do not realize that at this very moment the destruction of the Temple is being accomplished, and that the new Temple is rising up before them." The synoptics Mt 27:51, Mk 15:38, Lk 23: 45) all tell us that at the end of the Passion, as Jesus dies, the veil of the temple was torn into two immediately. This could probably be the inner temple veils that they referred to here, the one that seals off the Holy of Holies from human access. Ratzinger posits two important lessons from this: "On the one hand, it becomes apparent that the era of the old temple and its sacrifices is over. In place of the symbols and the rituals that point ahead to the future, the reality has now come, the crucified Jesus who reconciles us with the father. At the same time, the tearing of the Temple veil means that the path to God is now open."

## Jesus' Death and the Eschatological Temple

"Destroy this temple, and in three days I will raise it up." John comments (in 2:19–21): "But He was speaking of the temple of his body (ἐκεῖνος δὲ ἔλεγεν περὶ τοῦ ναοῦ τοῦ σώματος αὐτοῦ." Here, Jesus' words and response embodies multiple Old Testament eschatological allusions. This particular passage "has an evident eschatological thrust, the day of the Lord has come," and with it, a New Temple (Hahn 1970, 53). In this regard, Ferdinand Hahn notes that John introduces the theme of Jesus as the New Temple in John 2,13–21. This was "in order to pursue that theme as a key point throughout the remainder of his gospel" (Hann 2008, 107–44).

Eventually, they did destroy it. Jesus' last words are "It is finished!" (Jn 19:30). In the Greek text, this word (Τετέλεσται) which means "to the end" (telos) points back to the very beginning of the Passion narrative (Ratzinger, p. 223). It refers to the end or consummation of all thing in Christ, including the old temple whose end has come, giving way to the New Testament. "The new temple is the central idea of Jewish eschatology from its very beginning" (McKelvey 1969, 22). During the Second Temple period, the Jews looked for the coming of the new and glorious temple that had been prophesied, and that would be filled with the glory of God. This eschatological temple came to be considered as "entirely new in character and supernatural in origin. This eschatological interpretation of the temple has been seen as being reflected across all of the gospels" (Lohmeyer 1961, 41–42). One thing was astonishingly clear from the outset: with the cross and death of Christ, the old temple sacrifices were definitively surpassed. Something new has happened. The expectations expressed in the prophets' critique of the temple worship, and particularly in the Psalms, were now fulfilled (Ratzinger, vol. 1:230).

There has been a little debate over what the eschatological temple really signifies. The "fusion of the concept of the heavenly temple and the new temple found its logical outcome" in the belief that in the eschatological age, God would reveal His new temple and would dwell with His people "in a new and unprecedented way." Significantly, within this understanding, the Messiah is "a figure who stands not in His own right, but in relation to the divine dwelling," and all of these lines of thought converge on the hope of the coming of the eschatological temple (McKelvey 1969, 22).

Commenting on the fourth gospel, Alan R. Kerr (2002, 102) argues that "John is writing to demonstrate that Jesus is the answer for a Judaism that has lost its central institution." Another scholar, Walker P. L. (1996, 247) observes that "John's language may refer to the Jerusalem Temple, but his meaning does not" but, rather, refers to Jesus and the Church. According to the interpretation of John, the Church is essentially "the ongoing presence and action of Jesus in the world through His corporate body, the ecclesial community, which will salvifically reveal Him as He revealed God" (Schneider S. M, 2008: 47–83).

There is little doubt that Jesus' death inaugurated or was the advent of the "now eschatological" Temple, having ended the old. Christ is now the New Temple. Through this, we see him fulfilling also what he prophesied in his discourse with the Samaritan Woman by the pool in John 4: 7–26. In the context of worship, the Samaritan woman states something that no Jew or Samaritan could disagree with: "Our fathers worshiped on this mountain, but you say that Jerusalem is the place where people ought to worship" (καὶ ὑμεῖς λέγετε ὅτι ἐν Ἱεροσολύμοις ἐστὶν ὁ τόπος ὅπου προσκυνεῖν δεῖ— John 4,20). The reason the Samaritan woman explicitly mentions the Jerusalem temple is because the temple and its cult had been the subtext of Jesus' discourse all along. It was Jesus Himself who had implicitly introduced this theme (Stephen T. Um, 2006:2–14). Jesus' response was: "But, the hour is coming and now is here, when the true worshippers will worship the Father in spirit and truth (προσκυνήσουσιν τῷ πατρὶ ἐν πνεύματι καὶ ἀληθείᾳ). God is spirit and those who worship him, must worship him in spirit and truth (Jn 4:23–25).

Indeed, the death of Jesus opened the gate to this new temple of the spirit. It initiated the worship of the believers in this new temple and, at the same time, opened the new sanctuary of God in and to all who accept and believe in Christ, for wherever Christ lives, there lives the new Temple. Newton M. Newton (1985, 54–55) argues convincingly that Paul's use of the language of purity focuses on the concept that believers enjoy the presence of God in their midst because they comprise the Temple of God (Newton, p. 54–55).

This principle of the fundamental importance of the presence of God, as that which determines what is holy, applies throughout the New Testament. It is this principle that it is the personal presence of Christ that must be considered as a fundamental factor in determining what is God's Temple. Hence, the gospel of John demonstrates the ideal of the relationship that God wishes to have with humanity (Eliezer González, p. 59).

Jesus' response to the woman confirms this: "Whoever believes in Me, as the Scripture has said, 'Out of his heart will flow rivers of living water'"—ῥεύσουσιν ὕδατος ζῶντος—(vv.37–38.) Jesus was explicitly drawing attention away from the Jerusalem temple, and to Himself as the source of ὕδωρ ζῶν. Ezekiel 47 was a passage of Scripture that was actually read at this specific festival. Indeed, in one of his most striking passage, Jeremiah (17:12–13), describes a river of "living waters" which flows from the eschatological temple (τὰ ὕδατα αὐτῶν ἐκ τῶν ἁγίων ταῦτα ἐκπορεύεται) (Beasley-Murray 1987, 60). Hence, by using this symbolism, this should be understood as yet another declaration by Jesus of Himself as the One who takes upon Himself the functions of the temple.

The summary of Jesus' response to the woman with regards to worship could be framed thus: in His response, Jesus reveals Himself as the Messiah, the coming of whom signals that the time for transformation of worship, and for the replacement of the Temple, has now come: "Jesus said to her, I who speak to you, am He" (ἐγώ εἰμι)

(John 4:26). In other words, I am the new temple, you need not look elsewhere or walk for hours or suffer to go to Jerusalem or mount Gerizim to worship. The new temple is before you; believe now and worship in him, and he will live in you.

Brant Pitre (2008, 47–83, 56) based his analysis of the concept of the temple in the gospel of John on the understanding that "from a theological and liturgical perspective, for a first-century Jew, the Temple was at least four things: (a) the dwelling place of God on earth; (b) a microcosm of heaven and earth; (c) the sole place of sacrificial worship; (d) the place of the sacrificial priesthood." Jesus, accordingly, saw each of these aspects as being fulfilled in Himself and in His disciples. In representing this transition, the gospel of John demonstrates both the reverence of Jesus for the temple, as well as presenting the "unveiled glory of the divine presence" that has been manifested in the coming of the Son of Man.

## Conclusion

From the evidence we have seen so far, there is little doubt that there is a great relationship between the new Temple and the presentation of the death of Christ. The death of Christ inaugurated the new Temple. In short, Jesus embodies the wisdom, glory, presence, and name through which God has always been known, including in the Temple. He lives among us, and his death and resurrection are tied to the destruction and raising of the Temple. In fact, He not only fulfilled his words and prophecy: "destroy this temple and I will rebuild it in three days" (ἀπεκρίθη Ἰησοῦς καὶ εἶπεν αὐτοῖς Λύσατε τὸν ναὸν τοῦτον καὶ ἐν τρισὶν ἡμέραις ἐγερῶ αὐτόν" (Jn 2:19), but fulfills the hopes for the restoration of Israel celebrated and anticipated by the Temple festivals, preeminently in his death.

Finally, in the course of this work, two important concepts emerged. They include that of Jesus as the Temple and Jesus in the heavenly Temple. Neither concept should be denied or inappropriately overemphasized to the exclusion or detriment of the other. The connection between the two is significant since it illuminates important soteriological concepts not only in the fourth Gospel but in other parts of the New Testament. The concept of Jesus as the incarnational temple, focusing on His atoning sacrifice, is the fundamental soteriological point of connection between Christ's heavenly ministry and the lives of those who believe in and follow Him on this earth. This perfectly reconciles the notions of Jesus as the temple and of Jesus in the temple.

# THE THREE DIVINE PERSONS: ONE ESSENCE, ONE MISSION IN JOHN'S GOSPEL

*Trinity and Divine Economy*

## Introduction

I would like to begin this brief paper by perhaps posing the question: what are we looking for here? This helps us to streamline our search in this branch of theology (Trinitarian), where the risk of drifting into error or even heresy is highly probable. While the aim of this brief paper is not to write an apologetics for the theology or doctrine of the Trinity, it is a contribution to the ongoing conversation that the gospel of John bears great testimony to the trinitarian mystery. Though the three divine persons of the Trinity are distinct, in the Gospel of John one could see much evidence that they are of the same essence in the Godhead. They have one mission and are united in achieving this mission. The central focus of this mission is the creation and final salvation of the world. This is evident from the history of salvation which begins in the book of Genesis and continues in the gospel of John.

So this work shall try to draw a conclusion that the gospel of John is a credible place to turn to if one is really searching for the relationship between the three divine persons. This is captured in the theme of this paper, "The three divine persons: one essence and one mission." Simply put, we shall show that there is unity of essence and relation among the three divine persons, and in the words of Thomas Aquinas, that "the divine persons are not solitaries, they are inseparable (ST I, q. 36, a. 31, a. 2; cf. a.4).

Finally, we shall try to show that although the word *Trinity* (which came into common use as a religious term only after the Council of Nicaea in AD 325) may not be explicitly found in the fourth gospel, it is implicitly there. Although this paper is not a commentary on the gospel of John, however, for the purpose of our quest, we shall explore some important verses in the gospel which relate to the three divine persons. Also, shall use the following terminologies or names: "the gospel of John" or "John's gospel" and "the fourth gospel" interchangeably to refer to the one and only gospel according to John, different from the synoptic gospels (Matthew, Mark, and Luke).

## Three Divine Persons: One Divine Essence

The doctrine of the Trinity, simply put, teaches and means that there is one God who eternally exists as three distinct Persons: Father, Son, and Holy Spirit. Stated differently, God is one in essence and three in person. These definitions express three crucial truths: (1) Father, Son, and Holy Spirit are distinct Persons, (2) each Person is fully God, and (3) there is only one God. Without bothering much about historical antecedents or developments such as arguments, counterarguments, error, and even heresies that helped to shape and establish the doctrine and theology of the Trinity, we would like to take some time and space here to explore each Person of the Trinity, and their essence. This is important in understanding what we are looking for in the gospel of John. The three divine persons are the Father, the Son and the Holy Spirit. They are distinct persons.

However, it is worth mentioning that in regards to the Trinity, we use the term *person* differently than we generally use it in everyday life. Therefore, it is often difficult to have a concrete definition of person as we use it in regards to the Trinity (Desiring Gold, 2006). This is of course taking into due consideration the fact that the only way human beings can explain and have a glimpse of what God is like is simply through the use of their language.

Hence, as the doctrine of the Trinity teaches that there are three persons in one God, it means that each of the persons is truly and holistically a person, one distinct from the other. The term *person* has undergone much debate throughout the history of the church, especially with reference to the Greeks' use of *hypostasis* and the Latins' use of *persona*. While a historical synthesis and background would be helpful, space restricts us to limit our study on the basic meaning. The term "person" ultimately indicates that "this one" is not "that one." Hence, the term "person" signifies real distinction.

This brings us to another important concept: "essence," which is the core of what makes the Trinity what it is. God's essence is his Being, and in God there is no accidental. John says: "God is Spirit" (Jn 4: 24). Hence, we clearly should not think of God as consisting of anything other than divinity. The "substance" of God is God, not a bunch of "ingredients" that, taken together, yield a deity. The essence of a being is what makes a being what it is. It could be likened to the "form" of a being. This is what the three divine persons share in common, the same essence or form. In them, there is no accidental because they are what they are and need no extension or are not extensions or different modes of existence of one another. The divine persons cannot be separated from their essence. This is what they have in common. Therefore, they share real unity and are thus equal in being, essence, and divinity.

## The Gospel of John and the Trinity

The reason for the choice of the gospel of John for this quest and paper cannot be overflogged. It is simply because of its outstanding and implicit witness to the trinitarian mystery. From the patristic period until today, John's gospel has served as a major source for the church's knowledge, doctrine, and worship of the triune God. The Fathers found in the fourth gospel both a primary text concerning the trinitarian mystery of salvation and ammunition for the refutation of heresies such as Modalism (Sabellianism) and Arianism (Plantinga (1991, 305). In expounding their full-orbed trinitarianism, major fourth-century pastors and theologians were drawn like a magnet to John's Gospel.

The gospel of John is admittedly different from the synoptic gospels, Matthew, Mark, and Luke. However, that difference does not imply separateness. The Trinitarian slogan of the Church is useful here. This is not to suggest in any way that the synoptic gospels did not do an equally good job in presenting the relationship and mission of the three divine persons. However, it a known fact that most scholars have attributed more divinity to the fourth gospel than to the rest of the synoptics. Hence, as one could find, John's gospel has been referred to as the "spiritual gospel" and "the eagle that soars high." This is simply to highlight its distinctness in presenting the divinity of the three divine persons. This fact is also buttressed by the very high Christology attributed to the gospel of John. So the fourth gospel helps us to shade more light on this very important Christian mystery of the Trinity.

Scholars of John have long noted that John is like an "artist," weaving his story with increasing intensity and passion to get his readers to understand who Jesus is, what He has done, and what He now demands. John's Gospel is a never-ending oasis that beckons Christians to study it in order to help them to grow in the truth, beauty, and glory, not only of Jesus, but of the Trinity in general. God's people, through the work of the Trinity, are enabled to know and make known the "non-ontological supremacy" of God the Father and Jesus in the power of the Holy Spirit (David 2013). The gospel of John indicates that the Father, Son, and Holy Spirit are distinct Persons. For example, since the Father sent the Son into the world (Jn 3: 16), he cannot be the same person as the Son. Likewise, after the Son returned to the Father (Jn 6: 10), the Father and the Son sent the Holy Spirit into the world (Jn 14: 26). Therefore, the Holy Spirit must be distinct from the Father and the Son.

In spite of this, "The idea that God is the ultimate hat-trick, that is, that he is at once, the Father, the Son, and the Holy Spirit

224

is something that has always confused and challenged many. This is especially true for those who attempt to grasps this trinitarian mystery with only a binary-style brain" (John 2009). We have only to look at the opening (prologue) of the fourth gospel to learn all that we could and want to know about the triune nature of God: "In the beginning was the Word, and the Word was with God, and the Word was God. He was with God in the beginning. Through him all things were made; without him nothing was made that has been made. In him was life, and that life was the light of men."

This prologue of John immediately communicates to his reader to expect something most divine in the gospel. Although there is no explicit mention of the Trinity in the prologue of John's gospel, as it would not be found elsewhere in the NT, it is still one place that one must examine closely for the divine persons. Also, it suffices to note that just as there was no explicit mention of the word Trinity, there was no mention of the "Holy" Spirit here. This in no way, means that the Holy Spirit was absent in this entire process of the "Word becoming flesh" (Jn 1:14). This should not constitute much problem, given the facts of the events surroundings the virgin birth of the Christ, or the divine incarnation of the eternal *Logos*. The message of the angel Gabriel to Mary was clear: "Behold the Holy Spirit will overshadow you and you shall conceive and bear a Son..." (Lk 1: 25–38). From the prologue, one sees that with philosophical malice forethought, John sets up the whole of his prologue on the basis of a dialectic or dualism of being and becoming. Every time God or the Word is mentioned, some form of the verb "to be" is used. Every time something created is mentioned, some form of the verb "to become" is used.

## The Person and Property of the Father in John's Gospel

Following the doctrine of the Trinity and the works of the Patristic from which Aquinas developed his Trinitarian theology, the Father is the source and principle in the Trinitarian relation or "order." So simply put, the Father's person within the Trinity is through his paternity. He is constituted in his personal being by his character of paternity. This is, through his relation to the son (Emery 2010, 293). The designation "Father" reveals his role within the Trinity. In speaking of the relationship between the Father and the Son in the gospel of John, Andreas J. Köstenberger and Scott R. Swain (2008, 123) state: "The Father enjoys personal priority in the *taxis* (order) of the triune life, not ontological superiority, for the Father and the Son hold all things in common: one divine name (17: 11), one divine power (5:19, 21–22), one divine identity."

How does John's gospel present the Father to us? In the gospel of John chapters 14–16, "Father" appears forty-four times. In relation to God the Father, Holy Scripture also reveals Jesus as "God the Son." He is referred to as "Son" over forty times in the gospel of John alone. Jesus is called the "only begotten son" or "the one and only son" (Jn 3:16, 18: 1:14,18), (Wan and Penman, 2010). The name God signifies the divinity, but in a supposit and concrete way, whereas the name deity signifies divinity in an absolute and abstract way. From this, it follows that through its natural capacity and mode of signifying, the word deity cannot stand in for person; it can only be a placeholder for the nature. But from its own mode of signifying, the word God can naturally stand in for the person, just like the word man takes the place of a human-natured supposit. Thus, when it is said in Jn 1:1–2 that "the Word was with God," the word "God" must necessarily be standing in for the person of the Father, since the preposition "with" signifies a distinction from the Word which is said to be with God (Sweeney 1995, 267–90).

Thompson (1999, 28) argues that "there are distinct patterns of usage that illumine the meaning of 'Father' in the Gospel" and which suggests why it is such an important term for God. She further asserts that, "The primary understanding of God as Father in John comes from the expression in John 5:26: 'Just as the Father has life in himself, so he has granted the Son also to have life in himself.' Thus, what shapes the understanding of God as Father is "the fundamental reality that a father's relationship to his children consists first in terms of simply giving them life. What it means to be a father is to be the origin or source of the life of one's children. [A] son by definition is one who has life from his father" (Christopher 2006, 115–35).

## The Person and Property of the Son in John's Gospel

The Son's person within the Trinity derives from or is constituted by his filiation to the Father. The prologue of John tells us: "In the beginning was the Word and the Word was with God...the Word was made flesh and dwelt among us (Jn 1:1–14). Also, Christ himself said: "I came from the Father and entered the world; now I am going back to the Father." (Jn 16:28). This simply shows that the Son who comes from the Father still dwells in the Father.

Thomas's encounter with the risen Christ is worth reflecting upon here. After this encounter, his doubt left him and his spiritual eyes were opened. So caught up in great awe, he exclaimed, "My Lord and my God!" (Jn 20:20). At this point, he confirmed most of what Christ had earlier taught and told them. Earlier, in trying to help his disciples and the Jewish authorities understand where he came from and his relationship with the Father, Christ had told them that "no one has ever seen God, but the one and only Son, who is himself God, and is in closest relationship with the Father, and has made him known" (Jn 1:18). Later on, by way of explaining his mission and that of the Father to them, he declared: "For God so loved the world, that he gave his only begotten Son, that whoever believes in him should not perish but have eternal life" (Jn 3: 16). Instructing them on his relationship with both the Father and the Holy Spirit, He told them: "And I will ask the Father, and he will give you another advocate to help you and be with you forever" (Jn 14:6). Christ is the one sent by the Father to redeem the world. He did not achieve this in isolation of the Father and the Holy Spirit. The Father sent Christ, and the Holy Spirit accompanied him to accomplish his mission." He was led by the Spirit into the wilderness to be tempted by the devil (Mt 4:1).

The one that broke the camel's back was when Christ declared, "Truly, truly, I say to you, before Abraham was, I am" (Jn 8:58). In order to further clear their doubts, Christ vehemently told them: "Believe in God; believe also in me. In my Father's house there are many rooms...if I go and prepare a place for you, I will come again and will take you to myself, that where I am you may be also. And you know the way to where I am going." Thomas said to him, "Lord, we do not know where you are going. How can we know the way?" (Jn 14:16). Possibly, apart from doubting Christ's resurrection, all long Thomas had doubted all these declarations of Christ until his eyes were eventually opened. There and then, he saw and recognized Christ in his "pure form," not only as "my Lord" but also as "my God." He was privileged to see the Jesus who had the same essence with the Father, and the Jesus who is "I am" became real to him.

John buttresses Christ's filiation to the Father. He is the Son of God, or said in another way, God is his Father. "This was why the Jews were seeking all the more to kill him, because not only was he breaking the Sabbath, but he was even calling God his own Father, making himself equal with God" (Jn 5:18). This does not make any sense! How can the son of God be God? However, the Jews understood the implication of both his sayings that "before Abraham, I am" and "God is my Father." They knew that both amounted to the claim of being God himself. Christ was not just making empty claims because He knew he was of the same essence with the Father and the Holy Spirit.

## The Person and Property of the Holy Spirit in John's Gospel

The Synoptic Gospels have little to say when considering the person and work of the Holy Spirit. The gospel of John may be criticized on its structure and genre, but it is beyond dispute that John demonstrates a deep understanding of the person, role, and place of the Holy Spirit within the Trinity. In the fourth gospel, the Evangelist spends three chapters (John 14–16) teaching on the Holy Spirit's person and role in the life of the believer. From this, one could also see his place in the Trinity.

The person of the Holy Spirit refers to the attributes of emotions, will, volition, intelligence, sensibility, and personality, which relate to humanity (Towns 2002, 264). Jn 14:16–17 makes it clear that the Helper spoken of is the Spirit of truth. "The Holy Spirit is not merely a power but a person, just like the Father and the Son. He is another Helper, not a different Helper." The word "another" indicates one like myself who will take my place and do my work. Hence, if Jesus is a person, the Holy Spirit must be a person (Hendrickson 1953, 275). "John assigns personal attributes to the Holy Spirit (14:26; 15:26). Hence, His relation to the Father and the Son is described as of such a character that if these are persons, he too must be a person. Also, the Spirit, in Jn 14:17, is called another Paraclete (Greek—"*paraklētos*" called in aid; "*para*"—from, alongside). This is a term meaning to be called to the side in order to help. The Father and the Son called the Spirit to the side of the disciples in order to help, comfort, admonish, teach, and guide them. In other words, in order that in any given condition, the Paraclete may furnish whatever help that is necessary. The Father and the Son sent the Holy Spirit to not only comfort, teach, and guide believers into all the truth, but also to send and lead them on and in His mission. "Not only are Jesus and his disciples 'sent' in this Gospel, but also is the Spirit 'sent' (Keener 2009, 21–45). The Spirit comes to represent and carry on Jesus' work.

A comparison between Jn 14:26, "The Spirit whom the Father will send in my name" and 15:26, "whom I will send to you from the Father" makes it clear that the sending of the Holy Spirit at Pentecost is ascribed to both the Father and the Son. "The two should be viewed as concentric circles (Hendrickson, p. 286). John has intentionally demonstrated in his Gospel a view of the Holy Spirit that is relational, personal, and intimate. One who longs to breathe new life into those who come to Jesus and to sanctify the beloved in the Word by washing them with the sanctifying power of the Word of God.

## Relation and Order Within the Three Divine Persons

Thematic tension is a concept by no means foreign to the fourth gospel (Christopher 2006, 115). The apparent presence of contending themes such as divine sovereignty and human responsibility, the divinity and humanity of Jesus, and future and realized eschatology has been a frequent topic of discussion in Johannine scholarship (Carson 1981, 125–98). It would not necessarily be surprising then to find similar tension in the gospel's presentation of the relationship among the divine persons, or, using the predominant Johannine terminology, among the Father, the Son, and the Spirit (Morris 1995, 277). Numerous modern commentators understand John to ascribe deity to Jesus, though not as a challenge to Jewish monotheism. Rather, they interpret the evangelist as portraying the Father, Son, and Spirit who are distinct as having the same divine "nature," "essence," or "being." Commenting on John 1:1, Barret C. K. (1978, 156), writes: "θεος" is predicative and describes the nature of the Word. The absence of the article indicates that the Word is God but is not the only being of whom this is true. The deeds and words of Jesus are the deeds and words of God and of course, of the Holy Spirit."

If the three persons are distinct, so how are they related? "What does the 'Father-Son-Spirit' language in the fourth gospel imply regarding the relationship between God, Jesus and the Holy Spirit, or the three divine persons?" More specifically, "Do these terms necessarily imply a hierarchical relationship between the two?" Jesus consistently calls God "Father" when speaking of his actions of dependence and obedience in the relationship. "The Son can do nothing on his own, but only what he sees the Father doing; as the Father does, so the Son does" (5:19). The Father taught the Son (8:28), whose obedience is evident because he always does what pleases the Father (8:29) and speaks what he has heard from him (8:38). Jesus honors his Father (8:49, cf. Ex 20:12) and keeps his word (8:55). When his hour draws near, he tells his disciples that he is going to the Father "for the Father is greater than I" (14:28) (Christopher, p. 129).

One of the terms used to describe the Trinity is "economic." Economic, in this sense, means the way things are ordered. Each member of the Trinity has a specific role. Although each is fully God, the roles within the Trinity are distinct for each member. First, they are in full cooperation. The Father creates, the Son redeems, and the Holy Spirit sanctifies and sets apart. In spite of this, they perform these roles in full cooperation with the other members. In each mission, all three are active. From John's gospel, one way the three divine persons are related is through their mutual testimony to one another. Jesus gave them this answer: "I tell you the truth, the Son can do nothing by himself, he can do only what he sees his Father doing, because whatever the Father does the son also does" (Jn 5:19). In John 14:16–26, we read, "I will pray the Father, and He shall give you another Comforter, even the Spirit of truth." Again, "but the Comforter, the Holy Spirit, whom the Father will send in my name, He shall teach you all things." In John 15:26, "when the Comforter comes, whom I will send to you from the Father, even the Spirit of truth, who proceeds from the Father, He shall testify of me" (Watson 2012). In all three of these passages, we have a perfect statement of the three divine persons acting in perfect unity, yet each person in the same relative position: the Father as the source and principle of all; the Son as obeying the Father, revealing, and teaching, and praying, in His prophetic and priestly offices; and then the Holy Spirit proceeding from the Father and the Son, and by the command of the Father and the Son, is the powerful Advocate, Counselor, and Comforter.

The mere or literal thought of "order" linguistically and humanly speaking may imply antecedence or posterity among the divine persons. However, in spite of this, there is a way in which order exists within the Trinity. This order is the "order of nature (*ordo naturae*). This simply implies pure relation of origin. To deny any such ordering within the Trinity will lead to the construction of internal conflations which the distinctions in the Trinity should exclude (Emery, p. 228). One way to make sense of this order is by trying to understand the relation between the Father, the Son, and the Holy Spirit. The Father is the principle of the Trinity. The Son takes from the Father the breath with which to breathe (with him) the Holy Spirit. In order words, this formula puts the spotlight on the order amongst Father and Son. That is, the Son's relation of origin coming from the Father. So on the level of personal operation and within the limitations of linguistics, one can infer that this order, for example, expresses the "authority" belonging to the Father. That is to say, the Father's legitimate position within the Trinity as Source and Principle without principle (I Sentences d. 12, q. un., a. 3, ad 4; ST I, q. 36, a.3). Thomas Aquinas (ST I, q. 36, a. 3), puts it thus: "Since therefore, the

Son has it from the Father that the Holy Spirit proceeds from him, one can say that the Father breathes the Holy Spirit through the Son', or, what amounts to the same thing, 'the Holy Spirit proceeds from the Father through the Son." In spite of all this order talk, it is very important to eschew any ontological priority, authority, or superiority of one divine person over another.

How does the fourth gospel present the relation within or among the three divine persons? Some scholars have pointed to some verses in the fourth gospel as evidence of subordination not only of the Son to the Father, but of the Holy Spirit both to the Father and the Son. This includes some of the following examples: John 5:26: "Just as the Father has life in himself, so he has granted the Son also to have life in himself"; Jn 14: 26, "The Spirit whom the Father will send in my name" and 15:26, "whom I will send to you from the Father".

For Marianne Meye Thompson (2001, :72), John 6:57, which speaks of God as "the living Father," and the above statement from 5:26, "are essential to understanding John's delineation of God as Father and Jesus as Son." So she argues that when Jesus calls God "Father," he points first to the Father as the source or origin of life, and to the relationship established through the life-giving activity of the Father. The primary characteristic of the Father-Son relationship is the life that constitutes their relationship. So to label Jesus' words in John 14:28 ("The Father is greater than I") as an example of John's "subordinationism" is misleading, "in as much as it conceives of the relationship of Father and Son primarily in hierarchical terms." Thompson insists that since John stresses the function of the Father as the one who gives life to his offspring, rather than the role of the Father as the one who instructs or disciplines, statements such as "The Father is greater than I" ought not to be read against a backdrop of patriarchal hierarchy. The Father is the source of the Son's life; it is as the origin of the Son's very being that "the Father is greater than I." This relation no doubt extends to the Spirit who proceeds from both.

## Three Divine Persons of the Trinity: One Mission

The interconnectedness of the Godhead is revealed in many events and divine acts in the world. From Genesis, as the salvific history unfolds, major works of the Triune God such as redemption and salvation are seen to be works where the three divine persons of the Trinity are intricately involved together in achieving the end result. This is displayed in the salvation story, where the Father sends the Son. The Spirit fills and guides the Son. The Son embraces the cross and, through His death and resurrection, enables the reconciliation between God and humanity. As St. Augustine of Hippo puts it, the world was made by the Father, through the Son, in the Holy Spirit. Each Person stamps creation with something of its own specific property. That is why creation is so rich because behind it, and within it, is hidden the wealth of each divine Person, as that Person is, ever distinct and ever in communion" (Boff 2000, 104). The distinct persons of the Trinity work in their unique ways to fulfill the purpose and mission of the Triune God.

With regards to their mission, in John's Gospel, the distinct personal identities of Father, Son, and Spirit and their unity in being, will, and work are equally affirmed. While there are important personal differences in the roles of the triune God (or the three divine persons) along salvation-historical lines (the Father sends, the Son is sent and sends, the Spirit is sent) the *missio Dei* (God's mission) is characterized by a deep underlying unity among the participants in this mission. As the fourth evangelist puts it, the Father and the Son are "in" one another, and they are "one" (Jn 10:30, 38; 14:10–11). The unity and love that exists among the three divine Persons of the Trinity is expressed in many ways throughout Scripture (Andreas and Scott, p. 19). God's tripersonal reality is intrinsic to his existence as the one God who alone is God. He is a socially related being within himself. In this tripersonal relationship, the three persons love one another, support one another, assist one another, team with one another, honor one another, communicate with one another, and in everything respect, enjoy one another (Ware 2005, 21). Hence, they have one and the same mission. They are united by and for it.

## Conclusion

From the patristic period until today, John's Gospel has served as a major source for the church's knowledge, doctrine, and worship of the triune God. Among all New Testament documents, the fourth gospel provides not only one of the most material for the doctrine of the Trinity, but also the most highly developed patterns of reflection on this material, particularly patterns that seek to account in some way for the distinct personhood and divinity of Father, Son, and Spirit without compromising the unity of God.

Is there any tension among the three divine persons in the fourth gospel? Although many scholars might respond affirmatively to this, but the obvious is that viewed and analyzed well, all seeming tensions will disappear or diminish, and we are left with the obvious relation, order, unity, and role of the three divine persons. Hence, I have tried to show here in this brief paper that the fourth gospel presents a clarity of the three divine persons, having one essence, one mission. And that this mission is the salvation of the world. They act and work together to achieve this mission without any being less God than, or to the others, or having his "own separate time of reign." In other words, none of them have absolute dominance of a particular period of time. True, the Father as the source and principle of all things sent or "begot" the Son, and both (the Father and the Son) in turn sent the Spirit, who proceeds from them. Yet, they are one God, having one essence and one mission.

# A CATHOLIC PERSPECTIVE ON
# PAULINE GOSPEL AND THEOLOGY

*Pauline Epistles*

## Introduction

Saint Paul "shines like a star of the brightest magnitude in the Church's history, and not only in that, but of its origins" (Pope Benedict XVI, 2006). How did the church receive the gospel of Paul? How should a Catholic understand and explain Paul's message to a non-Catholic? What influence or effect does the gospel of Paul have in the formulations and teachings of the church? These and many more questions form the crux of Catholic view on the gospel of Paul. Hence, this work is my brief reflection and contribution on the Catholic view of this great Apostle Paul, his gospel, and theology.

Although much has been written about him, his gospel, and theology, this brief work matters, as any contribution would count in no small measure in trying to explicate what Paul means and stands for. Hence, it seeks to contribute to the age-long but inexhaustive discussion on Paul, his gospel, and theology. To begin this work, it is right and just to appreciate the work of Michael F. Bird and Stanley N. Gundry who in their book *Four Views on The Apostle Paul* assembled four erudite scholars to air their views and that of the various schools of thought they represent. This yielded a tremendous result.

It suffices to note that among these fours erudite scholars was Luke Johnson Timothy, a Catholic, and precisely a former Benedictine monk and priest. His contribution on the Catholic perspective on Paul will form the stepping stone of this brief work. Hence, one major aim of this work is to evaluate his contibution in order to see how he acheived the goal of presenting a Catholic view or perspective of Paul. Then I shall make my contributions, especially where there seems to be an apparent lacuna or lack. However, it is very important to note that this work is by no means an attempt to critique the work and contribution of Johnson on this topic.

As I have already pointed out, the essay of Johnson will serve as a stepping stone for this work. By this, I simply mean that this work will follow the four basic outlines trailed by the contributors in the work of Michael Bird and Stanley Gundry. That is, salvation, sigificance of Christ, framework for Paul's theological perpective, and Paul's vision for the Church. However, we shall not follow this chronological order in this work. Rather, I shall begin with the frame-work for Paul's theological perspectives immediately after a brief look at the person of the apostle Paul.

## The Apostle Paul at a Glance

Although this might seem unnecessary, however, it is important to say a few words about the great apostle Paul, who is the focus of this brief work. He is many things to many people, groups, denomi-nations, and even those labelled or perceived as heretics or the scorch of orthodoxy. Evidently, Paul was a "controversial and enigmatic" figure and continues to be for most of our time and history (Bird and Gundry 2012, 9). However, beyond his image as a controversial and enigmatic figure lies the great apostle who was responsible for shaping the early church in a significant way. Has Paul's influence on the church waned? I think the obvious response would simply lie in the negative.

Paul (originally known as Saul) was probably born in Tarsus (Acts 22:3). The most certain elements of Paul's biography are his encounter with Jesus Christ and his imprisonment in Rome in the years 60–62. He was martyred in Rome sometime between 63 and 67. Other points are difficult to ascertain; for example, the exact number of his journeys. Opinions vary from two to four, but three would appear to be the correct number (Edart, 2008). Major stages and events in his life were his formation in Jerusalem at the school of Gamaliel (Acts 22:3), his persecution of Christians in the years which followed, the encounter with Christ on the road to Damascus, meeting with the apostles in Jerusalem, mission to convert the gentiles, and his martyrdom in Rome.

Paul spoke about himself on various occasions, and this helps us understand who he is. He supplies us with important information: "Circumcised on the eighth day of my life, I was born of the race of Israel, of the tribe of Benjamin, a Hebrew born of Hebrew parents" (Phil 3:5–6). That he was circumcised on the eighth day after his birth shows the excellence of his origin. Paul was circumcised as prescribed by the law of Moses (Lev. 12:3). Paul also presents himself as one of the Pharisees who were well-known to love the law of Moses and oral law. "In the matter of the Law, I was a Pharisee" (Phil 3:5). This oral law, put into writing from the second century BC onward, became known as the Talmud. "The Pharisees have imposed on the people many laws of the tradition of the Fathers which are not written in the Law of Moses (Flavius Josephus 2005, lxxxii+208;13.297). We find this idea in Paul's letter where he says he fanatically "defends the tradition of the Fathers" (Gal 1:14).

Calling to mission, conversion, salvation, and justification are closely connected in Paul. This is why it is interesting to study the nature of his spiritual transformation in order to better understand him. Paul says little about this event in his letters. The principal epistles are 1 Cor 15:1–11, Gal 1:13–17, and Phil 3:2–14, but they contain few historical details. The apostle focuses more on the significance. He speaks of an experience which changed his life completely. However, rather than an isolated event, he sees it as a call right from his mother's womb: "God, who had set me apart from the time when I was in my mother's womb, called (Jer 1:5) me through his grace and chose to reveal his Son in me, so that I should preach him to the gentiles" (Gal 1:15–16).

What did Paul leave us with? Paul has thirteen letters to his credit. Seven (Romans, 1 and 2 Corinthians, Galatians, Philippians, 1 Thessalonians, and Philemon) are firmly believed by scholars as authored or written by Paul. Whereas six (Ephesians, Colossians, 2 Thessalonians, 1 and 2 Timothy, and Titus) are classified as disputed letters of Paul. Here, we shall not delve in to the reason for this classification for lack of space and time.

## Framework for Describing Paul's Theological Perspective

According to Johnson, the framework for describing Paul's perspecive is "probably a matrix consisting of Paul's grounding in Greco-roman culture, his religious sensibilities and his loyalty to his Jewish heritage pricipally through the jewish culture" (Bird and Stanley, p. 13). This was how Michael Bird sumarized Johnson's view on the best framework for describing Paul's theology. He was right. This could be seen from the work or presentation of Johnson himself.

Johnson sees all the thirteen letters attributed to Paul as "authored by Paul" thus stongly denying the general wideview by scholars that there are seven undisputed and six disputed letters of Paul (Thomas, p.16). "All the thirtheen letter should be considered as authored by Paul during his lifetime, in the sense that he 'authorised' their composition, even if he did not directly write any of them." Though he has his reason for this, I do feel that this is a shift from what is generally believed about the Pauline corpus. I do agree with him that Paul was not a systematic theologian, and so, it is very difficult to pinpoint or push his work into a particular theme. He was more of a pastor responding to concrete or certain pastoral issues at a given time and as the need of each community demanded him to respond. So he had to do this using his expirience, cultural and religious, (Graeco-Roman and Jewish) background in order to resolve isssues (Bird and Stanley, p. 72).

Johnson observed that three religious realities characterize Paul and the interpretation of his work. First, his personal expirience, which included not only his encounter with the risen Christ and his call to be an apostle, but also his mystical experience of prayer. Second, the religious experiences of his readers he saw as existing in the energy field of the Holy Spirit who consequently placed them in Christ (1 Cor 1:2, Gal 3:26). Finally, the complex of traditions and practices of the community already in place when Paul became a founder of churches and writer of letters. These include the practice of baptism (Rom 6:1), the Lord's Supper (1 Cor 11:1–34), confession of faith (Rom 10:9), and above all the tradition concerning Jesus (his life death and resurrection and the shape of his human character). These make Paul's letters distinctive.

Paul's teaching move into, out of, and around such experiential and traditional elements. This I stongly beleive, and there is no better way of describing Paul's theological motivation and perspective, which is christocentric as we read from Johnson. Theology proper deals with the question "who is God," so even though Paul was not a systematic theologian as has been widely said, throughout Paul's letters, and especailly in 2 Corinthians, Paul names God in various ways: "Our Father (2 Cor 1:2, Rom 8:15–15), Father of our Lord Jesus Christ (2 Cor 1:2).

## Salvation: Grace, Faith, Justification, and Good Work

With respect to salvation, Johnson emphasizes that salvation is chiefly about liberation and transformation, liberation from hostile powers, cosmic and social, transformation in the empirical state of human beings into renewed persons still awaiting the final triumph of God at the end of history (Bird and Stanley, p. 13). Thus, the living God for Paul, is acting on and for humanity through Christ, and the good news of Christ was the power of God for the salvation of every one who believes (Rom 1:16).

Two improtartant points emerge from Johnson's presentation. These incude, first, that salvation is both now and a future process. It is ongoing and will terminate at the final end of time. Second is that "salvation is not somethng accomplished by humans, by their own efforts, but is accomplished by God thtough the death and resurrection of Christ and the power of the Holy Spirit" (Bird and Stanley, p. 13). In other words, it it is through the "grace" of God. However, and surprisingly, Johnson did not employ this very important word in the Catholic understanding of salvation, especially in relation to Paul. The implication of this is that salvation is universal and a free grift of God. This perfectly coheres with the church's view of Paul's salvation. An important mark is Paul's perception of the universal character of salvation. He is the man of universality. In a world marked by divisions and barriers between peoples and cultures, he realizes that Christ's message is for every man and woman of whatever culture or religion, nationality or social condition. He realizes that "God is the God of everyone" (Pope Benedict XVI, General Audience 25 October 2006).

Johnson was right to point out that "liberation" (I agree), "is not from social or political oppression, but from forces that constrains and distorts personal freedom and community integrity." In this regard, for Paul, humans are either ruled by (evil) powers that hold them captive (Rom 5, 14–17; 6:12), or powers that established them in freedom by the reign of God. Also, salvation is not simply a matter of repair or of restoration in the human condition. Rather, it is a matter of elevation to a higher state of being.

Catholic view of salvation is unequivocally hinged and dependent on God's grace through faith. "Our Justification (Salvation), comes from the grace of God. Grace is a favor, the free and underserved help that God gives us to respond to his call to become children of God, adoptive sons, partakers of divine nature and eternal life" (CCC 1996). This is because we believe that grace is the *impetus agitat* and the ultimate ground for our existence and union with Christ and God, through the Holy Spirit. Salvation, thus, is Christocentric and means participation in Christ (Chrstosis and Theosis). That is simply is to say that it conforms us to the image of Christ and, consequently, to the image of God. In this regard, "ultimately, salvation involves communion with God in Christ" (Stanley and Stanley p. 68), and through the Holy Spirit.

All these are simply to say that through baptism (Titus 3:5; 1 Cor 6:11; 1 Pt 3:21), the grace of God covenantly unites us to the one family of the Trinitarian God. Hence, the following, in brief, summarizes this view: "The charity (χαρις: *charis*) of Christ is the source in us of all our merits before God. Grace, by uniting us to Christ in active love, ensures the supernatural quality of our acts and consequently their merit before God and before men. The saints have always had a lively awareness that their merits were pure grace." (CCC 2011). For Catholics, salvation is not simply being saved from wrath or forensically acquitted from wrath, but also from the power of sin and death. It is thus in this regard that one could see the relationship between salvation and righteousness. Salvation makes us live righteously by avoiding sin and escaping the pangs of spiritual death. It incorporates us into the life of Christ and God through the power of the Holy Spirit. It precisely makes us adopted sons of God, brothers and sisters of Christ, the first and only natural born son of the Father.

Does what the Catholic Church believe run contrary to Paul? Not at all! A brief dive in to the Pauline corpus will show that the Catholic view coheres with Pauline understanding of salvation which is both now or realized (Titus 3:5; Rom 8:4), as well as a future or an eschatological reality (Rom 10:13; 1 Cor 3:15; 1 Tim 2:15). Furthermore, in relation to work, the Catholic Church as the Pauline gospel teaches that while salvation or justification is purely a matter of God's grace, good works are criteria or evidence for salvation. They are necessary (Phil 2:12–13; Rom 2: 6; 2 Cor 5:10; Gal 2:20; Jas 2:22). Other biblical passages other than from Pauline corpus may suffice here (Ps 62:12; Prov 24:12; Mt 16:27; 25:34–46; 1 Pt 1:17; Rev 2:3, 20:12, 22:12). This is especially with regards to salvation as a future reality. So Catholics affirms that we are saved by grace through faith, and this faith is the result of God's work within the believer. This faith is to be understood as the act performed by the believer who truly believes through the grace or gift of God. Hence, this act of believing (faith) is what the *Catechism* defines as "a gift of God, a supernatural virtue infused by him" (CCC 1996).

Commenting on the "Assurance of Salvation," Michael Barber writes, and I agree in toto with him as representing the Catholic view of salvation: "In Catholic teaching, believers have the assurance not hope of certainty, but of 'hope.' Hope, not absolute certainty, is the language of scripture (Rom 8:24–25; Gal 5:5; Eph 4:4; Col 1:5). As

Aquinas explains, the object of the believer's hope is not in what one has attained, but in God's mercy and faithfulness to his promises" (Alan and Stanley, p.68). To buttress this point and to clear misconceptions, Michael adds: "This should not lead us to be paralyzed by anxiety. Attempts to portray the Catholic view of this matter in such terms are wide off the mark. Catholic teaching recognizes that in the scripture, the promise of salvation is linked to the sacraments (e.g., 1 Pt 3:21). While we do not have indubitable assurance that we are among the elect, we do have confidence in his promises" (Heb 10:23).

To conclude this reflection on the Catholic view of of Paul's salvation, let us draw from the wealth of Pope Benedict XVI's view:

> Christ justifies (saves) man "with God's mercy" entering into deep communion with him, forgiving his sins. This was the fundamental experience of the Apostle's conversion. Man is justified by faith. The second element which shows this Christ-centered aspect is the Christian identity. This Christian identity is composed of precisely two elements: This restraint from seeking oneself by oneself but instead receiving oneself from Christ and giving oneself with Christ, thereby participating personally in the life of Christ himself to the point of identifying with him and sharing both his life and his death. (Pope Benedict XVI, General Audience 8 November, 2006).

## Paul and the Significance of Christ

On this particular theme, I must say that Johnson did hit the nail right on the head. Again, Bird comments: "In Johnson's perspective, the significane of Christ for Paul lies in the fact that God's new creation is expirienced through the the expirience of Jesus." This is true, and rightly so, because Paul is purely Christocentric, as Johnson made very clear in his work. All these religious expiriences and traditions center on the figure of Jesus Christ. It is Christ who inuagurates the new age. Christ makes both the end and the goal of history: "He is the eschatological Adam, and he is the son of God."

Johson highlighted a very significant point that butresses the fact that the center of Paul and his theology is Christ as a whole. Specifically, what shaped Paul's perception of Jesus includes his resurrecction, the work of the Holy Spirit, his comparism of Christ with Moses rather than potraying him as the new Moses (Rom 9:1–3; 2 Cor 3:7–18) "as the one who reveals the new form of humanity and the 'new covenant.'" According to Johnson, Jesus' resurrection is more than resuscitation or simply vindication. With other early believers, Paul above all proclaims Jesus to be "Lord," with the term *kyrios* bearing all the theophoric resonance established by the LXX's use of the title for the proper name of God. This is in complete agreement with the views of Thomas D. Stegman (p. 25) who equally wrote: "Paul's fundamental gospel proclamation is Jesus Christ [is] Lord" (1 Cor 4:4). Both titles, Christ and Lord, are important. For Paul, Jesus' lordship is intimately linked with the resurrection (2 Cor 4:14; Phil 2:11), for it is the resurrection that reveals Jesus as Lord.

Johnson also heighted the fact that in Paul, there is a relationship between his understanding of Christ's resurrection and the work of the Holy Spirit. This is because, according to Paul, no one can proclaim that Jesus is Lord without being empowered by the Holy Spirit (1 Cor 12:3), just as the resurrection of Christ, in turn, has become a life-giving spirit (1 Cor 15:45) (Bird and Stanley, p. 75). Furthermore, that Christ even has a role in creation (1 Cor 8:6; Col 1:16) and participates fully in the divine, "being in the form of God" (Phil 2:6). The last point here which centers on Christ's participation in God, and our paticipation or conformity with Christ (Rom 12:1–2), no doubt represents fully the views of the Catholic Church. To drive this point home, it is important to pinpoint how this is related to the teaching of the church and Paul. This is through baptism. It helps us to parcicipate in the new life of Christ and in the new covenant that Christ initiated. It configures and conforms us to the image of Christ. Holy Baptism is the basis of the whole Christian life, the gateway to life in the Spirit. Through baptism, we are freed from sin and reborn as sons of God; we become members of Christ, are incorporated into the Church, and made sharers in her mission (Rom 6, 3:7–11) (CCC 1213).

Johnson noted a very important elelment that shaped Paul's perceptive of Christ. In this element, Johnson delves sharply into Christology or the theology of the nature of Christ and what this acomplishes for us. The frequent assertion in Paul's letters that Christ "gave himself for humans (Gal 14:2, 2:20; Eph 5:2; 1 Tim 2:6), therefore, can ligitimately be read also as God's giving him-sellf" to humanity through Christ (Rom 8:31–39). This also points to the last important aspect of Christ's significance in Paul's letters, namely, his human character (Bird and Stanley, p. 13). This aspect of Paul's perspective of Christ's nature both as divine and as human was very important in the formulation of the creed at the Council of Calcedon in 451: "We unanimously teach and confess one and the same Son, our Lord Jesus Christ: the same perfect in divinity and perfect in humanity, the same truly God and truly man, composed of rational soul and body" (CCC 464–9).

Johnson concludes this aspect of his essay by noting the signifi-cance of Christ's death on the cross which Paul numerously mentions in his letters as the climax of Christ's humble offering of himself for the sake of humanity (Phil 2:6–11). This is very signifiant not only for the paschal mystery we celebrate, but for the community of God's people. The Cross as a shorthand for the manner and disposition of Jesus in his death appears in Paul's letter as a pattern for com-munity behavior (Johson 1982,77–90). His recounting of the *keno-sis* of Christ (Phil 2:6–8) has the purpose of encouraging readers to think as Christ did in order to shape a community ethos. Hence, the understanding of Jesus in Paul's letters is richly complex, embracing Jesus' relationship with God even in creation and in Israel's history (Bird and Stanley, p. 81).

It suffices to note that none of Paul's letter contains a system-atic presentation of his Christology, nor does any letter embody the whole of his Christology. Like Paul's letters, his Christology is occa-sional in nature. This is not to say, however, that it is minimal or unimportant. (Frank 1999, 132). The most important point which Johnson highlighted very well is that Paul's letters are Christocentric. Paul's understanding of Christ and his work is integral to the gospel he preaches. He might be labeled "unsystematic" in his Christological presentations or thought, yet certain concepts in his letters are very crucial in understanding what he says and means.

## Paul's Vision of the Church

Paul's vision of the church according to Johnson is that New Testament church consisted of local assemblies that carefully tried to establish an identity in the Greco-Roman world and held on to their religious hereitage with Israel. It was more than a voluntary association of people. This is Bird's evaluation of Jonhson's paper:

> "I continued reading to find those great terminologies or metaphors the Church employed to express in concrete terms what Paul really meant by the church." Although he was quick to use the Greek terminology *ekklesia,* perhaps for the inevitability of definition, most important Catholic expressions or metaphors like, the "Church as the Body of Christ", the "Church as the people of God", the "Church as a mystery", the "Church as the kingdom of God." the Church as the "Temple of the Holy Spirit" (mentioned brifely at the end), the "Church as the bride of Christ" or the "Church as the Universal Sacrament of Salvation" were not fully visible in his paper. He avoided all the metaphors, and Thomas R. Schreiner really appluded him for that: 'When it come to Paul's Soteriology, I agree that no metaphor take center stage in Paul's thinking.' (Alan and Stanley 2013, 85)

Of course, this was expected. However, it is important to note that Paul himself employed them freely in order to help his readers.

Again, like his treatment of Catholic view of salvation, there was no single reference to any church or magisterial document or even scholars as to how we understand and convey what Paul means by the church. What then is a Catholic view with regards to the church in Paul's letters? Johnson's paper seems flat-footed in this area. He did a general exposition of the church in Paul without necessarily giving the crux of Catholic view. These metaphors and images are important and worth reflecting on. For instance, the church as the "Body" of which Christ is the head implies several important points that are indispensible for the speculative mind, as fundamental element of the (Catholic) faith (de la Soujeole 2014, 77). The body has a head, Christ, from whom everything comes. In the mystery that is the church, in its essential constitutive element, in its life, everything comes from above: the vertical and the descending motion are altogether primary. The Church conditionally receives itself from Christ her Head. Imageries like these help and make things easier to understand.

The Catholic Church (CCC 772) teaches and beleives that it is in the Church that Christ fulfills and reveals his own mystery as the purpose of God's plan: to unite all things in him (Eph 1:10). St. Paul calls the nuptial union of Christ and the Church "a great mystery." This is because she is united to Christ as to her bridegroom; she becomes a mystery in her turn (Eph 5:32, 3:9–11, 5:25–27). Contemplating this mystery in her, Paul exclaims: "Christ in you, the hope of glory" (Col 1:27). Believers or the church are those, who through baptism, have been washed, sanctified, and justified. They were cleansed from their sins when they were baptized. They were placed in the realm of the holy when they were sanctified. Justification means that they were declared to be right and counted as righteous via their union with Christ.

The Church is the last chapter of the Pope Benedict XVI's meditation on Paul, who "is converted to Christ and to his Church" (Pope Benedict XVI, Audience, 22 November 2006). Jean-Baptiste Edart (2008) thus summarizes Benedict's view on Paul's ecclesiology thus:

The Church rightly finds herself in the life of Paul, the Apostle. The various Churches are for him a source of joy and sorrow. He is for them father and mother. The Body of Christ received in the Eucharist (1 Cor 10:17). St Paul's call for unity and charity are the immediate result of his theological vision. The Church is the place of communion with God and among ourselves, the assembly of those who invoke the name of the Lord Jesus Christ. Pope Benedict's reflection on the figure of the Apostle is indeed a summary of the apostle's teaching. He puts us face to face with an author judged, even by Saint Peter, difficult to understand. This could be an excellent method for an analysis of the letters of Paul.

The Church also lives in the period of the already and the not-yet. That is the realized and the future eschatology. The Church is also part of the mystical body of Christ. Though we are individually many, we are one body in Christ (Rom 12:5). "Now you are the body of Christ and individually members of it" (1 Cor 12:27). God, according to Paul, has entrusted the churches with the ministry of the new covenant (2 Cor 3:6), which is also "the ministry of reconciliation" (2 Cor 5:18–19). This is very important for the harmonious and continuous existence of the Church until the Lord's coming (Thomas, p. 27). One concrete manifestation of the ministry of reconciliation is the collection for the Church in Jerusalem (2 Cor 8:4, 9:1).

## Summary and Conclusion

This was how Taylor Marshal (2010) introduced or began his work, *The Catholic Perspective of Paul*: "This site is an outgrowth of my book, The Catholic Perspective on Paul. It is based on the conviction that the Pauline epistles contain the primitive and pristine doctrines of the Catholic Faith. In the Pauline corpus, we discover a

Paul who is Catholic, a theologian who is sacramental, a churchman who is hierarchical, a mystic who is orthodox."

Although Johnson tried in his work by trying to present what seemingly is the Pauline Catholic perspective on Paul, yet he falls short of that forcefulness or conviction of someone speaking or presenting the view of his Church. Of course, he did sound what looked like a note of warning or doubt at the beginning of his paper: "I am perhaps the least likely person to able to identify what is distinctively Catholic in this reading of Paul." Perhaps, he was being humble like Paul (1 Cor 15:9), if we are to understand him as such.

I was stunned, for example, that in his presentation of salvation, there was no single mention of the word *grace* (although he alluded to it), which is very important in the Catholic understanding of salvation I later tried to show. It could have been more assertive or more Catholic had he related or cited some Catholic documents and how they convey what Paul was saying. His approach is completely contrasted with what we see in Michael Barber's presention on the Catholic perspective on the role of works at the final judgement. He mentioned specific Catholic teachings and through them made a very giant strive toward presenting what the church teaches and beleives on the issue. Barber was assertive in the use of words like: "The Catholic Church teaches that… Catholics affirm that…" tell a lot about a truly Catholic perspective on any issue. I know that one could respond that "it is implied" in Johnson's work, but how do we know what you are saying if you do not really speak or say it? I think his opening comment above says it all; he was reflecting generally on Pauline corpus.

Having said this, I must commend Johnson, for like his codebaters, he agreed that Paul sees salvation as intimately bound up with what God did in his son Jesus Christ. Most importantly, he pinpointed the progressive dimension of salvation. That is, the fact that salvation is both now and eschatological. This is very basic and important in explicating any Catholic view of salvation, whether in Paul or in the whole of Scriptures. This is why we often talk of our "salvific history." Historically speaking, it is traceable right from Adam to Christ. Christ is the initiator, as well as guarantor, of the new convent people, the Church of eschatological hope, justified by grace through faith in him, and marching toward the heavenly Jerusalem through the power of the Holy Spirit. It is the same Christ who lives in and works in the same Church (Gal 2:20).

He equally noted that though not systematized, Paul's letters are Christocentric. The nonsystematic nature of Paul's letter is not much of an issue, given the fact that Paul did not sit down to write his letters as though he was writing an academic thesis in theology. Though in a way, he sounded like someone debating his case, yet he was addressing pastoral issues which cropped up in the various communities he founded. On the church, though he carefully avoided important metaphors, Johnson equally did a good job here. However, I must reiterate that such metaphors or images or symbols are important for the understanding of Paul, who himself employed them freely.

Finally, in this work, I have tried to evaluate the contribution of Johnson's Catholic perspective of Paul's letters. Though I found his work very interesting and motivating, there were some areas or aspects of the Catholic view of Paul he did not emphasize. In these areas, and based on the outline followed, I have made contributions in order to strengthen and present a more integrated Catholic view of Paul. Ultimately, this work proved that the Catholic Church's formulations and teachings embraced the gospel and theology of the apostle Paul.

# CATHOLIC EPISTLES AND LETTER TO THE HEBREW: A VERY BRIEF EXCURSUS

## The Catholic Epistles and Hebrews

### Introduction

Catholic Epistles (CE) are a collection or group of seven letters in the New Testament. They include James, 1 and 2 Peter, 1 and 2 John, Titus, and Jude, believed to have been written for a wider audience, or with no specific or particular community in mind, but addressed to the universal church or Christians in general (M. G. Easton 1897). Also, some scholars hold that they are "catholic" because their tone is universal, and they address themes that affect the whole church. One major controversy that has surrounded the catholic epistles is the question of their coherence. While some scholars have argued that theologically they are not coherent, others like Robert W. Wall (2009, 13) argue in favor of both their theological coherence and canonical role in the entire canon of the New Testament. Another popular view or consensus about the Catholic Epistles is that they were formed into a second collection of letters "to provide a broader and more balanced literary representation of the apostolic witness than the letters of Paul furnished by themselves" (Niebuhr 2004, 1019–44).

The letter to the Hebrews is one interesting and very impressive work in the New Testament canon. It is carefully crafted in sound Greek and passionately appreciative of Christ (Brown 1997, 683). Till to date (even with its assignation by some scholars to Paul), the authorship of the letter to the Hebrews is still a question of great controversy and debate.

## The Epistle of James: Relationship to Pauline Soteriology

The letter of James is considered the first of the New Testament epistles. In the words of Robert Wall, it is the "frontispiece of the epistles." It is a letter because the author wrote to a community he was not close to. This could be seen from its outlook as a homily or sermon. This can be seen from the author's use of rhetorical questions and strategies in addressing his audience. The authorship of the letter is a bit controversial because it did not specifically tell us which James actually wrote, the brother of Jesus or the son of Zebedee? However, while he did not specifically identify himself (as to which "James" he was, James 1:1), the author is widely thought to be James the half-brother of Jesus. Like the authorship, the dating also is problematic. This is due to lack of historical or internal evidence within this letter. So its dating has been difficult to determine. Some scholars have suggested the early 60s as the most probable date. However, others who insisted that the author of the letter was another James and not the brother of the Lord are of the opinion that its dating should probably be between AD 80 and 100.

Concerning the audience, internal evidence stemming from the letter obviously demonstrates that the audience of the letter is a Jewish Christian community. Of course, given the fact that at the time, Jewish converts were expelled from the temple, the only option for their gathering was the synagogue. In other words, it was a synagogue community. Hence, in chapter 2, the author warns of partiality during assemblies or fellowships, which of course were traditionally held in synagogues. It is also believed that James' audience was not just a one-community audience. Rather, given the situation of the time where the Jewish converts faced enormous prosecutions, there was much dispersions of those fleeing persecutions. Of course, in their various places of dispersion, they formed communities and gathered to share the new faith they had in common.

Structurally, the letter is divided into five chapters, addressing different themes. James addressed important issues that affected the early church. These issues cover both moral and spiritual. That is, ranging from how best to practice the newfound faith in Christ to how to live a good moral life. All these were in a bid to help the Christian community live their new faith without at the same time losing sight of their good cultural heritage. Also, important, James wrote to help the members of the community live in harmony, peace, and justice with one another. Hence, he treats topics like justice, peace, partiality, taming of the tongue, good works, while at the same time emphasizing the importance of prayer, healing, or anointing of the sick and faith in God (James 5:13–18).

One of the major themes of James is the inseparable relationship between faith and action as the prerequisite for salvation. This is captured in his famous word that "faith without good works is dead" (James 2:17.) So James consistently focused on practical action in the life of faith. This is its strongest relationship to Pauline soteriology as read within the NT canon. Of course, many scholars believe that James wrote in order to help his community have a better understanding of Paul's teaching on faith (Gal 2:16), which they interpreted in terms of *sola fidei* (faith alone) as the prerequisite for salvation.

So it is important to mention that the James we see in Acts (though viewed by some as having a tint of Paul in his submission that Gentiles should be admitted based on their faith on Christ) is no different from the James of the epistles. What he wrote in the epistle was a way of throwing more light on the issue taken out of context from Paul's perspective. It was a kind of clarification of how the relationship between faith and good work should be understood. This is no different with what other epistles (Peter, John, and Jude) tried to do with regards to other important issues and themes. In them, we equally see a similar move to balance the reading and interpretation of Paul which at the time was certainly enigmatic. Finally, James also wrote to show that Christianity is not completely opposed to Judaism or that it came to abolish the Law rather than to fulfill it. So James is the "frontispiece" of the Catholic epistles.

## 1 Peter: Relationship to Pauline Soteriology

In terms of arrangement within the New Testament, First Peter follows the epistle of James, which has been described as the frontispiece of the epistles. Apart from this, 1 Peter also treats similar themes, like James. Also, it addressed the persecution of his audience. This letter, which is presumably attributed to Peter the apostle, has been enmeshed in a wide controversy over its real authorship. While most scholars and canonicity unequivocally attributed it to Peter the apostle, some scholars wielding strong arguments oppose the attribution of the authorship to him. Some of the reasons proposed for countering the Petrine authorship of 1 Peter include its language. That is, the Greek as being too sophisticated to be employed by a mere fisherman of that time. Also, that the persecution mentioned in 1 Peter possibly postdates the letter itself. The last but not the least, that 1 Peter had a lot in common with Pauline letters. In spite of all these, the popular opinion is that the letter is from Peter the apostle.

The audience of 1 Peter is a vast group of Christians who lived in different Roman cities of Asia Minor. That is, Christians scattered in "Pontus, Galatia, Cappadocia, Asia, and Bithynia" (1:1). From the tune of the letter, one point is obvious. This is the fact that these Christians were having difficult times of severe persecutions. In light of this, the letter is believed to have been written in the early 60s. That is before Peter's martyrdom. Yet, some scholars still argue that it could have been written between the 70s and 100s or after Peter's death. Probably, the author wrote the letter from Rome (1 Pt 5:13). Babylon certainly refers to Rome of the reign of Nero around AD 62–63.

1 Peter has a fivefold outline or structure. It begins with an introduction or opening address in chapter 1 and progresses to exalt on the dignity of the Christian vocation within chapter 1 and 2. The

duties of the Christian life and the difficulties of Christian persecutions forms the crux of chapters 3 to 5. The letter ended with a brief closing benediction in the last chapter, 5. Resounding themes in 1 Peter include the resurrection, baptism, new life, sobriety of holiness, and the dichotomy between good and evil, the temple and God, and of course, there is the theme of the church as the "new Israel." The climax and the principal theme is that those who persevere in faith while suffering persecution should be full of hope. They will certainly enjoy end-time salvation, since they already enjoy God's saving promises through Christ's death and resurrection. This is simply the summary of this letter, given the circumstances and the time in which it was written.

The soteriological language in 1 Peter is theologically rich in general. However, it has been suggested that there is a relationship between 1 Peter and Pauline soteriology. Some scholars have, like in the case of the letter of James, viewed 1 Peter as throwing more light or trying to clarify some misunderstanding orchestrated by Paul's teaching on salvation. Paul insisted that salvation is by *sola fidei* (faith alone, Gal 2:16). While Peter also, writing to a suffering and a persecuted community equally, agrees that faith is necessary for salvation. This faith, however, is that which endures suffering and persecution. In other words, through good works. For through endurance and conducting oneself properly in the face of suffering shall one prevail (1 Pt 3:13–22). 1 Peter's soteriology exhibits and inhabits a sort of salvation-historical framework. It is profoundly theological in that it springs from God's elective purposes through Christ's atonement directed toward eschatological salvation. Hence, people of other nations are invited to embody its worldview.

## 2 Peter: Relationship with Jude and Pauline Soteriology

Second Peter begins with the author identifying himself as Simon Peter (1:1). He uses the first-person singular pronoun in a highly personal passage (1:12–15). Most importantly, he claims to be an eyewitness of the transfiguration. In the church, 2 Peter was not as widely known and recognized as 1 Peter. However, some may have used and accepted it as authoritative as early as the second century and perhaps even in the latter part of the first century. It was not ascribed to Peter until Origen's time, and he seems to reflect some doubt concerning it.

Eusebius the church historian placed 2 Peter among the questioned books, though he admits that most accept it as from Peter. After Eusebius's time, it seems to have been quite generally accepted as canonical. Modern scholars have greatly questioned the authorship of the letter as Peter's. Hence, today many biblical scholars and exegetes maintain that 2 Peter is a pseudographical work or a letter written by an unknown figure some years after the death of the apostle Peter around the 60s. some objections to Peter's authorship of the letter arise from a secular reconstruction of early Christian history or misunderstandings of the available data. For example, some argue that the reference to Paul's letters in 3:15–16 indicates an advanced date for 2 Pt beyond the apostle's lifetime.

Also, there is controversy surrounding the dating of 2 Pt. Of course, this is understandable given the fact that the authorship itself is a matter of similar controversy. In other words, the dating is strongly tied to the authorship of the letter. Should one assume the authenticity of the letter as from the apostle Peter, then the dating of the letter around the 60s would be most probable. On the other hand, if one inclines to the pseudepigraphic authorship, then it must have been probably written after the death of the apostle Peter. This could be situated around the 80s. However, some scholars have suggested a later date because they interpret the reference to the Fathers in 3:4 to mean an earlier Christian generation.

Concerning the audience of 2 Peter, there is no explicit mention to it in the letter. However, scholars believe that the letter was addressed to the same audience of 1 Peter. So, unlike 1 Peter, there is little information in this epistle about its recipients. If 2 Peter 3:1 refers to 1 Peter, then Christians in Asia Minor were the recipients of both epistles. Having said this, and taking for granted that both 1 and 2 Peter were written by the same apostle Peter, in his first letter, he feeds his audience by instructing them on how to deal with and endure persecution for the sake of their salvation. In this second letter, he senses the threat posed by false teachers to community, and so he instructs them on how to deal with false teachers and evildoers who have come into the church to destroy it (2: 1). Like 1 Peter, 2 Peter begins with an introduction or opening address, but instead of ending with a benediction, 2 Peter ends with a doxology in 3:8. The simple outline or structure of the three-chapter letter parades the following themes on God's precious promises to his faithful people: denunciation of false prophets or deceivers, their punishment and their poison, and of course, the theme of the promised return of Christ.

With regards to soteriology, 2 Peter presents Jesus as savior in that he delivered his followers from slavery, corruption, and the defilements of the world. For him, human beings became slaves of corruption through erroneous thinking and following the desires of the flesh. Jesus' followers have been released from this servitude by their recognition that Jesus has purchased them from their previous owner and is now their master. 2 Peter's ethical teaching is based on continuing in freedom from slavery to sin that has come through Jesus. Also, the eschatological teaching of 2 Peter describes the completion of salvation. That is the culmination of both slavery to sin and following Jesus. So the Pauline character of the soteriology of 2 Peter is very marked (2 Pet 3:16). In view of the author's claim that Paul agrees with what the author has said, this is not surprising.

There are both striking similarities and differences between 2 Peter and Jude. These similarities hinge on the source theory of the two epistles. So it has been suggested that one copied from the other, or that they both drew on a common source. However, if there is copying, it has equally been suggested that it is not an unreasonable one, but one that adapts to suit the writer's purpose. While many have insisted that Jude used Peter, it is more reasonable to assume that the longer letter (Peter) incorporated much of the shorter (Jude). Such borrowing was, however, fairly common in ancient writings.

## Role of Suffering in the Catholic Epistles and Hebrews

In contrast to the apostolic or Pauline epistles addressed to individual churches or persons, the term *catholic*, in the sense of universal, was applied by Origen and the other Church Fathers to the seven epistles written by James, Peter, John, and Jude. James wrote to all Jews of the dispersion, who had embraced the Christian faith. In his first epistle, Peter addressed the same Christians, including Gentile converts resident in five provinces of Asia Minor. His second epistle is to all Christians everywhere. John's first letter was evidently written to a cycle of churches and intended for universal use. Jude also had in mind all Christians when he said "to them that are called beloved in God."

The seeming exceptions are 2 and 3 Jn, addressed to individuals, but included within the catholic epistles as properly belonging with John's first epistle. The authorship of the letter to the Hebrews remains a matter of controversy. Several theories regarding the author's identity have been proposed over the years, but all of them contain significant problems. Also, the letter does not clearly identify its audience by name, city, or region. However, the original audience of Hebrews was persecuted. There were two well-known times of persecution for Christians during the first century AD that may have impacted Hebrews' original audience.

One common denominator of the Catholic Epistles and the letter to the Hebrews is suffering, which was the direct consequence of their persecution due to their newfound faith in Jesus Christ. One point that is perhaps central or common with the theme of suffering in all these writings is that it is strongly related to the eschatological hope. Here, I shall focus on four epistles from this group of letters. These shall include James, Hebrews, 1 and 2 Peter.

James regards its addressees as suffering trials and temptation (1:2–4; 2:6–7) and as needing to avoid and escape from wickedness and sin. So their trials are intended to produce endurance. This is an important virtue for those who have hope for their salvation. Through this endurance in suffering, which suffices for good work, and coupled with the believer's faith, salvation is guaranteed. This eschatological hope that those who humble themselves before God will be exalted is focused on the imminent *parousia* as the author indicated in 5:7–8.

In the letter to the Hebrews, there is a notion that the people of God live in an awkward and tense relationship with the world. The situation for the addressees of Hebrews is apparently one in which martyrdom is not yet a reality (Heb 12:4). They are strangers and exiles on earth. They are a wandering people looking toward their heavenly country. So this world is a place of sin, not yet subject to Christ's rule. Indeed, Christ's followers who have suffered hostility from the world can expect to be with him in the future. Through suffering, believers experience a similar fate to that suffered by the "great cloud of witnesses" (12:1). Most importantly, believers who suffer are following Christ himself, who endured similar hostility from his persecutors. So unlike in James, where again the addressees endure suffering, in Hebrews, Christ explicitly represents a path for his disciples to follow. That is the path of enduring suffering for the prize that lies ahead. However, like in James, we see the same eschatological hope in play. With James and Hebrews, it is clear that the letter's addressees are suffering. This same theme is especially evident in 1 and 2 Peter. To what extent the nature and causes of suffering are the same across all three texts is harder to discern, not least since the provenance and date of James in particular are uncertain. The situation depicted by 1 and 2 Peter is one in which suffering arises not only from general and informal public hostility but also from the Roman judgment of Christianity as essentially seditious and criminal.

So sporadic and informal hostility against Christians, sometimes involving Jews, sometimes not, is evidently prevalent from the earliest days. 1 and 2 Peter focuses on the sufferings of Christ. Thus, they presented Christ as a model for discipleship, specifically for slaves suffering under wicked masters. The spirit of Christ was present among them, showing the glory that lay ahead from Christ. So loyalty to Christ entails alienation from the world. Hostility and persecution aim to persuade Christians to abandon this loyalty. So 1 and 2 Peter seek to sustain the endurance of their audience against the pressure to conform to this world. This is especially when it leads to suffering and death.

## Conclusion

The theme of suffering, either through physical persecution or that orchestrated by sin or sinners cuts across the catholic epistles and the letters to the Hebrews. In one way or the other, their audiences were passing through tough and challenging moments. Faith in Christ and endurance or resistance in suffering was the key to overcoming suffering. Importantly, these are what fuels and sustains the eschatological hope of the believers in Christ.

# THE SIGNIFICANCE OF Κοίνωνία IN JOHANNINE COMMUNITY: 1 JN 1:1–4

*Johannine Epistle*

## Introduction

Like in his gospel, John begins his epistle in a very interesting way. He begins with a prologue, introducing his readers to why he is writing and what he wishes them to achieve from his message. That is, to share with him the same message he himself has known and enjoyed. Thus, he employs the word κοίνωνία (fellowship) in order to express this sharing. The Greek word κοίνωνία may not be found in all the books of the Bible (i.e., as a term). However, words or phrases which connote or express its meaning are abundant. In 1 John, the word takes a unique meaning as it does in the Pauline writings. Within the richness of the New Testament, Johannine corpus maintains a distinctive and honored place. Shared idiosyncrasies of language and thought bind the gospel and epistles of John together. Despite a fundamentally different perspective and apparent background, the Apocalypse too seems to have established links with this tradition. However, while Johannine theology has long been recognized as a major voice in the NT, its historical place within the development of the early church has been vigorously disputed.

The aim of this work, therefore, is to take a close look at the term κοίνωνιά in order to find out what it really means and the significance of its usage in 1 John 1–4 for Christians and their communities. In this paper, we shall employ the term "Johannine corpus" and "Johannine community" to mean the works and the audience of John the apostle respectively. Also, we shall simply refer to the first epistle of John as "1 John."

## Authorship and Dating

From the outset, it is very important to note that from the internal evidence right from the beginning or prologue of the 1 John, the author identified himself as an "eyewitness" (1:1). This is very important, considering the controversies surrounding the authorship of the gospel of John. Who this eyewitness is has also been a source of great debate among scholars. Of course, for those who insist that John the apostle authored the fourth gospel, there is no qualms also pinning the authorship of 1 John to the same apostle. Their reason is obvious: similarities in vocabulary and style. Is this enough evidence to pin it to the same John? In literary writing, is it not possible for two or more writers to adopt similar vocabularies and style? Some scholars have suggested allusions to John's epistles in a number of noncanonical Christian works dating mostly from the second century AD (Hall III, 1, 2, 3).

Here, we shall make do with the fact of the canonicity of 1 John, which allotted it to John the apostle. Speaking of canonicity, here we rely strongly on the testimonies of the early Church Fathers like Irenaeus, Tertullian (who quoted 1 John numerous times, referring to it as the work of John the Apostle) (*Adversus Marcionem* 5.16; *Adversus Praxeam* 15, 28; *Adversus Gnosticos Scorpiace* 12), Clement of Alexandria, Origen, Dionysius of Alexandria, and even Eusebius the historian. For the dating of 1 John, we shall also stick to a period around AD 100. That is, after John's gospel (Brown 1997, 384).

## Audience or Community of 1 John

We must note first of all that the only evidence we have about the historical situation of 1 John comes from the epistle itself, and since the author did not need to describe that situation in details for his readers, what we learn of it is mostly by way of allusion. To most scholars, it seems clear that the occasion for the writing of 1 John was a crisis within the Johannine community caused by the people mentioned in 1 John 2:18–27 (Rensberger 1997, 25). Hence, Urban C. von Wahlde (1990, 105–106) strongly believes that 1 John was written at a time of great turmoil within the Johannine community. Just as the Gospel had been composed to deal with the split between Johannine Christianity and its parent Judaism, so 1 John was written to confront the problems caused by a rift within the Johannine community itself. However, Judith Lieu (1991, 15–16) believes that 1 John is primarily directed within the community to bring reassurance to its members and to lay out an understanding of different aspects of Johannine theology. 1 John is one of the shorter books of the New Testament, but within its few short pages, it contains a wealth of materials. 1 John is a handbook for the understanding of what may have been the Johannine's community greatest crisis. The epistle encapsulates a struggle for the understanding of the entire Johannine tradition.

## Literary Structure of 1 John

Although we commonly refer to all the three epistles of John as letters; however, scholars disagree on the issue, since 1 John has none of the features of the letter format. Pheme Perkins thinks they represent three different literary genres. 1 John is not a letter at all but an instructional track which may have been intended to be circulated among several communities. Plausibly, it is a written exhortation interpreting the main themes of the fourth gospel in the light of secessionist propaganda that had certain plausibility and continued to attract followers. Pheme Perkins's (1979, XVII) view of the structure of the epistle is that it contains four major divisions plus a prologue, a conclusion, and an appendix. Kenneth Grayson (1984, 12–13) sees the structure of the epistle as falling into six major sections. Stephen Smalley's (1984) view of the structure is the most elaborate so far. That is, two major sections, with each of these sections containing four divisions. The subdivisions of each half parallel each other thematically. Furthermore, Raymond Brown (p. 392), believes that 1 John is an interpretation of the fourth gospel and so favors a bipartite division that corresponds to the gospel division.

## The Text: 1 John 1:1–4 (Prologue)

[1]Ὃ ἦν ἀπ᾽ ἀρχῆς, ὃ ἀκηκόαμεν, ὃ ἑωράκαμεν τοῖς ὀφθαλμοῖς ἡμῶν, ὃ ἐθεασάμεθα καὶ αἱ χεῖρες ἡμῶν ἐψηλάφησαν, περὶ τοῦ λόγου τῆς ζωῆς—[2]καὶ ἡ ζωὴ ἐφανερώθη, καὶ ἑωράκαμεν καὶ μαρτυροῦμεν καὶ ἀπαγγέλλομεν ὑμῖν τὴν ζωὴν τὴν αἰώνιον ἥτις ἦν πρὸς τὸν πατέρα καὶ ἐφανερώθη ἡμῖν—[3]ὃ ἑωράκαμεν καὶ ἀκηκόαμεν ἀπαγγέλλομεν [a]καὶ ὑμῖν, ἵνα καὶ ὑμεῖς κοινωνίαν ἔχητε μεθ᾽ ἡμῶν· καὶ ἡ κοινωνία δὲ ἡ ἡμετέρα μετὰ τοῦ πατρὸς καὶ μετὰ τοῦ υἱοῦ αὐτοῦ Ἰησοῦ Χριστοῦ· [4]καὶ ταῦτα γράφομεν ἡμεῖς ἵνα ἡ χαρὰ ἡμῶν ᾖ πεπληρωμένη (SBL Greek New Testament, 2010).

[1]That which was from the beginning, which we have heard, which we have seen with our eyes, which we have looked at and our hands have touched—this we proclaim concerning the Word of life. [2]The life appeared; we have seen it and testify to it, and we proclaim to you the eternal life, which was with the Father and has appeared to us. [3]We proclaim to you what we have seen and heard, so that you also may have fellowship with us. And our fellowship is with the Father and with his Son, Jesus Christ. [4]We write this

to make our joy complete (New International Version, 2011).

Verses 1:1–4 is the prologue of 1 John. "In style and vocabulary there are so many similarities between the first epistle of John and the gospel of John that no one can doubt that at least, they are from the same tradition." Here, the author presents himself as an eyewitness. This is evident from verse 1: "That which was from the beginning, which we have heard, which we have seen with our eyes, which we have looked at…" Also, important is the author's reference to "In the beginning…" (1:1). Scholars seem to vary in their opinion to exactly what this "In the beginning" refers to here. While some, like Raymond Brown, argue that "In the beginning" (unlike "the beginning" in John 1:1) refers to the start of the writer's ministry, others, like Rosemary Bardsley, are of the opinion that "'In the beginning,' immediately brings to the reader's mind the 'in the beginning' of Genesis 1:1, and of course, the same in Johannine gospel 1:1 where God is assumed to exist in unique, independent, absolute, unconditional, eternal self-existence. For her, John repeats this divine 'in the beginning', affirming the eternity and the deity of Jesus Christ, the One who was there 'in the beginning" (Bardsley 2018, 48). In verse 2, John presents his "ἀπαγγέλλομεν" (message) as the word of God which is life. Also, like in the gospel, the Logos is the central figure and the source of divine life. Whoever receives Him has received the fullness of life.

## Purpose of John's Epistle

We now turn to why the author wrote 1 John, which is at the core of this paper. Verse 3 presents the author's purpose of writing: "ὃ ἑωράκαμεν καὶ ἀκηκόαμεν ἀπαγγέλλομεν [a]καὶ ὑμῖν, ἵνα καὶ ὑμεῖς κοινωνίαν ἔχητε μεθ᾽ ἡμῶν· καὶ ἡ κοινωνία δὲ ἡ ἡμετέρα μετὰ τοῦ πατρὸς καὶ μετὰ τοῦ υἱοῦ αὐτοῦ Ἰησοῦ Χριστοῦ." (We proclaim to you what we have seen and heard, *so* that you also may have fellowship with us. And our fellowship is with the Father and with his Son, Jesus Christ). In communicating his message to his community,

John has no doubt that this will be a source of great joy to it. Hence, κοινωνία (fellowship) in, and with the Word, is the source of the Christian joy (v. 4).

The word κοινωνία (fellowship) appeared twice in verse 3, and John seemed to have used it for two different purposes. First, "So that you may have fellowship with us." In other words, that you may "share or participate in our joy." The second purpose is, "And our fellowship is with the Father and with his Son, Jesus Christ." In other words, not only living in fellowship with us, but most importantly, with the Trinitarian God. So, as one could decipher, John wrote to strengthen the community in their fellowship with himself and with the tradition of Christological witnesses and active love that he represents. Thus, he assures them that by remaining in this fellowship, they indeed remain in relationship with the Trinitarian God, the guarantor of eternal life and joy. The nature of this "κοινωνία" is our next and ultimate quest.

## Κοίνωνιά: Etymology and Meaning

The term κοίνωνιά is Greek and literally translated means "fellowship." The following synonyms can also suffice for its meaning: sharing, companionship, participate, partnership, communion, etcetera. In this case, it could be understood as a group of like-minded people who share common interests, experiences, or views (Linder, 2000). Κοίνωνιά is a feminine and singular word. Although the word κοίνωνιά appears most abundantly in the New Testament, one could say that the Old Testament alluded to it by the use of other synonyms as "companion" (Ps 119:63); "To walk with" (Ps 13:20); "To dwell together" (Ps 133:1); and "to Partner with" (Ps 29:24). The prophet Amos sees fellowship as "working together" (Amos 3:3). Ecclesiastes uses the term in the following way: "Two are better than one... Again, if two lie together, then they have heat..." (Ecc 4:9–12).

In the New Testament, one finds a more direct use of the term, especially in Acts and in the letters of Paul. A summary in Acts 2:42–47 lists four features of the communal life of the early believers. First, koinonia as fellowship (communion). Second, koinonia as prayer for one another. Third, koinonia as breaking of bread. The risen Jesus showed himself present at meals. Fourth, koinonia as the teachings of the apostles. The scriptures were authoritative for all Jews, in particular the Law and the Prophets. This would have been true for the first followers of Jesus as well (Brown, p. 287–9). In other NT books or letters, there are also allusions to κοίνωνιά. "Therefore, comfort yourselves together, and edify one another…" (1 Th 5:11). Peter wrote: "Finally, be you all of one mind, having compassion one with another…" (1 Pt 3, 8–9). James emphasized community prayer: "Confess your faults one to another, and pray one for another…" (Jas 5, 16), and Hebrews encouraged meeting together, "Do not forsake the assembly of one another" (Heb 10, 24).

There are about three levels of "fellowship" that runs through the entire scriptures: (1) fellowship with God (Gen 5:22; Ex 29:45; John 17:23). Paul prayed: "And the God of love and peace shall be with you" (2 Cor 13:11). (2) Fellowship with Christ. "For where two or three are gathered in my name, there am I in their midst" (Mt 18: 20). (3) Fellowship with the Holy Spirit. "The grace of the Lord Jesus Christ, and the communion of the Holy Spirit, be with you all" (2 Co 13:14). In all these, fellowship among the believers is also embedded in the fellowship with the Father, the Son, and the Holy Spirit. This is because to be truly in fellowship with the them is to be in fellowship with fellow Christians.

The wide distribution κοίνωνιά in the NT shows that the believers in Jesus strongly felt that they had much in common. Something translated as "fellowship." More literally, it is "communion" (the spirit that binds them together), or "community" (the grouping produced by that spirit). Indeed, κοίνωνιά may reflect in Greek an early Semitic name for the Jewish group of believers in Christ. This is comparable to the Jewish group responsible for the Dead Sea Scrolls which designated itself as "yahad" (oneness unity)." For Bultmann (1974, 15), *κοίνωνιά* is the union in common faith brought about by the proclamation of the divine Logos.

## Koinonia in Johannine Corpus

In Johannine corpus, "fellowship" may be understood as communion, participation, or partnership. Here, it is set out as the goal of the proclamation of the Gospel. Moody D. Smith (1990, 37) views fellowship as both a vertical and a horizontal partnership. That is, fellowship with God and Christ, and with others. In the Johannine corpus, the fatherhood of God is constantly set over and against the sonship of Jesus. This is a way of expressing their most intimate relationship. This relationship is entered into and shared by believers. It can be called κοίνωνία, but it can also be spoken of in other ways, particularly in terms of "abiding in or with" God or Jesus, or the Holy Spirit (1 Jn 2:6–10, 14:10–11, 23, 15:7–10).

There is a mutual indwelling among the Father, the Son, the Holy Spirit and believers. This constitutes their fellowship. In common Christian parlance, κοίνωνία in the Johannine corpus is "the Church." Interestingly enough, the term, κοίνωνία is not found in the fourth gospel. However, the idea of mutual abiding or indwelling occurs frequently. In the Apocalypse, κοίνωνία is presented using "dinning with" and "to dwell with" (Rev 21:3, 20). Thus, in the Gospel, Jesus' final prayer stresses the importance of the unity of believers (17:21–23). The rich concept of κοίνωνία belongs to 1 John (Brown, p. 384). It is only in this epistle that the word κοίνωνία was used in the entire Johannine corpus. Fellowship in 1 John is the root of Christian joy and an essential feature of the community.

## Theology of Κοίνωνία in 1 John

The Johannine tradition is famous for its expressions of unity of believers with one another, and with the Father, the Son, and the Holy Spirit. When John speaks about God, or Jesus dwelling "in" the believer, he is not referring to some private or individual inner divine presence. He always uses that language when speaking about the community of believers that has been brought into being by Jesus' presence of outstanding holiness. It is shared equally by all who belong to the community, since for John, Jesus is the only real locus of light, truth, glory, and life from God. The ordinary sense of the word κοίνωνιά is sharing or partnership, a usage that may have been in common use in the early Christians mission. In 1 John, it corresponds to the language of mutual indwelling with Christ. It also strongly highlights the importance of community as a place of eternal life.

Conflict within the community threatens the unity or fellowship. Whereas mutual love is the hallmark of a good community. Since κοίνωνιά is totally absent from the Gospel, its appearance four times in 1 John 1:3–7 is noteworthy. The author reminds his audience that the basis of their unity is fellowship. Then he highlights the true root of any such fellowship. The most characteristic Johannine expression is "remain in" or "abide in." In the gospel, rather than being led to reject him by the Jewish opposition, that way of speaking can easily be carried over into this new situation in 1 John, where some Christians seem to form a separate group and to encourage other members of the Johannine community to follow their lead. Pheme Perkins (p. 11) notes that: "Two aspects of disciples are associated with the expression of remaining or abiding with the teachings about Jesus (1 Jn 2:24; 2 Jn 2:9), and leading a life of mutual love appropriate to believers (2, 6)." Sometimes, the author varies the metaphor by speaking of abiding in an attribute of the Father: his truth (1:8; 2:2); his word (1:10; 2:14); his seed (3:9); eternal life (3:15) and love (4:2).

So John's invitation to fellowship implies an invitation away from the dissident group. By putting themselves outside the tradition of witness to the incarnation, they have separated themselves from the fellowship and partnership of the community, and consequently, from fellowship with God. Also, the opponents are probably in view when the author speaks of God's Son, since a significant element in his Christological message is that Jesus is the Christ and the Son of God (2:22–24; 3:23). Those titles are deeply rooted in the Johannine tradition (Jn 11, 27, 20, 31), Their use here help to introduce the specific subject of 1 John. David Rensberger notes that the statement of the authors purpose for writing in verse 4 may be compared with others in 2:1; 5:13. The joy mentioned here is not merely an emotion, but an eschatological blessing (Jn 15:11; 17:13). The author's joy and that of the group he represents is complete if his readers are included among those who have fellowship with the Son and the Father by adhering to the tradition of witness to the incarnation (Rensberger 1979, 47–48). Hence, the carefully construed allusion to the fourth gospel in this section of 1 John stresses the fact that the fellowship shared by the author and his audience is grounded in Jesus Christ.

## Conclusion

In order to make sense of the need to live together, the circular world employs sayings as: "No man is an island," "Man is a gregarious being," "United we stand, divided we fall," and according to a quote ascribed to Aristotle: "He who is unable to live in society, or who has no need because he is sufficient for himself, must be either a beast or a god." So this paper highlights the significance and importance of κοίνωνιά to the body of Christ. This is especially for the "religious men and women" called to bear a special witness to Christ through community life. As the author of 1 John admonished his community to live in fellowship with him, the Trinity, and of course, with one another, so his message resounds to all of us today.

Christian fellowship is not some elective choice about doctrine or mere community organization. In 1 John 1:1–4, the author presents κοίνωνιά ("fellowship") as unity with the Father and the Son. It is the hallmark of any true Christian community. John reminds Christians that the basis of our own fellowship with one another is remaining in the community. Remaining in the community implies love for its members. It is the fellowship of those who walk in the light and truth of Christ, the incarnate word of God (1:6), of those who walk in union with the Trinitarian God and with fellow believers, and the fellowship of those whose hope is eternal life. It suffices to end this brief paper with these words from the Spiritan rule of life: "Fraternal life in community builds up the body of Christ. It is a living prove that a genuine fraternal unity in Christ is possible" (*SRL No. 28.1*).

# BIBLIOGRAPHY

*Abingdon Old Testament Commentaries*, Psalms 73–150. Nashville: Abingdon, 2003.

Ackroyd, P. R. et al. *The Book of Proverbs*. Cambridge: Cambridge University Press, 1972.

*Adversus Marcionem, Adversus Praxeam, Adversus Gnosticos Scorpiace.*

Afanassiev, N. "Una Sancta." *Irenikon* 36 (1963).

Kerr, Alan R. "The Temple of Jesus' Body: The Temple Theme in the Gospel of John." *Journal for the Study of the New Testament* 220 (2002): 102.

Alexander, T. Desmond. 1999. "The Composition of the Sinai Narrative in Exodus XIX 1–XXIV 11." *Vetus Testamentum* 49, no. 1: 2. *Academic Search Complete*, EBSCO host (accessed February 3, 2017)

McGrath, Alister E. *Christian Theology—An introduction*. Oxford: Blackwell publishing, 2001.

Allen, Leslie C. "Psalms 101–150." *Word Biblical Commentary*. Vol. 21. Waco: Word, 1983.

New Catholic Encyclopedia. "Analogy, Theological Use." Accessed November 2, 2017. http://www.encyclopedia.com.

"Ancient Greek." http://www.wikisearch.net/search?q. Aorist, =Future+tense&page.

Anderson, G. W. "Canonical and Non-Canonical." In *The Cambridge History of the Bible*. Cambridge: Cambridge University Press, 1970.

Köstenberger, Andreas J., and Scott R. Swain. "Father, Son and Spirit: The Trinity and John's Gospel." *New Studies in Biblical Theology* 24 ed., edited by D. A. Carson. Inter Varsity Press, Illinois, 2008.

Ceresko, Anthony R. *The Old Testament: A Liberation Perspective*. New York: Orbis Books, 1992.

Athanasius. *The Life of Antony and the Letter to Marcellinus*, translated by Robert C. Gregg. Paulist Press, New York.

Augustine of Hippo, *Ear. Ps. 49.2.*

———. *The City of God (Civitate Dei)*.

———. "Exposition on Psalm 149." Accessed, November 7, 2018. www.newadvent.org/fathers/1801149.htm.

———. *In Joannem Evangelium*.

Flannery, Austin. *Verbum Dei. A Vatican II Council*. St. Paul's: New Delhi, 2007.

Barret C. K. *The Gospel According to St. John: An Introduction with Commentary and Notes on the Greek Text*. 2nd ed., Philadelphia: Westminster, 1978.

Benedict XVI, *Post-Synodal Exhortation on the Eucharist as the Source and Summit of the*

De La Soujeole, Benoit-Dominique. *Introduction to the Mystery of the Church*. Catholic University of America: Washington DC, 2014.

Ben-Porat Z. "The Poetics of Literary Allusion, PTL." *A Journal for Descriptive Poetics and Theory of Literature* (1976): 105–28.

Bergsma, John, and Brant Pitre. *The Old Testament: A Catholic Introduction to the Bible*. San Francisco: Ignatius, 2017.

bible.org/series page/authorship-1-John, 2004.

Biser, E. *Die Glaubensgeschichtliche Wende: eine theologische Positionsbestimmung*, 2nd ed. Graz: Styria, 1987.

Harrod, Bloom. *Huxley Aldous: Blooms Modern Critical Views*. InfoBase publishing, New York, 2010.

Brainyquote.com/quotes/Aristotle -10174.

Pitre, Brant. "Jesus, the New Temple, and the New Priesthood." *Letter and Spirit 4, Temple and Contemplation: God's Presence in the Cosmos, Church, and Human Heart*, 2008.

Reuven, Brauner, and Shimush Pesukim. *Comprehensive Index to Liturgical and Ceremonial Uses of Biblical Verses and Passages*, 2nd ed, 2013.

Shanley, Brian J. OP. "Divine Causation and Human Freedom in Aquinas." *American Catholic Philosophical Quarterly* 72:1 (1998).

Stephen, Brock L. *The Philosophy of Saint Thomas Aquinas, A Sketch.* Cascade Books, Eugene, Oregon, 2015.

Brown, Raymond E. *An Introduction to the New Testament.* Yale University Press: New Haven, 1997.

———. *The Virginal Conception and Bodily Resurrection of Jesus.* Paulist Press, 1973.

———. "Communicating the Divine and Human in Scripture." *Origins* 22:1 (May 14, 1992).

Brown, Raymond. *Response to 101 Questions on the Bible.* Mahwah: Paulist Press Limited, 1990.

———. et al, *The New Jerome Biblical Commentary* (Hardback). New Delhi; St. Paul's, 2007.

———. *Introduction to the New Testament.* New York: Doubleday, 2007.

Brown, T. Ken. "Temple Christology in the Gospel of John Replacement Theology and Jesus as the Self-Revelation of God." MA in Biblical Studies at Trinity Western University, Langley, B.C., Canada, 2010

Bruce A. Ware. *Father, Son, & Holy Spirit Relationships, Roles, & Relevance.* Wheaton, Ill.: Crossway Books, 2005.

Waltke, Bruce K. "The Phenomenon of Conditionality within Unconditional Covenants." *Israel's Apostasy and Restoration: Essays in Honor of Roland K. Harrison*, edited by A. Gileadi. Grand Rapids: Baker, 1988.

Morrill, Bruce T. "Anointing of the Sick as Sacrament within a Larger Pastoral Process of Faith." *Liturgical Ministry* 16 (Fall 2007).

Hassel, Bullock C. *Encountering the Books of Psalms: A Literary and Theological Introduction.* Baker Academic, Grand Rapids, 2001.

Walter, Burghardt and Lawler C Thomas (eds). *St. Augustine on Faith and Works,* translated by Gregory Lombardo CSC, STD. New York: The Newman Press, 1988.

Cardinal Bellarmine. *Commentary on the Psalms,* translated by John O'Sullivan, new edition. London, Peterson Row, 2008.

Olson, Carl E. "Eschatological Fact and Fiction: Catholicism and Dispensationalism Compare." http://www.ignatiusinsight.com/features2006/colson_eschatology_jun06.asp.

Carlson, R. A. David. *The Chosen King.* Uppsala, Sweden: Almqvist and Wiksell, 1964.

Brooks, Carol. *The Resurrection Account,* edited by Vicki Narlee. http://www.inplainsite.org/html. Accessed 20/07/18.

Dempsey, Carol J. *The Prophets.* Minneapolis: Fortress Press, 2000.

Carson D. A. *Divine Sovereignty and Human Responsibility: Biblical Perspectives in Tension.* Atlanta: John Knox, 1981.

————. *Scandalous: The Cross and Resurrection of Jesus.* Crossway Books, USA, 2010.

————. "Matthew." *The Expositor's Bible Commentary* Edited by Frank E. Gaebelein. Grand Rapids, MI: Zondervan, 1984.

*Catechism of the Catholic Church,* 2nd ed. Washington, DC: United States Catholic, 1997.

Ceresko, Anthony R. "Psalm 149: Poetry, Themes (Exodus and Conquest), and Social Function." *Biblica* 67 (1986): 177–94.

Cha Kilnam. "Psalms 146–150: The Final Hallelujah Psalms as a Fivefold Doxology to the Hebrew Psalter." Graduate Faculty of Baylor University, 2006.

Charles Pope, "Making Sense of the Resurrection Accounts: Are There Discrepancies?" Accessed 20/07/2018.

Brevard, Childs S. *The Book of Exodus; a Critical, Theological Commentary.* Philadelphia: Westminster Press, 1974.

Robert, Chisolm. "When Prophecy Appears to Fail, Check Your Hermeneutics." *JETS* 53/3 September 2010: 561–77.

Arevalo, Chito. "The Eucharist and the Church." http://www.clerus.org/ clerus/dati/ 2002-03/25.

Hayes, Christine. "Introduction to the Old Testament." http://oyc.yale.edu/religious-studies/rlst-145, 2017.

Church's Life and Mission Sacramentum Caritatis. http://www.catholicliturgy

McCann, Clinton. "The Psalms as Instructions." *Interpretation: A Journal of Bible and Theology,* 1980 No. 4. Vol. XXXIV.

Viscichini, Cole. "The Mount Sinai Covenant" (Exegesis). http://www.academia.edu/7894894/ (accessed, February, 3 2017)

Humphreys, Colin J. and Waddington W. G. "The Date of the Crucifixion." *Journal of the American Scientific Affiliation, 37.* (March 1985).

Congar, Yves. *The Meaning of Tradition.* Ignatius Press: San Francisco, 2004.

———. *The Mystery of the Temple* trans. Reginald F. Trevett. Westminster: Newman, 1962.

———. *Divided Christendom: A Catholic Study of the Problem of Reunion.* London; Centenary Press, 1939.

———. *Lay people in the Church: A Study for a theology of the Laity.* Westminster, MD; Newman Press, 1957.

Congregation for the Clergy. "Biblia Clerus, The Holy See, 2007. http:/www.clrerus. org/bibliaclerus/index_eng.html; EE21

Constitution on the church, no 5. *The Document of Vatican II*, edited by Walter M. Abbott. New York, 1966.

Jean, Corbon. *The Well Spring of Worship.* Ignatius Press, San Francisco, 2005.

Courson, Jon. "Exodus 24." *Blue Letter Bible Audio/Video Commentaries.* October 2013.

Christopher, Cowan. "The Father and the Son in the Fourth Gospel: Johannine Subordination Revisited." *JETS* 49/1 (March 2006). 115.

Jesse, Coyne. "The Later New Testament Writings and Scripture: The Old Testament in Acts, Hebrews, the Catholic Epistles, and Revelation." Grand Rapids: Baker, 2012. *Journal of the Evangelical Theological Society*, 56 no 1 Mar 2013, p 178–180.

Keener, Craig S. "Sent Like Jesus: Johannine Missiology (John 20:21–22)." *Asian Journal of Pentecostal Studies* 12, no. 1 (January 2009).

"Creative Fidelity, the Observations." *Heythrop Journal* 39 (1998) 18–36.

Crenshaw J. L., "Proverbs Book of," *Anchor Bible Dictionary*, edited by D. N. Freeman, vol. 5, p. 531–20.

Murray. "The Temple in Jerusalem." Accessed July 22, 2018. https://www.ancient.eu/article/852/the-temple-in-jerusalem/.

Keating, Daniel A. *Deification and Grace: Introduction to Catholic Doctrine.* Sapientia Press, Ave Maria University, Naples, Florida, 2007.

———. *First and Second Peter, Jude, Catholic Commentary on Sacred Scripture.* Grand Rapids: Baker, 2011.

Gallagher, Daniel B. "Review of Grabowski's Plato, Metaphysics and the Forms," *Journal of the History of Philosophy*, (48) 2010:2.

Bock, Darrell L. "The Covenants in Progressive Dispensationalism," *Three Central Issues for Today's Dispensationalist*, edited by Herb W. Bateman, IV (Grand Rapids: Kregel, forthcoming).

Garner, *David B. Sons in the Son: The Riches and Reach of Adoption in Christ.* Phillipsburg, NJ: P&R Publishing, 2016.

Clines, David J. "The Ideology of the Writers and Readers of the Hebrew Bible." *Interested Parties, JOST Supply*, 205, Sheffield: Sheffield Academic Press, 1995.

———. "Story and Poem: The Old Testament as Literature and as Scripture Study of the Old Testament." *Interpretation: A Journal of Bible and Theology*, 1980: No. 2. Vol. XXXIV.

David M. S. *The Gospel of Matthew.* Minnesota; Liturgical Press, 1960.

Reid, David P. *What Are They Saying about the Prophets?* New York: Paulist, 1980.

Rensberger, David. *Abingdon NT Commentaries, 1, 2, & 3 John.* Abingdon Press, 1979.

Meconi, David V. *The One Christ: St Augustine's Theology of Deification.* The Catholic University of America Press, Washington DC, 2013.

Franz, Delitzsch. *Biblical Commentary on the Proverbs of Solomon.* Edinburgh: T&T Clark, 1880.

de Lubac, Henri. *Catholicism: Christ and the Common Destiny of Man*, trans. Lancelot C.

de Lubac, Henri. *The Church: Paradox and Mystery*, trans. James R. Dunne. New York: Alba House, 1969.

Dobkins, Rebecca J. *1997 Memory and Imagination: The Legacy of Maidu Indian Artist Frank Day. With Carey Caldwell and Frank La Pena*. Oakland: Oakland Museum of California, 1997.

Dodd C. H. *According to the Scriptures. The Sub-Structure of New Testament Theology*. London, 1952.

Dogmatic constitution on Divine Revelation, III.12 (A. Flannery [ed.], Vatican Council II, p. 669

Doorly W. J. *Understanding the Book of Amos*, Mahwah, New Jersey: Paulist, 1989.

Dennis, Doyle M. "Henri De Lubac and the Roots of Communion Ecclesiology," *Theological Studies* 60 (1999).

Driver S. R. *An Introduction to the Literature of the Old Testament*. Edinburgh: T & T Clark, 1961.

Dumbrell, William J. *The Reformed Theological Review*, 39 no. 2 May–Aug 1980.

Durham, John. *Exodus*. Waco, Tex.: Word Books, 1987.

Easton M. G. *Illustrated Bible Dictionary*, 3rd Edition. Thomas Nelson, 1897.

Easton, B., "The Pharisees." *Easton's 1897 Bible Dictionary, Bible CD*, 2008.

González, Eliezer. "Jesus and the Temple in John and Hebrews: Towards a New Testament Perspective." *DavarLogos* 2016, vol. XV–N. º 2

Ellicott, C. J. *Ellicott's Commentary on the Whole Bible: A Verse by Verse Explanation*. Grand Rapids, 1954.

Ellis E.E. *The OT Canon in the Early Church*. Philadelphia: Fortress Press, 1988.

Towns, Elmer. *Theology for Today*. Belmont, CA: Wadsworth/ Thomson Learning, 2002.

Gilles, Emery. *The Trinitarian Theology of St Thomas Aquinas*. London: OUP, 2010.

Wan, Enoch and Kevin P. Penman. "The Trinity: A Model for Partnership in Christian Mission." *Trinitarian Study*. April 1, 2010. Accessed, 23 May 2018. www.GlobalMissiology.org.

Lohmeyer, Ernst. *Lord of the Temple: A Study of the Relation Between Cult and Gospel,* translated by Stewart Todd. Edinburgh and London: Oliver and Boyd, 1961.

Gilson, Étienne. *The Unity of Philosophical Experience.* New York: Scribners, 1937.

Biser, Eugen. "Wisdom," *Encyclopedia of Theology* edited by Karl Rahner, p. 1817–21.

Eusebius' Church History (6.26.14; 6.25.2ff) in *The Catholic Encyclopedia* (New Advent), Volume III. New York: Robert Appleton Company.

Ferguson, Everett et al. "Canon," *Encyclopedia of Early Christianity.* London: Garland Publishing Inc., 1990.

*Faithful.* Collegeville: The Liturgical Press, 2003. Francisco: Ignatius Press, 2004.

Lawrence, Feingold. *Faith Comes from What Is Heard: An Introduction to Fundamental Theology.* Emmaus Academic Steubenville, Ohio, 2016.

Hahn, Ferdinand. "Der urchristliche Gottesdienst," *Stuttgartner Bibel-Studien 41.* Stuttgart: Verlag Katholisches Bibelwerk, 1970.

Ferguson, E. *Canon Muratori: Date and Province, Studies in Religion.* New York: Oxford Publishers, 1978.

Findlay, A. F. "Meekness." *A Dictionary of Christ and the Gospels,* Vol. 2. Edited by James Hastings. Edinburgh, Scotland: T. & T Clark, 1990.

Flavius Josephus, *Les Antiquités juives.* Volume IV, Livres VIII et IX Édition, trad. et notes par Étienne Nodet. Paris, Éditions du Cerf, 2005.

Filson, Floyd V. *A New Testament History.* Philadelphia: Westminster Press Limited, 1952.

Fortescue, Adrian. "Liturgy." *The Catholic Encyclopedia.* Vol. 9. New York: Robert Appleton Company, 1910. Accessed November 14, 2018. www.newadvent.org/cathen/09306a.htm.

Bertoldi, Francisco. "Henri de Lubac con Dei Verbum," *Communio: International Catholic Review* 17. Spring, 1990.

Thompson, Frank Charles (ed.). *Thompson Chain Reference Bible, NIV.* U.S.A: Kirkbirde Press, 1983.

D. N., Freeman (ed.). *Anchor Bible Dictionary.* Vol. 5, NY: Doubleday, 1992.

Fretheim, Terence E. *Exodus.* Louisville: John Knox Press, 1991.

Rachel, Friedman. "Searching for Holiness: The song of the Seas in the Bible and in the Liturgy," *Sanctification* edited by Birnbaum, David; Blech, Benjamin. New Paradigm Matrix, 2014.

Gaillardetz, Richard R. "The Ordinary Universal Magisterium: Unresolved Questions"

———. *By What Authority? A Primer on Scripture, the Magisterium, and the Sense of the Faithful.* Collegeville: The Liturgical Press, 2003.

Garrigou-Lagrange, Reginald, *Grace: Commentary on the summa Theologia of St Thomas, Ia, IIae. q.109–14.* B. Herder Book Co. St. Louis Missouri, 1952.

Gosewehr, Gene. "Dismantling Alleged Discrepancies. Part 4: The Resurrection," author. Accessed March 9, 2016. www.clearlens. org/.

Reid, George J. "The Canon of the NT in the Catholic Church," *The Catholic Encyclopedia (New Advent)*, Volume III. New York: Robert Appleton Company, 2007.

Klubertanz, George P. *St. Thomas Aquinas on Analogy: A Textual and Systematic Analysis.* Chicago: Loyola University Press, 1960.

Beasley-Murray, George R. *John.* Waco: Word, 1987.

Kittle, Gerhard. *Prophecy in the Theological Dictionary of the Old Testament.* Grand Rapids Michigan: WM. B EERDM Publishing Company, Vol. VI, 1983.

Gerstenberger, Erhard S. *Psalms, Part I with an Introduction to Cultic Poetry. The Forms of the Old Testament Literature.* Grand Rapids: Eerdmans, 1991.

Grisanti, Michael A. "The Davidic Covenant," *The Master's Seminary Journal,* 10/2 (Fall 1999).

Gunkel, "Psalm 149: An Interpretation," 303; Cohen, 477; Allan Harman, Psalms. Ross-shire: Mentor, 1998.

Hahn, Scott, and Curtis Mitch. *Covenant and Communion: The Biblical theology of Pope Benedict XVI*. Brazos Press, Michigan, 2009.

————. *Exodus with Introduction, Commentary, and Notes*. San Francisco, CA: Ignatius Press, 2012.

Hahn, Scott W. "Temple, Sign and Sacrament: Towards a New Perspective on the Gospel of John," *Letter and Spirit 4, Temple and Contemplation: God's Presence in the Cosmos, Church, and Human Heart*, 2008.

————. *Kinship by Covenant: a Canonical Approach to the Fulfillment of God's Saving Promises*. New Haven; London: Yale University Press, 2009.

Hahn, Scott and Curtis Mitch (eds.). *Ignatius Catholic Study Bible: New Testament*. San Francisco: Ignatius Press, 2010.

————. and Benjamin Wiker. *Politicizing the Bible: The Roots of Historical Criticism and the Secularization of Scripture 1300–1700*. New York: Crossroad, 2013.

————. *Covenant and Communion: The Biblical Theology of Pope Benedict XVI*. Brazos Press, Michigan.

Betz, Hans Dieter. "Hellenism," *Anchor Bible Dictionary*, Vol. 3, edited by D. N. Freedman.

Harrington J. Daniel. *Interpreting the New Testament. A Practical Guide*. Wilmington: Michael Glazier, 1979: and Dublin: Veritas, 1980.

Harris W. Hall III. *1, 2, 3 John Comfort and Counsel for a Church in Crisis*.

Bateman, Herbert W. "Christ and Son of God in Mark's Narrative Presentation of Jesus," *JETS* 50/3 (September 2007).

Higgins A. J. B. *The Lord's Supper in the New Testament, Studies in Biblical Theology, no.6*. Chicago: Henry Regnery company, 1952.

Hobbes, Thomas. *Leviathan: Or, The Matter, Form, & Power of a Common-wealth Ecclesiastical and Civil*. New York: Barnes & Noble Books, 2004.

Clark, Howard K. *Understanding the New Testament*, 4th Ed. 1997.

Hubbard, Benjamin J. "Exegetical Studies of Early Christian Resurrection Accounts." *Religious Studies Review*, 7 no 1 Jan 1981.

Kant, Immanuel. *Critique of Pure Reason* edited by Paul Guyer and Allen W. Wood. Cambridge University Press, 1999.

"Introduction to the Psalm," *The New Jerusalem Bible Study Edition*.

Irenaeus, *Against Heresies* 5.

Kingsbury, Jack Dean. *Matthew as Story*, 2nd ed. Minneapolis: Fortress, 1988.

Jackson, Wayne. "Messianic Previews in the Book of Zechariah." *ChristianCourier.com*. https://www.christiancourier.com/articles/ 1423.

Sanders, James A. "Canon of the NT," *Anchor Bible Dictionary* edited by D. N. Freeman. Oxford, 1971.

Hastin, James D.D. "Proverbs," *Dictionary of the Bible*. Edinburgh: T and T Clark, 1963.

———. "How is Adam the son of God in Luke 3:38?" https:// hermeneutics. stackexchange.com/ questions/7677.

Mays, James L. "Psalm 144: Praise in their Throats and Sword in their Hands," *Psalms*. Westminster John Knox Press.

Edart, Jean-Baptiste. "Greatest Missionary of all Times," FIDES News Service, Rome, June 28, 2008. catholicculture.org/culture/library/view. Cfm. recnum=8330: 2008.

Jenkins David. "The Work and Person of the Holy Spirit in the Gospel of John." Accessed May 18, 2018. blueletterbible. org / blb/2013/03/05.

Murdoch, Jessica. "On the Relationship between Sanctity and Knowledge: Holiness as the Epistemological Criterion in St. Thomas," *Pro Ecclesia* Vol. XXIII, No. 4: 418–434.

Conn, Joann W. "Spirituality," *The New Catholic Encyclopedia of Theology*, England, Liturgical Press: 2006.

Kincaid, John A. and Michael P Barber. "'Conformed to the Image of His Son': Participation in Christ as Divine Sonship in Romans 8." *Letter and Spirit* 10, 2015.

Bergsma, John and Brant Pitre, *The Old Testament: A Catholic Introduction to the Bible*. San Francisco: Ignatius, 2017.

Wippel, John F. *The Metaphysical Thought of Thomas of Aquinas: From Finite Being to Uncreated Being*. Washington, DC: Catholic University of America Press, 2000.

McDermott, John M. "On Theological Significance of the Indulgence," *L Observatore Romano*, 17 March 1999.

Oakes, John. "Are Zechariah 3:8–9, 6:11–13 and 12:10–13:3 messianic prophecies? Is Joshua a figure of Jesus?" http://evidence-forchristianity.org/are-zechariah-38-9-611-13-and-1210-133-messianic-prophecies-is-joshua-a-figure-of-jesus/.

Heil, John Paul. *The Letter of James: Worship to Live By*. Eugene, OR: Cascade, 2012.

John Paul II. *Ecclesia de Eucharistia*. http://www.vatican.va.

———. *Encyclical Evangelium Vitae*. March 25, 1995

———. *Encyclical Letter Ecclesia de Eucharistia*. www.vatican.va/ holy father /special features/encyclicals/ *documents/hf_jp-ii_enc_20030417 ecclesia_eucharistia_en.html*.

———. *Encyclical, Ecclesia De Eucharistia*. April 17, 2017.

John S. K and Michael L. B. "Introduction to Psalms," *The Jerome Biblical Commentary* edited by Raymond E. Brown et al. London: Burns and Oates, 2007.

Johnston, David. *The Rhetoric of Leviathan; Thomas Hobbes and the Politics of Cultural Transformation*. Princeton: Princeton UP, 1986.

Levenson, Jon D. "The Davidic Covenant and Its Modern Interpreters," *Catholic Biblical Quarterly* 41 (1979).

Aumann, Jordan. *Christian Spirituality in the Catholic Tradition*. London: Ignatius Press, 1989.

———. *Spiritual Theology*. Great Britain: Continuum Press, 2006.

Frey, Jörg. "New Testament Eschatology, An Introduction: Classical Issues, Disputed Themes, and Current Perspectives," *Eschatology of the New Testament and Some Related Documents* edited by Jan G. Van Der Watt. Tübingen: Mohr Siebeck, 2011.

Sudbrack, Josef. "Spirituality: Biblical Foundations and Historical Development," *Encyclopedia of Theology* edited by Karl Rhaner. Indiana, Paul Press.

Owens, Joseph. *An Elementary Christian Metaphysics*. Houston: Center for Thomistic Studies, 1985.

Ratzinger, Joseph (Pope Benedict XVI). *Jesus of Nazareth, vol. 1: From the Baptism in the Jordan to the Transfiguration*. New York: Doubleday, 2007.

Josephus. *The Complete Works of Josephus: Antiquities of the Jews* translated William Whiston. 1987.

Lieu, Judith. *New Testament Theology, the Theology of the Johannine Epistle*. Cambridge University Press: 1991.

Walter, Kaiser C. *The Messiah in the Old Testament*. Zondervan Publishing House, Grand Rapid, Michigan, 1995.

Broussard, Karlo. "Biblical Resurrection Reports Are Not 'Hopelessly Contradictory.'" Accessed July 18, 2018. https://www.catholic.com/magazine/.

Niebuhr, Karl-Wilhelm. "A New Perspective on James? Neuere Forschungen zum Jakobusbrief," *TLZ* 129, 2004.

Dell, Katharine. *Get Wisdom Get Insight: An Introduction to Israel's Wisdom Literature*. London: Darton, 2000.

DycKaman, Katherine and Patrick Carroll. *Solitude to Sacrament,*. Minnesota: The liturgical Press, 1970.

Tanner, Kathryn. *God and Creation in Christian Theology: Tyranny or Empowerment?* Oxford: Basil Blackwell, 1988.

Ogden, Kelly D. "Jesus And the Temple" Accessed, 21/7/18. https://www.lds.org/ensign/1991/04/.

Grayson, Kenneth. *Epistles*. Grand Rapids: Erdmann, 1984.

Irwin, Kevin W. *Sacraments in The New Dictionary of Theology* edited by Joseph A. Komonchak et al. Bangalore: Theological Press, 2006.

Komonchak, A. Joseph. "The Ecclesiology of Vatican II," *Origins*, 28, April 22, 1999.

Clayton, Kraby K. "Five Covenants of the Old Testament." http://reasonabletheology. Org/5covenant.

Boat, Lawrence. *Reading the Old Testament—An Introduction*. New York: Paulist Press, 1984.

Morris, Leon. *The Gospel According to John,* rev. ed. NICNT; Grand Rapids: Eerdmans, 1995.

Boff, Leonardo. *Holy Trinity, Perfect Community*. Maryknoll, New York: Orbis, 2000.

Leske M. Adrian. "Context and Meaning of Zachariah 9:9," *The Catholic Biblical Quarterly* I 62, 2000.

Levenson, Jon. "The Davidic Covenant and Its Modern Interpreters," *The Catholic Biblical Quarterly*:14, 1979:206.

Life and Mission *Sacramentum Caritatis*. http://www.catholicliturgy. com/index.cfm/Life and Mission, Sacramentum Caritatis.

Lilly L., Joseph. "Alleged Discrepancies in the Gospel Accounts of the Resurrection," *The Catholic Biblical Quarterly* 2, no. 2, April 1940.

Lloyd Strickland (ed). *Leibniz and the Two Sophies: The Philosophical Correspondence*. Toronto: Iter, Inc., 2011.

Lockett, Darian. "Are the Catholic Epistles a Canonically Significant Collection?: A Status Quaestionis," *Currents in Biblical Research*, 14 no 1 October 2015.

*L'Osservatore Romano*, "Final Report, II.C.110," December 1985.

Regis, Louis-Marie. *St. Thomas and Epistemology*. Whitefish, MT: Kessinger, 2010.

Loux J. Michael. "Aristotle: Metaphysics," *The Blackwell Guide to Ancient Philosophy* edited by C. Shields. Malden MA: Blackwell Publishing, 2003.

Johnson, Luke T. "Romans 3: 21–26 and the Faith of Jesus," *CBQ* 44, 1982.

*Lumen Gentium*: *Pastoral Constitution on the Church in the Modern World*. Washington: United States Catholic Conference, 1965.

"Magisterium," *Theological Studies 64*, 2003.

Manson T. W. *The Sayings of Jesus (Study Ed.)* Britain; Billing and Sons, 1975.

Marianne M. Thompson *The God of the Gospel of John*. Grand Rapids: Eerdmans, 2001.

Marianne M. Thompson. "The Living Father," *Semeia 85*, 1999.

Powell, Mark A. "Introducing the New Testament." cdn.bakerpub-lishinggroup.com /processed/esource-assets/files/796/2009.

Marshall, Taylor. *Catholic Perspective on Paul* (Kindle Location 26). Saint John Press. Kindle Edition.

Matera J. Frank. *New Testament Christology.* Westminster John Knox Press: Louisville, London, 1999.

―――. *New Testament Christology.* Westminster John Knox Press: Louisville, London.

Perman, Matt. "What Is the Doctrine of the Trinity?" Accessed, 18 May, 2018. www.desiringgod.org/articles/01/26, 2006.

McKelvey R. J. *The New Temple: The Church in the NT.* London: Oxford University Press, 1969.

Meier, John P. *A Marginal Jew. Rethinking the Historical Jesus. Vol. 1. The Roots of the Problem and the Person; 1994. Vol. 2. Mentor, Message, and Miracles; 2001. Vol. 3. Companions and Competitors.* New York: Doubleday, 2001.

Melina, Livio. "The Role of the Ordinary Universal Magisterium: On Francis Sullivan's"

Menken, J. J. Martinus J J. "Striking the Shepherd. Early Christian Versions and Interpretations of Zechariah 13,7," *The Catholic Biblical Quarterly*, 55 no 3 Jul 1993.

Metzer B. "Canon of the NT," *Anchor Bible Dictionary* edited D. N. Freeman. Oxford, Vol. 6, 1971.

Downey, Michael (Ed). *The New Dictionary of Catholic Spirituality.* India: 1995.

Marmura, Michael E. (trans.). *The Incoherence of the Philosophers.* Provo, Utah: Brigham Young University Press, 1997.

Bird, Michael F. and Joseph A. Dodson (eds). *Paul and the Second Century.* LNTS 412; London: T&T Clark, 2011.

―――. and Stanley N. Gundry (eds.). *Four Views on the Apostle Paul.* Zondervan, Grand Rapid, Michigan, 2012.

Homan, Michael M. "The Tabernacle and the Temple in Ancient Israel." Wiley online library. First published: 27 October 2006. Accessed, 23 Jul 2018. https://onlinelibrary.wiley.com.

Peppard, Michael. "Adopted and Begotten Sons of God: Paul and John on Divine sonship," *The Catholic Biblical Quarterly*, 73 no 1 Jan 2011.

Microsoft Encarta. 1993-2008. Microsoft Corporation. All rights reserved.

Miller, Patrick D. *Interpreting the Psalms*. Philadelphia: Fortress, 1986.

*Modern Biblical Criticism, Christianity and Literature* Vol. 61, No. 1 (Autumn 2011).

Moody D. Smith. *Interpretation, A Bible Commentary for Teaching and Preaching*. USA: John Knox Press, 1990.

Morrow L Jeffrey, *Leviathan and the Swallowing of Scripture: The Politics behind Thomas Hobbes' Early Modern Biblical Criticism*

———. *Three Skeptics and the Bible La Peyrère, Hobbes, Spinoza, and the Reception of Modern Biblical Criticism*. Pickwick Publications, Oregon, 2016.

———. "The Untold History of Modem Biblical Scholarship's Pre-Enlightenment Secular Origins," *Journal of Theological Interpretation* 8.1 (2014).

Moseman R. David. "Reading the Two Zechariah As One," *Review and Expositor* 97, (Fall 2000)

Moshe Weinfeld, "The Covenant of Grant in the Old Testament and in the Ancient Near East," JAOS 90 (1970):185; Waltke, "Phenomenon of Conditionality."

Murphy R.E, "Wisdom in the OT" *Anchor Bible Dictionary*, Vol. 6, edited by D. N. Freeman.

Neile M. "The Pharisees," *Robertson's NT Bible Commentary, Bible CD*, 2008.

Nelson H. H. Graburn. "What is Tradition?" Museum Anthropology of American Anthropological Association.

Nelson, T. *The Holy Bible (NRSV Catholic Ed.)* India; Cath. Bible press, 1990.

New Advent. "Son of God." http://www.newadvent.org/cathen/14142b.htm.

*New Revised Standard Version Bible, Catholic Edition*. Bangalore: Theological Publication, 2005.

Newsome J. D. *The Hebrew Prophets*. Atlanta: John Knox Press, 1984.

Newton, M. Newton. *The Concept of Purity at Qumran and in the Letters of Paul*. Cambridge: Cambridge University Press, 1985.

Noah W. *Webster's Universal Unabridged Dictionary,* 2nd Ed. NY; Dorset and Balt, 1964.

Gottwald, Norman K. *The Hebrew Bible: A Socio-Literary Introduction.* Philadelphia: Fortress Press, 1985.

Perrin, Norman. *The Resurrection According to Matthew, Mark and Luke.* Philadelphia Fortress Press, 1976.

Norris Clarke, "The Meaning of Participation in St. Thomas," *Proceedings of the American Catholic Philosophical Association* 26 (1952).

Odendal, F.F. *Handwoordeboek van die Afrikaans taal.* Johannesburg: Perskor, 1991.

Onwudufor F. O. F. *Mmanu E Ji Eri Okwu (Igbo Proverbs),* Vol. II, Enugu: Snaap Press Limited, 2008.

Eissfeldt, Otto. *The Old Testament. An introduction.* Oxford: Basil Blackwell, 1974.

Packer, J. I. *Knowing God.* InterVarsity Press. Downers Grove, IL, 1973.

Painter, John. *James as the First Catholic Epistle.* Waco, Texas: Baylor Univ Press, 2009.

Patrich, Joseph. "The Temple of Herod," *Bible Review.* October 1988.

Deterding, Paul E. "Eschatological and Eucharistic Motive," *Concordia Journal,* 1979.

Evdokimov, Paul. *The Struggle with God.* Glen Rock, New York: Paulist Press, 1966.

Paul VI. Encyclical *Marialis Cultus* (February 2, 1975)

———. Encyclical *Mysterium Fidei* (September 3, 1965)

Fredriksen, Paula. "Gospel Chronologies, the Scene in the Temple, and the Crucifixion of Jesus." Presented to the Department of Religion, Boston University.

Lagrange, Père. *Evangile de Jésus Christ.* Librairie Lacoffre, Paris.

Hailey, O. L. "The Three Prophetic Day: A Harmony of the Apparent Discrepancies in the Gospel Narratives about the Resurrection of Jesus Christ," *Review & Expositor,* 6 no 1 Jan 1908.

Miriam, Perlewitz. *The Gospel of Matthew; Message of Biblical Spirituality.* Wilmington; Michael Glazier, 1988.

Perkins, Pheme. *The Johannine Epistles*. Willington, Michael Glazier, 1979.

Linder, Phil. "Bible Power CD Programme," *Strong's Greek Dictionary*, 2000 Bronson: Online Pub.

Igbo, Philip. *New Testament Era, Class Handout for the Course: The Close of New Testament Era*, 2010.

Plantinga, citing Hilary of Poitiers, the Nicean homoousios clause and Tertullian's refutation of Sabellianism. Pollard documents the use of John 10:30 in early trinitarian controversies, 1991.

Pomerleau M. Julie. "Yves Congar's Ecclesiology and the Role of the Church in the World."

Pope Benedict XVI. Audience, November 22, 2006.

———. Audience, November 8, 2006.

———. Audience, October 25, 2006.

Pope John Paul II, Homily during Mass, 24 April 1981 *L' Observatore Romano*, English, May 4, 1981.

Power S. J. "Exodus," *A Catholic Commentary on Holy Scripture* edited by Orchard, B., & Sutcliffe, E. F. Toronto; New York; Edinburgh: Thomas Nelson, 1954.

Schulte, Raphael. *Sacraments in Encyclopedia of Theology* edited by Karl Rahner. London: Burns and Oates, 1975.

Ratzinger, Joseph. *Eschatology: Death and Eternal Life*, trans. Michael Wildstein. The Catholic University of America Press, Washington DC, 1988.

———. *The Spirit of the Liturgy*, translated by John Saward. San Francisco: Ignatius Press, 2000.

Stamper, Ray and Casey Chalk. "The Shaping of Biblical Criticism: A Catholic Perspective on Historical Criticism." www.calledto-communion.com. 2014/11.

Règle de saint Benoît, chapitres XII et XIII, traduction par Prosper Guéranger. (Abbaye Saint-Pierre de Solesmes, réimpression, 2007.

Rendtorff R. *Reflection on the Earthly History of Prophecy in Israel: History and Hermeneutics*. New York: Harpers and Row, 1967.

Richard P. M., "The Pharisees," *Harper Collins Encyclopedia of Catholicism* edited by Harper Collins San Francisco, 1989.

Gaillardetz, Richard R. *By What Authority? A Primer on Scripture, the Magisterium and the Sense of the Faithful.* Liturgical Press: Collegeville Minnesota, 2003.

Richards, W L. "Present Status of Text Critical Studies in the Catholic Epistles." Andrews University Seminary Studies, 13 no 2 Aut 1975.

Robert A. and Feuillt A. *Introduction to the Old Testament.* New York: Images Books, Vol. II, 1970.

Robert J, B., "Mtt. 23, 2" *Robertson's NT World Pictures*, Bible CD, 2008.

Russell, Robert J. "Special Providence and Genetic Mutation: A New Defense of Theistic Evolution," *Evolutionary and Molecular Biology: Scientific Perspectives on Divine Action*, edited by Robert J. Russell, William R. Stoeger, and Francisco J. Ayala.

Gordon, Robert P. *I & II Samuel: A Commentary.* Grand Rapids: Zondervan, 1986.

Wall, Robert. "A Unifying Theology of the Catholic Epistles," *The Catholic Epistles and Apostolic Tradition* edited Karl-Wilhelm Niebuhr and Robert W. Wall. Waco, TX: Baylor University Press, 2009.

Murphy, Roland E. *Introduction to the Wisdom Literature of the Old Testament.* Collegeville: Liturgical Press, 1952.

Youngblood, Ronald F. "1, 2 Samuel," *The Expositor's Bible Commentary* edited F. Gaebelein. Grand Rapids: Zondervan, 1992.

Bardsley, Rosemary. God's Word or You.com/bible-studies/the-gospel-of-john/425-study-1.html.

Roth W. M. W. "The Numerical Sequence x / x + 1 in the Old Testament, VT 12." 1962.

Bultmann, Rudolf. *The Johannine Epistles.* Philadelphia, Fortress Press, 1974.

Sailhamer, John. *The Pentateuch As Narrative: A Biblical-Theological Commentary.* Grand Rapids, Mich.: Zondervan, 1992.

Sanderson J. E. "Amos." *Woman Bible Commentary.* Louisville: Westminster John Knox Press, 1998.

Schneider S. M. "The Raising of the New Temple: John 20.19–23 and Johannine Ecclesiology," *New Testament Studies* 52 (2006).

Frayne, Sean. *The World of the New Testament*. Wilmington: Michael Glazier, 1980.

Second Vatican Council, *Dei Verbum*, Dogmatic Constitution on Divine Revelation.

*Shepherd's Note, Old Testament: Proverbs*. Tennessee: Broadman and Holman Publishers, 2000.

*Sheppard and Sister Elizabeth Englund*. Ignatius, San Francisco, 1988.

Shore, John. "The Mystery of the Holy Trinity Explained in Four Sentences: A Look at John 1:1–4." Accessed May 21, 2018. www.patheos.com/blog/2009/01.

Mowinckel, Sigmund. *He That Cometh*. New York: Abingdon, 1954.

Van den Bergh, Simon (trans.) *Tahfut al-Tahfut* 452. Cambridge: E.J. Gibb Memorial Trust, 1987.

Simon-Prado (Praelectiones Biblicae, N. T. I4, p. 612) quotes Lyranus: "Sol potest intelligi oriri dupliciter: uno modo perfecte…alio modo quando lux ejus incipit apparere, seil., in aurora, et sic accipitur hic ortus solis."

Russell, Sisson. *Not by Paul Alone: The Formation of the Catholic Epistle Collection and the Christian Canon*. Waco, Tex: Baylor Univ Pr, 2007.

*Biblica*, 90 no 4 2009.

Garrett, Smith. "The Two Messiahs," *Zechariah. Issues, a Messianic Perspective*, Vol. 15.5, 2004.

Smith P. and Charles M. Jacobs (eds.), *Luther's Correspondence*. United Lutheran Publication House: Philadelphia, 1918.

Smith, W. S., "The Pharisees," *Smith's Bible Dictionary*, Power Bible CD, 2008.

"Some Recent Observations," *Heythrop Journal 39*, 1998.

Baruch, Spinoza. *A Political Treatise. In A theologico-Political Treatise and A Political Treatise* translated by R. H. M. Elwes. NY: Dover, 1951.

Springborg, Patricia. "Hobbes' Biblical Beasts: Leviathan and Behemoth!" *Political Theory*. 1995.

Porter, Stanley E. and Craig A. Evans. *Dictionary of New Testament Background: A Compendium of Contemporary Biblical Scholarship.* Downers Grove, IL: InterVarsity Press, 2000.

Stanley P Alan and Gundry N. Stanley (eds.). *Four Views on The Role of Worlds at the final Judgement.* Zondervan, Grand Rapids, Michigan, 2013.

Stegman D. Thomas. *Second Corinthians: Catholic Commentary on Sacred Scriptures.* Barker Academic, Grand Rapids, Michigan.

Smalley, Stephen. *1, 2, & 3 John.* WBC: Waco Word, 1984.

Um, Stephen T. "The Theme of Temple Christology in John's Gospel," *Library of New Testament Studies.* London: T & T Clark, 2006.

Stewart Don. "How Do the Different Members of the Trinity Work with Each Other? (Economic Trinity)." Accessed May 21, 2018. www.blueletterbible.org/.

Sweeney E. "Supposition, Signification and Universals: Metaphysical and Linguistic Complexity in Aquinas," *Frei Z Philosophical Theology* 42(3) (1995).

*The New Jerusalem Bible Study Edition*: "Introduction to the Proverbs" Greek is Bible Works (2003), Greek LLX/ BNT LLC.

C. Pegis, Thomas Anton, James F. Anderson, Vernon J. Bourke, and C J. O'Neil. *Summa Contra Gentiles.* Notre Dame, Ind.: University of Notre Dame Press, 1975.

C. Pegis, Thomas Anton, James F. Anderson, Vernon J. Bourke, and C J. O'Neil. *The Summa Theologica of St. Thomas Aquinas.* London: Burns Oates & Westbourne, 1912.

Thomas Aquinas. *Sentences* d. 12, q. un., a. 3, ad 4; ST I, q. 36, a.3.

———. *Summa Theologiae.* Taurini: Maritti, 1948, I-II, q. 112, a. 4.

McCreesh, Thomas P. "Introduction to Proverbs," *The Jerome Biblical Commentary* edited by Raymond E. Brown et al. London: Burns and Oates, 2007.

*Thomas Pazhayampallil Sacraments in General (in Pastoral Guide).* Bangalore: Kristu Jyoti Publication, 2006.

"Train Marketing. Israel, God's son through adoption." www.nightlight.org/2007/10/israel-gods-son-through-adoption.

Tucker G. "Prophetic Authenticity: A Form Critical Study of Amos 7, 10–17", *Interpretation Journal* 1973: Vol. XXVII.

Turro J. C. and Raymond Brown. "Canonicity," *Ferom Bible Commentary*, Englewood Cliffs: Prentice-Hall, 1968.

Ulrich Wilckens. *Resurrection: Biblical Testimony of the Resurrection. An Historical Examination and explanation* translated by A. M. Stewart. Atlanta, John Knox Press, 1978.

United States Conference of Catholic Bishops: Psalms, Chp.149. Accessed, 7 November, 2018.

Urban C. Wahlde. *The Johannine Commandments—1 John*. John Knox Press, USA, 1990.

VanGemeren, Willem A. "Psalms," *The Expositor's Bible Commentary*. Vol. 5. Edited by Frank E. Gaebelein. Grand Rapids: Zondervan, 1991.

Vatican II. *Sacrosanctum concilium* 7 § 2–3

Vosloo, R. R. 2004. "Anderkant etiek: tradisie, dekonstruksie en verdere weë." *NGTT* 45 (3&4):936–955.

Walker P. W. L. *Jesus and the Holy City: New Testament Perspectives on Jerusalem*. Grand Rapids: Eerdmans, 1996.

Brueggemann, Walter. *First and Second Samuel*. Louisville: John Knox, 1990.

Kaiser, Jr., Walter C. "The Blessing of David: The Charter for Humanity," *The Law and the Prophets: Old Testament Studies Prepared in Honor of Oswald Thompson Allis*, edited by John H. Skilton. Philadelphia: Presbyterian and Reformed, 1974.

Watson G. D. *Our Own God*. Harvey Christian Publishers, UK, 2012.

Wattson F. *The Rhetoric of Oppression*. Grand Rapids: Eerdmanns, 1994.

Welch J. Lawrence. "The Infallibility of the Ordinary Universal Magisterium: A Critique of"

———. "Quaestio Disputata Reply to Richard Gaillardetz On the Ordinary Universal"

Wepener, C. J. *Liturgy on the Edge of Traditon*. Society for Practical Theology in South Africa, 2008.

Whybray R. N. *Proverbs, New Century Bible Commentary*. London: Marshal Pecking, 1994.

wikipedia.org/wiki/Psalm 149.

Carroll, William E. "Creation, Evolution, and Thomas Aquinas." *Revue des Questions Scientifiques* 171 (4) 2000.

Hendrickson, William. *NTC: The Gospel of John*. Grand Rapids, MI: Baker House, 1953.

"William Lane Craig vs. Bart D. Ehrman debate. Is There Historical Evidence for the Resurrection of Jesus?" College of the Holy Cross, Worcester, Massachusetts, United States— March 2006. Transcript at www.reasonablefaith.org/media/debates/is-there-historical-evidence-for-the-resurrection-of-je-sus-the-craig-ehrman. Accessed, 20 Jul, 2018.

Placher, William. *The Domestication of Transcendence*. Louisville, KY: Westminster Press, 1996.

William R. Farmer et al. *Proverbs in International Bible Commentary*. Collegeville: The Liturgical Press, 1998.

William Whitson F. *The Works of Josephus Complete and unabridged; New Updated Edition*. Peabody, Hendrickson, 2006.

Wright, N. T. *The New Testament and the People of God*. Minneapolis: Fortress, 1992.

Zargar A Nazi. "What is Wrong with Perennial Philosophy?" http//kashmirreader.com/2017.

Zimmerli N. *The Law and the Prophets: A Study of the Meaning of the OT*. New York: Harper Torch Books, 1993.

# About the Author

Fr. Canice Chukwuemeka Njoku, C.S.Sp. is a Catholic Priest and a member of the Congregation of the Holy Ghost Fathers and Brothers, also known as the Congregation of the Holy Spirit (Spiritans). He has been a Missionary in Puerto Rico (The Island of  Enchantment) since 2014, where he is the Chancellor of the Dioceses of Fajardo-Humacao as well as the Parish Administrator of Parroquia la Resurrección del Señor, Canóvanas, Puerto Rico.

In addition to his qualification in Food Science and Technology (FST), he has a Dip. in Philosophy; B.A in Religion and Cultural Studies: M.A in Divinity; M.A in Biblical Theology.

He is the author of: God's Word from my Heart to my Lips—Homilies for Sundays and Solemnities, Year C; La Palabra de Dios desde mi Corazón a mis Labios - Homilias para los Domingos y Solemnidades, Año C; The Divine Sonship of Christ and the *Totus Christi* (The whole body of Christ); and Peace Upon Our World.

Lightning Source UK Ltd.
Milton Keynes UK
UKHW041026071219
354907UK00002B/113/P